Bloomsbury Professional Law Insight

Cannabis Law and Regulation

Preface

This book has been written with the aim of providing insight for anyone who wishes to develop a more in-depth knowledge of global cannabis laws, as we enter the most significant period of regulatory upheaval since the 1920s prohibition era.

It is my hope that lawyers, consultants, business executives, government officials, academics, pharmaceutical and healthcare specialists will come away with everything they wish to know about the current landscape and how quickly it is advancing.

No prior knowledge of cannabis or the law is required, nor presumed, and at the front of the book I have laid out the absolute basics necessary to help the reader put everything else into context, including international definitions of cannabis, and some drug law terminology.

The book begins and ends with the United Nations and the existing international drug control regime, and there are questions for policymakers at every level to consider. Global treaty agreements are crumbling; why is this happening, is it time to reform the system, and what can we do differently next time?

This book covers activity in the most significant global territories where medicinal and recreational cannabis regulations and laws are evolving, and where possible, it looks ahead to important legislative updates earmarked for the next 12 months. In truth, things are moving at such a pace there are consequential developments occurring almost every day.

The nexus of law and business will have a profound impact on the shape of the industry in the coming years, as regulation of cannabis is happening quickly and, in some cases, unevenly.

More than one international official I spoke with off the record admitted they are looking to the cannabis sector to produce reliable, honest research to help them shape policy.

It is clear that if we are going to regulate, we need sensible, evidence-based rules that protect public health, young and vulnerable people, and the environment, along with business, consumers, and investors. It will take strong, pragmatic and informed governments to deliver this.

This book also investigates emerging trends along the cannabis supply chain, from cultivation and production to research and testing, sales, marketing, intellectual property and trademarks, all the way to the legal ramifications for financial investors.

The business of cannabis has been all over the financial press in the last 12 months, and the subject of some truly astonishing market projections for both individual companies and indeed entire continents. M&A activity is soaring, and 2020 promises to be a record-breaking year for deals. There are questions for cannabis businesses and market analysts too; are you being realistic in your valuations?

It is quite remarkable that a single plant has the potential to upend so many sectors, including (but not limited to) pharmaceutical, alcohol, food and beverage, tobacco, wellness, and cosmetics.

With so many commercial interests at stake, it would be easy to lose sight of the medicinal promise that cannabis holds, as this may prove to be the most valuable and worthy outcome of such widespread reform.

During the course of my research I heard from families who travel abroad to obtain cannabis-based medicines for their epileptic children, spending money they cannot afford in the process. There are others who choose to continue sourcing from the black-market because it is simpler than dealing with convoluted healthcare systems.

Physicians and general practitioners respond that they are reluctant to prescribe drugs they are unsure about, and that do not come with the levels of testing they would feel comfortable with. The reader will find a recurring message from governments that more testing of medicinal cannabis, particularly full-scale clinical trials, is a necessity.

With all of this in mind, why did I, a journalist, decide to write this book? A life-altering 3,000-mile road trip down the United States west coast from Washington state to San Diego in 2018 with the lady I would later call my wife was the catalyst.

I knew that certain states were allowing people to smoke cannabis, but I had no idea how ubiquitous the dispensaries were. As we drove down Highways 1 and 101, we lost count of the shops and signs in seemingly every town, no matter how remote and sparsely populated.

It was not a stretch to observe how this nascent industry resembles the online gambling sector of 15 years ago; namely explosive growth, piecemeal regulatory regimes and fruitless attempts to put the genie back in the bottle. Can we avoid some of the regulatory mistakes that industry made?

The cannabis sector is at the precipice of something truly extraordinary, and to me, the time is right to stop and capture the scene.

I hope you enjoy this book; your feedback is encouraged, as are any relevant updates or interesting stories from wherever you are in the world. If you want more information and the URLs collated are too much to bear in the written edition, do get in touch and I am happy to send any link you wish to follow up on.

You can contact me at any time on mark@mktmedia.co.uk.

Mark Taylor
January 2020

Acknowledgements

This book would not have been possible without Andy Hill and Greg Kilminster from Bloomsbury Professional; I am truly grateful for their support and help. Their colleagues Jenny Lank and Jane Bradford also deserve my eternal gratitude. Indeed, without Jane's editing skills this book would not have been readable.

I must also thank the law firms, regulatory officials and other industry experts around the world who contributed with analysis, assistance and links to research. This includes Dr Gilles Forte, secretary of the Expert Committee on Drug Dependence at the World Health Organization, Brendan Hughes, principal legal analyst at the European Monitoring Centre for Drugs and Drug Addiction, and Sir Norman Lamb.

Any errors are mine, not theirs.

Special thanks also to Dylan Kennett of DLA Piper, and top cannabis lawyer Robert Jappie, who have been a constant source of guidance, along with Sean Hocking at Cannabis Law Report.

Finally, thanks to Juno for being there every day, and to my incredible wife Georgia for her patience and belief.

Contents

Chapter 1

The global framing of cannabis

CANNABIS TERMINOLOGY AND DEFINITIONS

1.01 Drug terminology can be extremely confusing, even without the element of slang. The terms 'legalisation', 'decriminalisation' and 'depenalisation' are frequently misused and misunderstood, and as this book concerns their deployment in law, we will address them at the start to add clarity.

In many jurisdictions around the world there is no legal definition of 'cannabis', and 'medicinal cannabis', and there are also contrasting definitions of what constitutes 'a small amount', 'personal amounts' and 'personal consumption', with the discretion often left up to arresting officers or the judiciary.

Before we look at the legal detail of individual nations, we must also remind ourselves of the standards agreed under international law, with which every country party to the United Nations treaties once agreed.

CANNABIS AS DEFINED IN INTERNATIONAL LAW

1.02 The international drug control regime as laid out in the 1961 Single Convention on Narcotic Drugs gives the following definitions of cannabis the plant and its by-products:

- Cannabis: 'The flowering or fruiting tops of the cannabis plant (excluding the seeds and leaves when not accompanied by the tops) from which the resin has not been extracted, by whatever name they may be designated.'
- Cannabis plant: 'Any plant of the genus Cannabis.'
- Cannabis resin: 'The separated resin, whether crude or purified, obtained from the cannabis plant.'

Different laws were drawn up around the world, using these definitions as a platform, to determine what behaviours involving the plant would be controlled.

The regulatory prohibition of cannabis later included the central psychoactive component, tetrahydrocannabinol (THC), and cannabidiol (CBD) which is not mentioned above.

'Cannabis and its derivatives': all products derived from the cannabis plant. This includes the flowering tops (marijuana), compressed cannabis resin (hashish), cannabis oils, concentrated cannabis extracts (waxes) and edible preparations (eg, infusions, cookies and chocolates).

'Cannabinoids' are substances found only in the cannabis plant. There are estimated to be 104 unique, naturally-occurring cannabinoids. The two most extensively studied and of interest are THC and CBD.

- THC produces the psychoactive effects, such as euphoria, relaxation and heightened sensory experiences; the 'high' sought by recreational users;
- CBD has almost no psychoactive effects. It may moderate the psychoactive effects of THC and is believed to have antioxidant, anti-inflammatory and neuroprotective effects.

Approved pharmaceutical cannabinoids include dronabinol, nabilone, nabiximols and CBD. Research is ongoing into the potential uses of other cannabinoids.

Shades of legality

1.03 The European Monitoring Centre for Drugs and Drug Addiction (EMCDDA), the EU's drug agency, has noted that while all countries in Europe consider possession for personal use an offence, prison is not a penalty in over one third of countries in certain circumstances; of those remaining, many have lower-level guidance advising against prison for that offence.

Decriminalisation is the removal of criminal sanctions from a certain behaviour or action. Non-criminal sanctions may still be applied, and the activity is not legal. In regard to cannabis, decriminalisation is becoming more common in jurisdictions where authorities do not punish individuals who may be in possession of an amount of cannabis below a certain weight. It is almost always used in law to address acts of possession rather than selling or transporting. Countries which have decriminalised cannabis use for personal possession include Luxembourg, Croatia, Georgia, and Colombia, along with US states such as Maryland and Delaware.

Legalisation is to make a previously illegal act lawful. Cannabis legalisation usually involves the stripping away of all sanctions both criminal and non-criminal (fines etc). There may still be limits applied in regard to the permissions, however legalisation will also often cover possession amounts, sales and transporting of the product. Cannabis has been fully legalised in Canada, Uruguay, and 11 US states.

Depenalisation is the removal of criminal punishments in given examples. An individual may be allowed to hold an amount considered minor, and the authorities do not wish to pursue prosecution. In Europe, this is the position in Germany and Austria.

On the same page

1.04 EU member states have been asked by Brussels to agree on a legal definition of 'medicinal cannabis'. This is the first step towards drawing up an overarching bloc-wide set of rules that will 'standardise and unify products that contain cannabis-based medicines'.

These guidelines will be handed down to member states to transpose into their domestic legislation, ensuring all countries in the single market developing medicinal cannabis programmes have equal standards.

In theory, the regulatory, financial and cultural barriers that are hindering the advancement of medicinal cannabis in Europe can then be addressed.

Presently, multiple medicinal cannabis products are licensed across Europe, yet in most countries it is almost impossible for patients to access them.

Some countries lawfully allow patients access to medicinal cannabis, but do not, or will not, allow the licensing of medicinal cannabis products.

In the US, the picture is even more fragmented due to the number of states that have created their own set of cannabis rules, running counter to federal guidance and often clashing with each other.

There are no standardised definitions of 'medical marijuana', and 'high-CBD' or 'low-THC' products, yet media reports commonly use these terms interchangeably.

In the US, 'medical cannabis' does not mean a specific variety or strain, or a mode of preparation, or dosage form, and yet cannabis is often classified by the purpose of its use 'medical' or 'recreational'.

Medical cannabis products often contain various cannabinoids, however most are predominantly comprised of THC. 'High-CBD' products contain more CBD than other medicinal marijuana products, but some of these products may have levels of THC ranging from 0.3% to 5%, depending on the jurisdiction.

Sovereignty is of primary importance for governments, and this book will discuss, many countries are stepping outside of the boundaries of international law to create their own unique cannabis regulatory systems.

If we are to create effective, consistent and supportive regulations, however, and this applies to both the medicinal and recreational cannabis sectors, a degree of international harmony will be required when it comes to the definitions of standards.

The UK's decision to leave the EU means British businesses will have to align with the EU standards on medicines in order to continue selling products into the single market. Theoretically, once it is no longer an EU member, the UK could tailor its approach to match the needs of other cannabis markets, such as Canada, should it wish to explore areas of trade currently off-limits within the EU.

INTERNATIONAL OVERSIGHT OF CANNABIS

1.05 Cannabis is one of the psychoactive substances covered in the United Nations drug control regime, which is comprised of three treaties: the 1961 Single Convention on Narcotic Drugs[1] (Single Convention), the 1971 Convention on Psychotropic Substances, and the 1988 Convention against Illicit Traffic in Narcotic Drugs and Psychotropic Substances.

Prior to the 1961 agreement, drug treaties were narrower in focus, including formal control of opium, coca, and opiate derivatives, such as morphine, heroin and cocaine.

The Single Convention, adopted in 1961, merged nine separate multilateral drug control treaties negotiated between 1912 and 1953, widening the scope to include cannabis and other similar substances.

It is considered to be an international version of the US drug laws of the period.[2] Today, the agreement has been signed by 186 countries.

Classifications

1.06 There are 250 substances listed in the three agreements. Their purpose of which is to control and limit the use of the listed substances according to a classification of their therapeutic value, risk of abuse and health dangers, and to reduce the diversion of precursor chemicals to illegal drug manufacturers.

Cannabis is a Schedule I and IV narcotic; the most strictly controlled of the four categories. This grouping is for substances that have addictive properties, and present a serious risk of abuse.

Schedule I drugs are subject to all measures of drug control applicable under the agreements. This includes cannabis derivatives, along with cocaine, heroin, methadone, morphine and opium.

Schedule IV drugs are already considered the most dangerous substances and are already listed as Schedule I. They are considered particularly harmful and of extremely limited medical or therapeutic value.

Control is very strict, and these substances are subject to a total ban on 'the production, manufacture, export and import of, trade in, possession or use of any such drug except for amounts which may be necessary for medical and scientific research' (art. 2.5.b). Cannabis and cannabis resin are covered, alongside narcotics such as heroin.

Under the Single Convention, cannabis use within the signatory countries is limited 'exclusively to medical and scientific purposes the production, manufacture, export, import, distribution of, trade in, use and possession of' (article 4c).

International cannabis law guidelines

1.07 The Single Convention on Narcotic Drugs can be considered as a baseline for domestic laws. Every country signing the treaty must implement it in their law; they can make the law stricter, but they can't make the law weaker. The Single Convention is therefore present in the laws of every nation that has accepted it as binding international agreement. It must not be violated, reformed, or ignored by any individual nation.

After that, it becomes a matter of interpretation. The United States and Argentina are both signatories, but have both implemented the law differently.

In the United States, federal implementation of the Single Convention in the Controlled Substances Act criminalises possession of any amounts of cannabis.

In Argentina, for example, growing, producing, and selling are illegal, but the courts have decriminalised possession of small amounts, circumventing the international law. Recreational use of cannabis in Argentina, as in many other countries, is accepted, despite technically being illegal.

Treaty adherence

1.08 The International Narcotics Control Board (INCB) is the 'independent and quasi-judicial' body responsible for monitoring member states' implementation and adherence to the drug treaties.[3]

As far as international drug control is concerned, the INCB is the top global watchdog.

The INCB was established in 1968 in accordance with the Single Convention, although it had predecessors in previous drug control treaties under the League of Nations (1920–1946).

The INCB has 13 individual members serving in their personal capacity, elected for five-year terms. Its primary functions consist of:

- ensuring that there is adequate supply of legal drugs for scientific and medical purposes;
- helping to stop legal drugs and precursor chemicals funnelling into illicit supply channels;
- identifying weaknesses in international and national drug control systems, and recommending measures to address those weaknesses; and
- maintaining a permanent dialogue with governments to assist them in complying with their obligations.

The INCB investigates apparent violations of the treaties, proposes appropriate remedial measures for governments not in compliance or having difficulty complying.

Countries who routinely ignore or flout the treaties are referred to the Commission on Narcotic Drugs (CND) and the Economic and Social Council.

The CND is one of the United Nations organs with prime responsibility for drug control matters. In line with its mandates, the CND monitors the world drug situation, develops strategies on international drug control and recommends measures to address the world drug problem.

As a last resort, the treaties empower INCB to pressure members to stop importing, exporting drugs, or both, from a defaulting country. In all cases, INCB works in close cooperation with the governments.

Criticisms and controversy

1.09 Little is known about the operation of the INCB. Its missions, communications and letters remain confidential. It doesn't allow observers at any meetings and no minutes are available, even to member states.

It appears to lack any accountability procedure and is the least transparent and most secretive body within the UN system. The secretariat of the INCB argues that its unique status within the UN system empowers it to operate this way.

No public mechanism exists for member states or community organisations to contest claims, seek clarification, or offer amendments when a Board member makes an inaccurate statement.

The INCB Secretariat, funded by the UN, does not respond to requests for information from affected communities, non-governmental groups, or questions from the media. The INCB Secretariat did not respond to multiple attempts from this author to contact it via email and telephone.

WORLD HEALTH ORGANISATION EXPERT COMMITTEE ON DRUG DEPENDENCE AND CANNABIS RESCHEDULING

1.10 The World Health Organisation's Expert Committee on Drug Dependence (ECDD) carries out medical and scientific evaluations of the abuse liability of dependence-producing drugs falling within the terms of the 1961 Single Convention on Narcotic Drugs and the 1971 Convention on Psychotropic Substances.

It then makes recommendations to the United Nations Commission on Narcotic Drugs (CND) on the control measures, if any, that it considers appropriate. In the 50 years since its first meeting, in 1969, the ECDD has played a central role in the international drug control system, it is in effect the UN's health committee.

Until 2018 however, the ECDD had never carried out a full review of cannabis and cannabis-related substances since the International Drug Control Conventions were first established in 1961 and 1971.

Cannabis has been under the strictest controls, Schedules I and IV (the same brackets as heroin and cocaine), ever since the categories were drawn up to regulate narcotic drugs.

UN drug experts recommend rescheduling cannabis

1.11 The number of countries embarking on regulated access to cannabis and cannabis preparations has grown so significantly in recent years the WHO began to face mounting pressure to consider the evidence and potentially reschedule cannabis. Doing so would ultimately make research and laboratory testing easier, and would remove some of the stigma around conducting cannabis trials.

In November 2018, the ECDD met in Geneva to conclude its review of cannabis and cannabis related substances, and the outcomes were communicated to the UN in January 2019.[4]

After studying what amounted to decades of research, the ECDD recommended removing cannabis and cannabis resin from Schedule IV as it is not 'particularly harmful', and not associated with a significant risk of death.

It also said that products containing predominantly CBD and not more than 0.2% Delta-9-THC should not be under international control, as there is no relevant risk to public health.

It said the term 'extracts and tinctures' should be removed from the Conventions as they are too complex to be interpreted accurately. They would be replaced by a new entry in Schedule III of the 1961 Convention referring to pharmaceutical preparations of cannabis that do not pose a risk to public health.

The committee recommended Delta-9-THC/dronabinol be deleted from the 1971 Convention Schedule II and moved to the 1961 Convention, Schedule I (with cannabis and cannabis resin). Previously considered a pharmaceutical preparation, this primarily refers to the main psychoactive component of cannabis. This would be a similar approach as for coca leaf/cocaine and opium/morphine.

In its rationale, the ECDD found cannabis was considerably less harmful than other Schedule IV substances, that medical use had been proven, and in the case of CBD, it is used to treat childhood epilepsy, is not psychoactive and there is no evidence of dependence or abuse.

Delays

1.12 These proposals were due to be voted on by the CND at its March 2019 session, however the vote was postponed as the recommendations were delayed. Dr Gilles Forte, the secretary of the ECDD, said:

> 'It starts from a scientific process, where the committee will review specific aspects of substances, based on science, published and unpublished literature, along with lots of information provided by UN agencies and member states. Then it moves to political forums for the vote. It becomes political.'

The ECDD scientists felt as far back as 2014 that there was enough information to carry out the first review of cannabis, Dr Forte said, and by this time they had been fielding questions from a number of countries.

> 'We were asked by a number of member states, because they were struggling in their own country, trying to figure out how to get medicinal cannabis off the ground. They could see the potential, but they didn't know enough about it. There wasn't enough information, they were lost and the issue had become polarised.'

It was felt that the ECDD carrying out a purely scientific review of the cannabis plant and components would help. At the same time, the committee was responding to the opioid crisis in the US, and Forte said the tensions around cannabis were a lot stronger.

> 'When profiling opioids for pain, but also profiling the harms that can be caused, it is easier. It is simpler to communicate. Cannabis is a much more complex issue. We get asked questions about social care and public health impacts, legislation, etc, but these are not within our mandate. We are purely scientists.'

The committee looks at the harm posed to an individual and quantifies it. It does not look at the impact cannabis scheduling has on a population, and does not measure socio-economic factors.

Forte said by his count there are approximately about 200 global medical trials currently being performed to assess the impact of cannabis products on pain and other conditions. He said this is a large number, but the details are not being made public.

> 'Let's make the results more accessible, easy for people, but let's also acknowledge the harms of cannabis. The harms are not as important as opioids, because cannabis doesn't kill. We have to defend the scientific arguments, demonstrating that cannabis-derived medicines are useful. Let's continue the research and see how it can be even more used in medicine.'

As of October 2019, almost a year on from the first review ever into cannabis scheduling, the recommendations had not been passed, there is no fixed date for the vote to alter the scheduling, and the issue of cannabis reform at international level remains as polarised as ever.

Diplomatic balancing act

1.13 Some countries have continued to support the committee's work, but others, such as Russia, have stood in its path, said an ECDD official speaking on condition of anonymity. The scientists have done their part, but the countries who do not view the progress of medicinal cannabis as a good thing are refusing to budge.

> 'Each country has its own regulations and they are all different. 'How do global recommendations fit within a country context? This is part of the difficulty that some countries have. Privately they know the recommendations make sense, but they don't want to change their own domestic laws.' the official said. 'Other countries do not want the WHO to touch cannabis at all. They don't want to change anything because they are afraid of the impact; that the interpretation of the recommendation is to loosen control.'

There is a group of countries are very aggressive and reluctant for the WHO to touch this subject, the official said.

> 'Other countries are silent. They don't know what they are going to do. Some countries are quietly supportive, and others openly supportive. That is four very different groups for the WHO to deal with. It's incredibly complex and we are not sure how this will get resolved.'

ENDNOTES

1. The Single Convention on Narcotic Drugs: https://www.unodc.org/pdf/convention_1961_en.pdf.
2. Jay Sinha: 'The history and development of the leading international drug control conventions' (2001).
3. International Narcotics Control Board mandate: http://www.incb.org/incb/en/about/mandate-functions.html.
4. WHO review of cannabis scheduling letter: https://www.who.int/medicines/access/controlled-substances/UNSG_letter_ECDD41_recommendations_cannabis_24Jan19.pdf?ua=1.

Chapter 2

The Americas

CANADA

2.01 In 2018, Canada became the first G7 nation to open a fully legal recreational cannabis market. It became the second country globally after Uruguay to do so, with similar justifications that prohibition did not work, did not stop youngsters smoking marijuana, and often left many otherwise honest citizens with criminal records.

Prior to legalisation, Canada's black-market cannabis trade was worth around $7bn.[1] In July 2019, Canada's cannabis industry contributed approximately $8.26bn to GDP.[2]

The country's strong infrastructure and network of knowledgeable and connected entrepreneurs has combined well with a supportive government, and the industry is maturing quickly.

By virtue of its status as an early adopter, Canada is home to nine of the world's ten largest cannabis companies by market capitalisation, and it has become the global leader of an emerging industry.

The clearest sign of Canada's current dominance of the global market can be found in the presence of major names such as Aurora, Canopy, and Tilray, in almost every international market where cannabis is a potential opportunity.

Given the pace at which Canada's legal cannabis market launched, ferocious competition and interest from disruptive forces in adjacent sectors such as tobacco, food and drink, and biopharmaceuticals have contributed to the growing pains the sector has endured.

Although not the first country to fully legalise cannabis for adult recreational and medicinal use, the eyes of the world are on Canada as the most developed nation to do so.

The country has a ready-made financial services and supply chain infrastructure, and domestic companies are not bound by the cross-border restrictions US firms are subject to, given the US federal ban in place. Canada is a test case for other nations who are closely observing the impacts on public health, employment, and tax generation.

Legal background

2.02 Prime Minister Justin Trudeau's Liberal government announced in 2015 the intention to regulate the sale and use of cannabis, and a year later launched the Task Force on Marijuana Regulation and Legalization in 2016, led by former health and justice minister Anne McLellan.

Consultations with provincial, territorial, municipal and indigenous governments in Canada were held, and it was decided that total legalisation was the best option, and merely decriminalising cannabis would not work.[3]

Decriminalisation would not rid cannabis of the stigma of illegality, criminal sanctions would simply be replaced with other punishments, and dealers would have more incentive to sell openly, the task force concluded.

Prior to 2018, Canada's drug laws aligned with international agreements and cannabis was listed as a controlled substance in Schedule II to the Controlled Drugs and Substances Act. Individuals in possession of up to 30g of cannabis (without a medical exemption) risked a fine of up to CA$1,000 (US$758) and up to six months in jail.

Trafficking and producing cannabis carried more severe penalties. Approximately 53% of all drug offences in 2017 were for the possession and/or trafficking, production and distribution of cannabis, according to government statistics. In 2017, nearly 48,000 such offences were reported in Canada.

In April 2017, the government introduced Bill C-45[4] (the Cannabis Act) to legalise and regulate the production and sale of cannabis. The law received royal assent on 21 June 2018 and came into force on 17 October 2018.

Under the law, Canadians aged 18 and over can buy cannabis in provincially regulated retail stores or via mail. Adults can grow up to four cannabis plants at home, and to have up to 30g of dried cannabis (or the equivalent in non-dried form) in their possession in public. Growing at home for the purpose of selling to others is not allowed under the law.

Criminal offences for the sale of cannabis to young persons' carry penalties of up to 14 years in prison, along with penalties for the 'illicit' production, distribution and sale of cannabis.

On 14 June 2019, the new regulations for edible cannabis, cannabis extracts, and cannabis topicals were published in the Canada Gazette, Part II,[5] and entered into force on 17 October 2019.

They cover:

- Regulations Amending the Cannabis Regulations (New Classes of Cannabis);
- Order Amending Schedules 3 and 4 to the Cannabis Act;
- New Cannabis Tracking System Order.

The Cannabis Act did not set maximum THC potency levels; however, government research shows that current THC levels are around 12%–15%; more than quadrupling since the 1980s.

Regulation and monitoring

2.03 Canada's provinces and territorial governments are responsible for regulation of cannabis within their jurisdictions, and can vary the amounts individuals are allowed to hold or grow (Quebec forbids home-growing, for example[6]).

Each province and territory also has its own rules on the legal minimum age; where adults may buy it; where adults may use it, and how much adults may possess.

The provinces have powers to carry out inspections to determine compliance with relevant legislation and regulations, and share any relevant or necessary information with Health Canada or law enforcement.

Overall monitoring falls within the remit of Health Canada, the government's health ministry. Health Canada issues licences and has the power to businesses that are non-compliant with financial penalties or by revoking licenses and banning operators.

Medicinal cannabis

2.04 Canadians could legally access medicinal cannabis under Health Canada regulations established in 2001, and the recreational cannabis laws did not alter anything materially.

Following the introduction of the Cannabis Act, new regulations[7] replaced the Access to Cannabis for Medical Purposes Regulations (ACMPR) in Canada.

Patient access schemes were improved to allow individuals to buy directly from a federally licensed seller; by registering with Health Canada to produce a limited amount of cannabis for their own medical purposes, or designating someone to produce it for them.

Subject to the legal age limit in their province or territory, patients can buy cannabis at provincial or territorial authorised retail outlets, or through provincial or territorial-authorised online sales platforms

As of 2016, about 70,000 Canadians had registered with their health-care practitioner as medical-marijuana users.

Licensed users can grow marijuana for their own medical use or order it from one of approximately 116 licensed producers and have the drug posted to them.

In September 2019, Health Canada closed a consultation on the issue of individuals being able to purchase medicinal cannabis without first requiring a doctor's permission. The 'cannabis health products' in question, extend to sleep aids, or pain relief for muscle injuries. The purpose is to apply standards to the products and reduce the harm to vulnerable patients or the young by controlling the sale of such items.

Industrial hemp laws

2.05 Industrial hemp is cannabis that contains 0.3% THC or less in the flowering heads and leaves. The Industrial Hemp Regulations[8] under the Cannabis Act set out the requirements for cultivators of industrial hemp. Cultivators of industrial hemp must grow from the hemp varieties approved for commercial cultivation.[9]

While the Industrial Hemp Regulations are generally consistent with the previous rules under the Controlled Drugs and Substances Act, some alterations aligned licence requirements to the relatively low risk posed by industrial hemp as compared with other varieties of cannabis.

One of the updates is that the sale of hemp plants (flowers, leaves and branches) to licensed cannabis processors is now permitted, to provide a source of low-THC, high-cannabidiol (CBD) products.

Supply shortages

2.06 Retailers in Canada reported running low on supplies from the very first day of legalisation, and the shortage dragged on into late 2019.[10]

Health Canada said there had been enough cannabis grown to satisfy the country's demand, but it had been held up by 'logistical bottlenecks'.

Figure 1 Total Inventories and Sales – Dried Cannabis (kilograms)

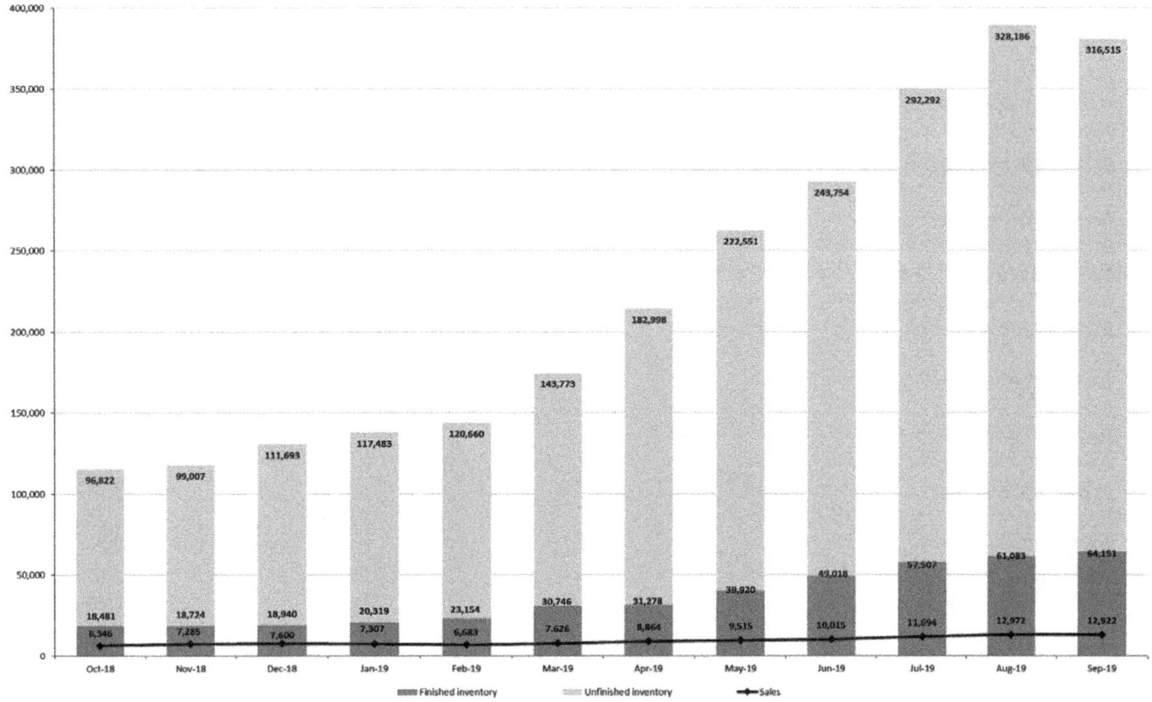

More than 85% of Canada's cannabis inventory is unfinished, meaning raw cannabis product that has not been processed, packaged and made ready to sell, and may never sell, either due to contamination or other factors. Licensed producers cannot sell it under law, but there is also no guidance on destroying it.

Health Canada acknowledges the supply issues are not down to the creation of the product, but rather with the production process itself.

What exactly is wrong with the production process is uncertain and industry experts point to producers not growing high enough volumes of quality cannabis that can be turned into dry cannabis, insufficient production facilities, or issues with shipping.[11]

John Fowler, president of Supreme Cannabis and vice-chair of the Cannabis Council of Canada, a cannabis business association, believes it is the growing pains of a new market:

> 'I think, overall, things have been working pretty well. Perhaps there was a lack of understanding of the complexity, not just regulatory complexity of license approvals, but just building the businesses and the supply chains to go from a market that literally didn't exist on October 17th.'

Fowler said every part of the industry was stretched, the licensing procedure was slow, and licenses to expand growing spaces, and packaging and equipment manufacturers are also being weighed down by a huge surge in demand.

Following a modest start, sales of recreational cannabis began to increase markedly and from October 2018 to July 2019 almost doubled.

Licensed store sales as recorded by Statistics Canada (price in $USD):

- October: $40.48m
- November: $40.52m
- December: $43.24m
- January: $41.39m
- February: $38.96m
- March: $45.96m
- April: $56.24m
- May: $64.71m
- June: $68.97m
- July: $78.80m

Recreational cannabis sales have totalled $519.27m since October 2018. Given the steady incline in sales, Canada's first trailing year of full legalisation will likely come in shy of $1bn, but most forecasts believe Canada will record around $5bn in annual sales within five years.

Consultants EY at said the Canadian sector could be worth $11bn by 2025. They feel increased competition will bring commodity prices down, and put even more pressure on producers to maximise output in the most cost-effective and efficient manner.

A 2019 survey conducted by the consultancy along with cannabis technology firm Lift & Co. estimates three million new consumers are likely to enter the Canadian market in the near future, which would make 20 per cent of the entire adult Canadian population customers.

Employment boom

2.07 The cannabis industry almost immediately become one of Canada's largest employers in its first year, with jobs nearly quadrupling in the past year, according to Statistics Canada. In August 2019, there were 9,200 people currently working in the Canadian cannabis sector, up from 2,630 in the fiscal 2018 year and 1,438 in 2017.

Of those jobs, about 60% were tasked with cultivation, harvesting, processing, manufacturing and administration duties. Another 20% were identified as working in packaging, marketing, and sales.

Marketing and branding

2.08 Given the excitement and the rush to market, Canadian businesses have found it a challenge to differentiate their products and establish their unique identities.

Health Canada restricts branding activities and is still reticent to allow new product forms/formulations. Most producers have concentrated on offering a variety of cannabis strains, with some also trying to create brands that register with consumers as 'premium' lifestyle products.

How consumers react to the sophisticated branding and marketing techniques employed by other consumer packaged goods companies[12] will also impact the evolution of the cannabis sector in the coming years.

Such is the size of the market at stake, there remains a risk certain firms are racing to become global corporations before they have established sustainable domestic businesses, which can cause compliance issues later on.

Export

2.09 The domestic market is so strong it is all but closed to outside firms, and now Canada's largest companies are stepping up overseas exports as they attempt to establish strongholds in emerging medical markets.

Shipments of dried cannabis tripled to 1,460kg (3,219lb) in 2018, compared with 500kg in 2017 and only 44kg in 2016.[13]

Canada currently ranks third in global exports of legal cannabis, behind the United Kingdom, where Sativex-maker GW Pharmaceuticals is based, and the Netherlands, where Bedrocan is headquartered.

From 2017 to 2019, Canada's firms fought each other to land one of the very few licenses handed out by the German government,[14] knowing that the European country's medicinal market alone would outstrip Canada's recreational and medicinal markets combined.

Germany, the largest and most important European market, has no capacity or experience growing its own cannabis for medicinal use, and will only look to established entities in the Netherlands or Canada for supply.

The scenes playing out in Germany are echoed all over Europe, Asia and Africa, as Canadian firm partner with local names to hoover up licences and get ahead of any regulatory adjustment.

International Treaty controversies

2.10 Canada is signed up to the three UN conventions on narcotic drug use, which oblige it to criminalise cannabis, amongst the other listed substances, for non-medical and non-scientific use.

The International Narcotics Control Board (INCB), tasked with monitoring adherence to the international laws, has twice criticised Canada for its violation of the Treaties. On passage of the Cannabis Act in October 2018, the INCB said Canada was 'undermining the rules-based international order'.[15]

In its 2018 annual report, the INCB also criticised apparent weaknesses in the Canadian medicinal cannabis system.

In a similar vein to the response penned by Uruguay, Richard Walker, a spokesperson for Canada's foreign ministry, said the legalisation did not weaken Canada's commitment to meeting the goals of the top UN drug conventions.

> 'Canada remains a strong supporter of the international drug control framework and will continue working with our international partners to advance the objectives of the drug control framework including through efforts to combat drug trafficking and to promote evidence-based solutions to mitigate the harms of problematic substance use.'

MEXICO

2.11 A regulated recreational cannabis market is imminent in Mexico, having been approved by legislators, and is likely to have become law by the time this book is published.[16]

The country's Supreme Court set a deadline of 24 October 2019, for the government to legalise recreational use of cannabis along with cultivation and sales, having ruled prohibition was unconstitutional earlier in the year.

Under Mexican law, if the Supreme Court issues the same decision five times, the rulings set a precedent and the court may order the establishment of a regulatory framework as well as further legal action.

Mexico would become the third country after Uruguay and Canada allow for the full legalisation of cannabis, overturning a federal prohibition law. The government launched a website to provide information for the public and to feedback on progress: https://cannabis.senado.gob.mx.

Several pieces of legislation aimed at legalising cannabis have already been introduced in the country, the government noted that, prior to any legislature acts on those proposals, committees:

> 'will initiate various legislative activities of open parliament … in order to know and listen to the opinions that they reflect the environment and the feeling of society with respect to such an important issue and, with that, contribute to obtaining a regulation according to the reality of our country.'

Mexico legalised medical cannabis in June 2017, but only imported cannabis derivatives with low-THC content were permitted, and medical products are still not readily available to patients. The possession of small amounts of marijuana for recreational use was decriminalised in 2009.

American drug war

2.12 Cannabis is a very popular social drug in Mexico, and for hundreds of years the plant was grown in the country for industrial hemp.[17]

When the US began to tax cannabis out of existence in the 1920s and put pressure on other countries to do so, Mexican drug laws moved in line, and hemp exports were banned in 1927.

A few abortive attempts at decriminalisation followed in the intervening decades, with the threat of US sanctions and embargoes enough of a deterrent for Mexico to rein in any liberalisation.

Mexico's drug war escalated throughout the 1980s and 1990s, and eventually in 2006, the army was called in to deal with the cartels.[18] The Mexican government has received billions of dollars in US funding over the course of the conflict, modernise security and to overhaul the legal system.

It has been a brutal and bloody war, with thousands of Mexicans, including politicians, students, and journalists, killed every year. The murder rate hit new heights in 2018 with more than 28,000 deaths linked to drug cartel activity.

A cornerstone of US President Donald Trump's election campaign and subsequent leadership has been criticism of the southern border, and the perceived failings of the physical barrier. Trump's administration is by no means the first to make these claims, however.

The legislation for cannabis-related substances (THC and CBD) in Mexico is the General Health Law, supplemented by guidelines and official norms published by or the Federal Committee for Protection from Sanitary Risks (Comisión Federal para la Protección contra Riesgos Sanitarios), the government department that deals with the importation of medical devices and issues advertising permits for these products.[19]

Medicinal cannabis

2.13 The Mexican Ministry of Health oversees medicinal cannabis regulation, but there is currently not much to regulate following a series of bureaucratic delays. Mexico began issuing medicinal cannabis identification cards in 2015, with regulations first expected to be in place by 2018.

It proposed to grant authority to the health body to design and execute policies aimed at regulating the production and use of medicinal products derived from cannabis, as well as the importation of cannabis-based medicines from abroad.

A law allowing the use of medical cannabis was signed in June 2017, but by 2019 products were still unavailable in pharmacies.

The country intended to rely on imported cannabis derivatives with low-THC content. Currently, only one company exports cannabis to Mexico, and commercial cultivation within the country is illegal.

On 14 August 2019, Mexico's Supreme Court stepped in and ordered the Mexican Health Ministry to issue regulations for marijuana 'within six months'.[20] It chastised the government for putting ill children at risk.

Recreational legalisation

2.14 In August 2009, a rule was enacted to decriminalise small amounts of recreational cannabis.[21] Later, between 2015 and 2018, the Supreme Court issued a series of rulings repealing various restrictions on the use of cannabis for recreational purposes. Ten bills to legalise cannabis have been put forward in Mexico's parliament in the last handful of years without success.

The most significant update occurred in 2018 when the Supreme Court ruled the ban on recreational cannabis violated free expression.[22] Under Mexican law, the Supreme Court must make five rulings on the issue to ensure it is binding across all courts, as occurred in this case.

The Supreme Court deadline for the government to comply with its ruling was 24 October 2019.

'The end of the prohibitionist policy is good for the country,' said Sen. Ricardo Monreal, the leader of Lopez Obrador's MORENA party in the upper chamber of Congress. He told Reuters that the bill would regulate personal use and sale of marijuana as well as research into the plant. It also contemplates creation of cooperatives that would grow marijuana plus a new regulatory agency.[23]

In mid-October, lawmakers unveiled the draft plan – a week before the court's deadline.

Here are some of the key points, according to a translation:[24]

- Adults aged 18 and older could possess cannabis for personal use, cultivate up to four plants and purchase marijuana from licensed retailers.
- An independent body called the 'Cannabis Institute' would regulate licensing, set potency limits and monitor the implementation of the law, among other responsibilities.
- Low-income individuals, small farmers and indigenous people would have licensing priority.
- Cannabis packaging would be nondescript, with containers that did not feature depictions of real or fictional people or testimonials.
- Cannabis could only be consumed in private spaces.
- Only medical cannabis patients would be allowed to purchase infused edibles and beverages.
- Unregistered seeds or plants could be seized by police.
- No pesticides could be used on cannabis plants.

The Bill seeks to:

> 'improve the living conditions of people living in the United Mexican States, combat the consequences of the problematic use of cannabis and reduce the crime incidence linked to drug trafficking [while] promoting peace, the security and well-being of individuals and communities.'

UNITED STATES

2.15 Cannabis is a controlled substance under US federal law, and it is illegal for individuals to produce, hold or sell, for any purpose, per the Controlled Substances Act of 1970. This law classifies cannabis as a Schedule I narcotic, with no recognised medical use, and with a high potential for abuse.

The US at federal level is aligned with international drug treaty laws that require countries to treat cannabis as an illegal narcotic that can only be used for scientific or medical purposes with strict approval.

At a state level the story is very different, however, and as of October 2019, recreational cannabis has been legalised in 11 states; Alaska, California, Colorado, Illinois, Maine, Massachusetts, Michigan, Nevada, Oregon, Vermont, and Washington.

At time of writing, 15 states have decriminalised cannabis, and a handful are going through public votes to loosen laws even further. By the time of publication more US states may indicate an intention to decriminalise, or open medicinal or even fully regulated recreational regimes.

Currently, 33 states permit individuals to obtain medical cannabis through a doctor.

The following chart shows the state-by-state picture of cannabis laws in the US, breaking out the recreational and medicinal status of each, decriminalisation information, along with the years where appropriate, and links to either the regulations and regulator, or latest status where applicable.

State	Recreational status	Medicinal cannabis	Decriminalised	State laws and more information
Alabama	Illegal	No	No	https://www.bamapolitics.com/alabama/bills/2019rs/sb/sb-236/
Alaska	Legal (2014)	Yes (1998)	Yes (1975)	https://www.commerce.alaska.gov/web/amco/marijuanaregulations.aspx
Arizona	Mixed	Yes (2010)	No	https://www.azdhs.gov/licensing/medical-marijuana/index.php#faqs-dispensary
Arkansas	Mixed	Yes (2016)	No	https://www.mmc.arkansas.gov/application
California	Legal (2016)	Yes (1996)	Yes (1975)	https://cannabis.ca.gov/laws-regulations/
Colorado	Legal (2012)	Yes (2000)	Yes (1975)	https://www.colorado.gov/marijuana
Connecticut	Mixed	Yes (2011)	Reduced	https://portal.ct.gov/DCP/Medical-Marijuana-Program/Medical-Marijuana-Program
Delaware	Mixed	Yes (2011)	Reduced	https://dhss.delaware.gov/dph/hsp/medmarhome.html
District of Columbia	Legal (2014)	Yes (2013)	Yes (2014)	https://mpdc.dc.gov/marijuana
Florida	Mixed	Yes (2016)	No	https://www.flgov.com/2019/03/18/governor-desantis-signs-medical-marijuana-bill-and-files-joint-motion-to-dismiss-states-appeal-and-vacate-lower-court-decision/
Georgia	Mixed	CBD Oil	No	http://www.legis.ga.gov/Legislation/en-US/display/20192020/HB/324

(continued)

(Continued)

State	Recreational status	Medicinal cannabis	Decriminalised	State laws and more information
Hawaii	Mixed	Yes (2000)	Reduced* (pending)	https://health.hawaii.gov/medicalcannabisregistry/general-information/marijuana-laws-and-related-documents/
Idaho	Illegal	No	No	https://idahonews.com/news/local/medical-marijuana-petition-filed-for-2020-idaho-ballot
Illinois	Legal* (pending)	Yes (2013)	Yes* (pending)	https://www2.illinois.gov/IISNews/20242-Summary_of_HB_1438__The_Cannabis_Regulation_and_Tax_Act.pdf
Indiana	Mixed	CBD Oil	No	http://iga.in.gov/legislative/2018/bills/senate/52#document-6a10d137
Iowa	Mixed	CBD Oil	No	https://idph.iowa.gov/omc/For-Patients-and-Caregivers
Kansas	Illegal	No	No	https://www.khi.org/policy/article/19-24
Kentucky	Mixed	CBD Oil	No	https://apps.legislature.ky.gov/record/19RS/hb136.html
Louisiana	Mixed	Yes (2015)	No	http://cityofno.granicus.com/MetaViewer.php?view_id=3&clip_id=2288&meta_id=318863
Maine	Legal (2016)	Yes (1999)	Yes (1975)	https://legislature.maine.gov/lawlibrary/recreational_marijuana_in_maine/9419
Maryland	Mixed	Yes (2003)	Reduced	https://www.marylandcannabispolicy.org/files/2019/MD%20Bill%20Summary%202019.pdf
Massachusetts	Legal (2016)	Yes (2012)	Yes (1996)	https://www.mass.gov/info-details/massachusetts-law-about-marijuana-possession#news-
Michigan	Legal (2018)	Yes (2008)	Yes (2018)	https://www.michigan.gov/documents/lara/Adult_Use_Marihuana_Establishments_659804_7.pdf
Minnesota	Mixed	Yes (2014)	Reduced (1976)	https://www.health.state.mn.us/people/cannabis/
Mississippi	Illegal	No	Reduced	https://www.medicalmarijuana2020.com
Missouri	Mixed	Yes (2019)	Reduced (2014)	https://health.mo.gov/safety/medical-marijuana/rules.php
Montana	Mixed	Yes (2004)	No	https://dphhs.mt.gov/marijuana
Nebraska	Illegal	No	Reduced	https://nebraskalegislature.gov/bills/view_bill.php?DocumentID=37628
Nevada	Legal (2016)	Yes (2000)	Yes (2001)	http://marijuana.nv.gov

(continued)

(Continued)

State	Recreational status	Medicinal cannabis	Decriminalised	State laws and more information
New Hampshire	Mixed	Yes (2013)	Reduced	http://gencourt.state.nh.us/bill_status/Results.aspx?q=1&txtbillnumber=hb481&txtsessionyear=2019
New Jersey	Mixed	Yes (2010)	No	https://www.njleg.state.nj.us/2018/Bills/A0500/20_I1.HTM
New Mexico	Mixed	Yes (2007)	Reduced (1978)	https://www.nmlegis.gov/Legislation/Legislation?Chamber=S&LegType=B&LegNo=323&year=19
New York	Mixed	Yes (2014)	Reduced (1977)	https://www.health.ny.gov/regulations/medical_marijuana/
North Carolina	Illegal	No	Reduced	https://www.arnoldsmithlaw.com/decriminalization-of-marijuana.html
North Dakota	Mixed	Yes (2016)	Reduced (2019)	https://www.ncagr.gov/hemp/
Ohio	Mixed	Yes (2016)	Reduced	https://www.medicalmarijuana.ohio.gov
Oklahoma	Mixed	Yes (2018)	No	http://webserver1.lsb.state.ok.us/cf_pdf/2019-20%20SUPPORT%20DOCUMENTS/BILLSUM/House/SB1030%20CCR%20A%20BILLSUM.PDF
Oregon	Legal (2014)	Yes (1998)	Yes (1973)	https://www.oregon.gov/olcc/marijuana/pages/default.aspx
Pennsylvania	Mixed	Yes (2016)	No	https://www.legis.state.pa.us/cfdocs/billinfo/billinfo.cfm?syear=2019&sind=0&body=H&type=B&bn=1899
Rhode Island	Mixed	Yes (2006)	Reduced (2012)	http://www.health.ri.gov/healthcare/medicalmarijuana/
South Carolina	Illegal	No	No	https://www.scstatehouse.gov/billsearch.php?billnumbers=3660&session=123&summary=B
South Dakota	Illegal	No	No	https://www.marijuanamoment.net/former-federal-prosecutors-marijuana-legalization-measure-advances-in-south-dakota/
Tennessee	Illegal	No	No	https://www.tmcta.com
Texas	Mixed	CBD Oil	No	https://guides.sll.texas.gov/cannabis
Utah	Mixed	Yes (2014)	No	https://medicalcannabis.utah.gov
Vermont	Legal (2018)	Yes (2004)	Yes (2013)	https://legislature.vermont.gov/statutes/section/18/084/04230
Virginia	Mixed	CBD Oil (2017)	No	https://law.lis.virginia.gov/vacode/title18.2/chapter7/section18.2-250.1/
Washington	Legal (2012)	Yes (1998)	Yes	https://lcb.wa.gov/mj-education/know-the-law

(continued)

(Continued)

State	Recreational status	Medicinal cannabis	Decriminalised	State laws and more information
West Virginia	Mixed	Yes (2017)	No	https://dhhr.wv.gov/bph/Pages/Medical-Cannabis-Program.aspx
Wisconsin	Illegal	No	No	https://www.wisconsinwatch.org/series/cannabis-question/
Wyoming	Illegal	No	No	https://legiscan.com/WY/bill/HB0171/2019

South Dakota was the only state to record no forward progress on cannabis policies in 2019. The state lacks a medical cannabis, decriminalisation, and legalisation law, and no legislator put forth a proposal to improve marijuana policies in 2019. While the legislature did pass a hemp bill in 2019, governor Kristi Noem (R) vetoed the measure, and the legislature could not obtain the votes to overturn. South Dakota does not permit the non-psychoactive CBD, which all states other than Idaho allow in some form, except in products that are FDA-approved. According to Karen O'Keefe, director of state policies at the Marijuana Policy Project lobby group:

> 'The Mount Rushmore State is also the only state that criminalises 'internal possession' — meaning a person could legally use cannabis in Canada, but face jail time if they test positive in South Dakota. However, change may be on the horizon: South Dakota is one of the 23 states with the ballot initiative process, meaning voters could take matters into their own hands in 2020.'

Pendulum swing

2.16 The United States has a complex history in regard to its relationship with cannabis, and only in recent years has it moved away from the draconian prohibition stance it takes not just at home, but forces on others internationally.

The Marihuana Tax Act of 1937 was one of the first attempts to regulate cannabis, although steps to outlaw public consumption in the US have been recorded as far back as 1906.

Post-Second World War, the US was the driving force behind the UN treaty agreements, and the Conventions have their roots in US drug laws. It considered cannabis a dangerous narcotic, and demanded it be banned around the world even in areas which it had been grown and used freely for thousands of years, such as Southern Asia.

Decriminalisation domestically began in Texas in the early 1970s, but the most significant date and arguably the point at which the genie emerged from the bottle was 7 November 2012.

On that day, voters in Washington and Colorado approved the first two laws in the US to end prohibition and legally regulate cannabis production, distribution and sales.

The watershed moment was marked with wild celebrations that stretched way beyond both states as campaigners across the US acknowledged 'the beginning of the end' for prohibition.

By December 2012, cannabis possession and use by adults 21 years of age and older was legal in Washington, and a year-and-a-half later, the first retail marijuana stores opened their doors, on 8 July 2014.

During 2014, the first year of implementation of Colorado Amendment 64,[25] Colorado's legal marijuana market (comprising both medical and recreational) reached total sales of $700m.[26]

Since that date, nine more US states have opened recreational markets. Illinois is the latest, with business due to begin 1 January 2020.

Medicinal cannabis

2.17 California was the first US state to pass laws approving medicinal cannabis through Proposition 215, or the Compassionate Use Act of 1996. It allowed the use of medical cannabis despite the lack of the normal Food and Drug Administration (FDA) testing for safety and efficacy. California's medicinal cannabis laws have been updated three times since 1996.[27]

There are currently 33 US states with medicinal cannabis laws. The allowable concentration of THC, the main psychoactive component of cannabis, varies from state to state. The laws were enacted to allow for the use of cannabidiol (CBD), a non-psychoactive cannabinoid effective in the treatment of seizure disorders, particularly in children. Currently 14 states are considered to have low-THC, high-CBD laws. The THC content peaks at 5% in some states such as Georgia, Virginia, and Kansas.

In June 2018, the FDA approved Epidiolex, a CBD oral solution for the treatment of seizures associated with two rare and severe forms of epilepsy, Lennox-Gastaut syndrome and Dravet syndrome, in patients two years-of-age and older.

It was the first FDA-approved drug that contains a purified drug substance derived from marijuana.

Regulatory arbitrage

2.18 Cannabis companies operating in the US rely heavily on state-specific regulations, they are forbidden from conducting cross-border trade due to the federal ban. According to Chris Barry, of counsel at Dorsey & Whitney, head of the firm's Canada cross-border practice group and co-chair of the firm's cannabis practice group:

> 'Although the trend in some states has been a process of liberalisation (eg, Colorado has slowly relaxed some of its geographic prohibitions related to investment in or ownership of cannabis companies), new regulations often take months or longer to come out. So, what may be prohibited now could quickly become permissible as states issue new regulations to better balance the need of serving the industry and addressing valid public safety and other concerns.'

Guidance for businesses

2.19 Licensed cannabis businesses in Colorado and Washington, for example, cannot be publicly-traded companies, nor can they have public-traded owners, Barry said:

> 'A variety of structures have been developed to allow investors to participate in financing the industry in these states without owning an equity interest in a cannabis business.'

Other jurisdictions, such as California, Nevada, Oregon and others, do not restrict foreign ownership of licensed cannabis businesses or ownership by public companies, but certain county or city regulations may limit or forbid foreign ownership.

Due to the federal restrictions, companies have reported significant problems acquiring or maintaining bank accounts in the US.

The Financial Crimes Enforcement Network (FinCEN) provided guidance on February 14, 2014[28] about how financial institutions can provide services to cannabis-related businesses consistent with their Bank Secrecy Act obligations (BSA).

The SAFE Banking Act, sometimes referred to as the Marijuana Banking Bill, may be on its way to becoming federal law, which would ease some of the banking problems referred to. We discuss this in greater detail in our Americas chapter wrap.

The legislation wouldn't change the legal status of cannabis under federal law, but the bill would ensure marijuana businesses can open accounts, take out loans, accept credit cards and deposit money into banks without repercussions from the federal government.

The patchwork of individual state laws promises an enormous compliance burden for any business hoping to become major domestic players in the US market should full legalisation one day occur, and it is the hope of many that federal guidance will standardise as much as possible.

According to US Cannabis Pharmaceutical Research and Development (USCPRD) chief executive Michael Patterson:

> 'Every US state is like a different country, the rules and laws are very different. For example, flower is allowed in Pennsylvania, but it's illegal in New York State where only oil products are permitted, and yet they are both medical cannabis states.
>
> 'Also, Oklahoma has a medical marijuana program and allows for unlimited licenses to own a marijuana operation (cultivate, process, dispense). It currently has over 6,500 licensed marijuana business. A total contrast is Florida, which has strict limit on the number of licenses marijuana businesses.
>
> 'There are currently about 300,000 patients and only 22 licensed marijuana businesses in Florida, which is a medical cannabis state. 'A licence in Florida is worth around $50m, while an Oklahoma licence is worth around $5000.'

The Farm Bill and emerging standards

2.20 In 2020, a number of trends are emerging that will help to shape the US cannabis industry into a more corporate, standardised sector. These include more stringent laboratory testing laws, sustainability and environmentally-focused rules, and further taxation.

The Farm Bill 2018,[29] which passed in December 2018, is viewed as a precursor for future recreational laws that appear from the federal government. The Bill standardised guidance for hemp and all of its constituent components such as CBD, ensuring they became broadly lawful throughout the US.

Under the Bill, hemp cannot contain more than 0.3% THC, per section 10113. Any cannabis plant that contains more than 0.3% THC would be considered non-hemp cannabis under federal law and would thus face no legal protection under the law.

There are also significant, shared state-federal regulatory powers over hemp cultivation and production. Under section 10113 of the Farm Bill, state departments of agriculture must consult with the state's governor and chief law enforcement officer to draft a plan that must be submitted to the Secretary of the United States Department of Agriculture (USDA).

A state's plan to license and regulate hemp can only commence once the Secretary of USDA approves that state's plan. USDA will construct a regulatory program for states that do not draw up their own, under which hemp cultivators in those states must apply for licences and comply with a federally-run program.

This system of shared regulatory programming is similar to other areas such as health insurance marketplaces, or workplace safety plans, both of which had federally-run systems for states opting not to set up their own systems.

The Farm Bill also addressed actions that are considered violations of federal hemp law (including such activities as cultivating without a license or producing cannabis with more than 0.3% THC). The law details possible punishments for such violations, pathways for violators to become compliant, and even which activities qualify as felonies under the law, such as repeated offences.

'What the federal government does in other sectors is put in public safety standards,' said Patterson. 'There are nursing homes in all 50 states, for example, but there is a federal standard then a state standard. You must follow whichever is the most stringent. I think this is what we will see with cannabis.'

Also, according to Patterson:

> 'In terms of physically selling the product, I think we can expect what we see now with alcohol. The federal government won't get involved so much in how you sell it, how many stores you open or how many licences, but they will have the basics such as background checks for anyone that has a licence.'

There has also been talk of a federal cannabis tax on sales of around 2%.

> 'This is happening with the hemp sector. The government set a federal rule of how it would work, and then rolled out guidelines, so make sure you are aligned with the most stringent aspects.'

The US Food and Drug Administration (FDA) are expected to draw up regulatory standards in regard to laboratory testing of cannabis products and cleanliness of labs.

Toward the end of 2019, panic swept over the vaping sector when the FDA warned consumers[30] not to purchase or use any vaporisers that contain THC following an outbreak of vaping-related illnesses and reported deaths.

> 'The vape crisis is going to have a knock-on effect, but we were already seeing movement in terms of standards and accountability. Tougher laboratory testing regulations are the number one issue that states are moving towards; either updating their rules or converting their old ones. Colorado is updating its requirements, for example, and they were one of the first states to go recreational.'

Colorado regulators required medical and recreational marijuana concentrates to be tested for mycotoxins as of 15 September 2019. The state's Marijuana Enforcement Division sent a notice to the industry that any concentrates made from marijuana on or after that date that failed microbial contaminant testing will be tested for mycotoxins.[31]

Public support

2.21 Gallup has recorded four consecutive years in which support on the measure to legalise cannabis in the US has increased. The polling company has documented a sharp increase in the percentage of Americans favouring legal marijuana in the past decade, from 44% in 2009 to 64% in the current survey.

Gallup has measured support as high as 66% in an October 2018 update; in 1969, the first time Gallup polled on the issue, just 12% were in favour of legalising marijuana.

In June 2019, Gallup found 86% of US residents backed legal marijuana saying its medicinal benefits were the main reason they supported legalisation. Freeing up police resources to focus on other crimes, respecting people's personal freedom, and generating tax revenue for state and local governments were other key reasons for their support.

Opponents, though smaller in number, point more to the societal risks, including those related to car accidents and the gateway nature of cannabis leading to harder drugs for those types of users susceptible to addiction.

The US states which have legalised recreational cannabis have done so on the back of public votes. More states are considering making recreational use legal through either the legislative process or voter referendums. Also, nearly every Democratic 2020 presidential candidate is in favour of full legalisation.

The trends in public policy are consistent with public opinion on the issue, and point towards a fully-legal federal market in the near future.

International drug treaty controversy

2.22 Unlike its neighbours Canada and Uruguay, the US has not been the subject of any statements directly criticising its tolerance of non-medical cannabis in its borders from the United Nations' International Narcotics Control Board's (INCB).

Instead, the Board, which is responsible for monitoring adherence to international drug treaties including the 1961 Single Convention on Narcotic Drugs, saved its barbs for an attack on the US medical marijuana laws in its 2018 annual report.

The INCB said the programmes were weak, testing was poor, and that an increase in medicinal cannabis availability would inevitably lead to non-medicinal use and abuse in young people.

Next steps

2.23 The modern era of prohibition began with the US, and it may be that Washington DC heralds the end of it too. Canada's legalisation project is young but has been viewed largely as successful, and now Mexico stands on the brink of reform. As industrious as the US is, it will not want to fall too far behind its neighbours given cannabis is a genuine 'home-grown' made-in-the-US opportunity.

The passage of the Farm Bill has been widely viewed as a federal endorsement of the US cannabis sector and an indicator that acceptance and expansion of the marketplace is imminent. The wheels of Congress move slowly however, and there is no rush to regulate despite the current levels of hype and excitement.

Towards the end of 2019, the House of Representatives passed its version of the SAFE Banking Act, which would give cannabis companies access to the US banking system including retail banking, credit card processing and access to institutional lending.

Lobby groups are doing all they can to force the Bill through – an NCIA spokesman said:

> 'In addition to broad reforms, the National Cannabis Industry Association supports the Secure and Fair Enforcement (SAFE) Banking Act, bipartisan legislation that would provide safe harbour to financial institutions doing business with the state-legal cannabis industry. No matter where one stands on the broader issue of marijuana legalisation, it's clear that nobody benefits when much of our nation's existing $10bn+ legal cannabis industry is forced to operate outside the banking system.'

In October 2019, Bank of New York Mellon Corp (BNY), one of the largest custody and clearing banks in the world, announced it would stop accepting positions or trading with US marijuana-related businesses. This restricts trading of large cannabis companies that are listed on Canadian exchanges, but have US operations. Canadian-listed firms without US operations can still be traded.

A US company that employs North Americans and provides legal cannabis products to North Americans must publicly list its shares on the Canadian Securities Exchange.

US retail investors must execute cross-border trades in order to invest in cannabis stocks with all of the capital and fees flowing away from Wall Street to Bay Street in Toronto. The oversight of US exchanges and securities laws does not apply.

The move by BNY is an indicator large US banks are still not comfortable dealing with cannabis businesses, despite the guidance they have been given.

ARGENTINA

2.24 Argentina's population is pro-cannabis, but a series of vague rule modifications have vexed users of both recreational and medicinal marijuana. The country's top court ruled a decade ago that prohibition was unconstitutional in the case of individuals who hold a small amount, but subsequent legal reforms to clarify the wording of the law have stuttered.

The country's medicinal cannabis regime was announced three years ago and has almost ground to a halt following political and legislative deliberations. It is hoped that through 2020 relations between regulator and cannabis businesses can improve.

Neither situation has done much to stem Argentina's black-market trade.

Legal background

2.25 The Argentine senate approved the use of cannabis oils in medicines, via unanimous vote in March 2017.[32] The wording of the law took two years to thrash out before it was eventually published in the *Official Gazette.*[33]

Argentine cannabis supporters have said while the law is supposed to guarantee that the state oversee the import and supply of medicinal cannabis, as well as promoting the domestic production and research, none of this had occurred by late 2019.

The government granted regulatory oversight to the National Agricultural Technology Institute (INASE), a federal extension agency, to authorise companies to cultivate, diffuse, handle, distribute and import cannabis.

INTA, which shares regulatory duties with the Ministry of Security, did not begin any cultivation for two years, reported *El Tribuo.*[34]

The regulations state any company engaged in cannabis cultivation must appoint a technical manager to report how much is produced to the government. This individual must be a scientist with a background in agriculture or plant-based research.

It also states that a fine of up to 100,000 pesos ($2,421) will be handed out to anyone that breaches the regulations. INASE can carry out unannounced inspections on any cannabis production operation to check their compliance.

Medicinal cannabis has also proved difficult for patients to access even with the latest ruling. Home-growing remains a crime and carries a hefty penalty of up to 15 years in jail under Argentina's drug laws.

Recreational cannabis and personal freedom

2.26 Cannabis was decriminalised for individuals holding 'small amounts' in 2009. The Narcotic Drugs Law 23.737,[35] which has been in force since 1989, replaced Law 20.771 of 1974, the country's first specific law on psychoactive substances. The law was broadly similar to its predecessor, but also raised the length of prison sentences to between 4 and 15 years.

It also made possession for personal use an offence punishable with jail time.

In 2009, a Supreme Court judgment known as the Arriola Ruling[36] declared that it was unconstitutional to enforce the second paragraph of Article 14 of 1989 Law 23.737, namely:

> 'The prison sentence will range from one month to two years when the small quantity of the drug and other circumstances suggest unequivocally that possession is for personal use.'

The Supreme Court ruled that possession of small quantities of marijuana for personal use is protected by Article 19 of Argentina's Constitution, which states:

> 'private actions that in no way offend public order or morality, nor are detrimental to a third party, are reserved for God and are beyond the authority of legislators.'

'The state cannot establish morality,' said Argentine Supreme Court President Ricardo Lorenzetti. He added that private behaviour is legal 'as long as it doesn't constitute clear danger.'

In April 2016, the government announced that it would send a bill to Congress that would amend Law 23737 to set clear limits and amounts on drugs for purposes of establishing personal use, to clear up confusion created by the Arriola decision.[37]

The unanimous (58:0) vote paved the way for patient access to cannabis oil and ended the ban on importing the plant. The country's Congress approved the move in late 2016, however reform is still pending.

Foreign investment

2.27 Despite the frequent revisions to the laws and general air of uncertainty, Canada's Aphria and Player's Network of Nevada in the US became the first major international companies to enter the Argentinian market in 2018.

Aphria is the exclusive supplier to the Argentinian medicinal cannabis market, and has set out plans to cultivate domestically.

Player's Network announced a partnership with Cannava SE to cultivate 15 hectares of land in Argentina's Jujuy Province. The same day INASE published the new cultivation guidelines, Player's Network announced approval from the Argentinian government to import seeds to their cultivation plot in Jujuy. The Nevada firm is the only international firm to receive such permission.

BERMUDA

2.28 Cannabis was decriminalised in Bermuda in 2017 following a vote in the house to allow persons to hold under 7g without being arrested.[38]

The Misuse of Drugs (Decriminalisation of Cannabis) Amendment Act, tabled by Zane DeSilva, the Minister of Social Development and Sport, was voted through.[39] A campaign was quickly launched to explain to citizens and tourists it was not OK to start smoking marijuana in public.

The Ministry of Labour, Community Affairs and Sport said:

> 'It is very important to recognize that cannabis remains a controlled drug under the Misuse of Drugs Act 1972. The Misuse of Drugs (Decriminalisation of Cannabis) Amendment Act 2017 does NOT legalize the use of cannabis in Bermuda. What the Misuse of Drugs (Decriminalisation of Cannabis) Amendment Act 2017 actually did, was to remove criminal offences for the simple possession by any person of 7 grams or less of cannabis.
>
> 'The Misuse of Drugs (Decriminalisation of Cannabis) Amendment Act 2017 does NOT make it legal for a person to consume, cultivate, traffic or import cannabis in any quantity.
>
> 'The benefit of the decriminalisation of cannabis is that a person cannot be subjected to criminal prosecution for simple possession of 7g or less of cannabis. It is our hope and our belief that taking this important action will help to prevent more young black men from being placed on the proverbial 'stop list' and have their lives completely altered by virtue of not being able to travel to the United States to pursue further education or to seek other opportunities.'

Bermuda is moving forward with reforms to its medicinal cannabis controls. Doctors can prescribe medical cannabis, but the country has no domestic supply and has not bid to raise its International Narcotics Control Board import quota from the current 1g.

Local patients have limited options, and the matter has been brought up in court.[40]

Bermuda's government has been in talks with Canadian firms such as Canopy Growth to discuss how to create a domestic cultivation programme.

BRAZIL

2.29 Brazil's prisons are so overcrowded that deadly riots are a frequent occurrence, with gang activity over drug trafficking at the centre of the violence. The government is attempting to take action, and the current hard-right ruling party has promised greater penalties for even minor drug offences.

Brazil does not want to be viewed as going soft on cannabis; however, this position is in contrast to most of its Latin American neighbours and pressure is building from the public, and the health-care sector to better support medicinal cannabis following moves in 2018 to legalise it.

Legal background

2.30 Possession and cultivation of cannabis for private use, in small amounts, was decriminalised by Drug Law 11.343,[41] which passed on August 23, 2006, but a number of restrictions to access still apply.

Cultivating large amounts, selling or transporting is classed as trafficking and carries a jail term of between 5 and 15 years.

Brazil legalised CBD for therapeutic use in January 2015,[42] but the matter has not been straightforward.

In November 2018, Brazilian lawmakers approved a bill to allow the use and cultivation of marijuana for medical purposes. It came about in response to an online petition that received about 119,000 votes calling for the removal of criminal penalties for growing, possessing and consuming cannabis for patients who receive prescriptions from doctors.

In 2019, two public consultations were held as legislators sought to further alter the cannabis laws to better support the medicinal side and cut harm to the public.

On 14 June 2019, ANVISA (the Brazilian Health Regulatory Agency) sought an opinion on the technical and administrative requirements for cultivating cannabis for medicinal and scientific purposes.

Henrique Frizzo, a partner in Trench Rossi Watanabe law firm in Brazil, said:

> 'According to the draft, the cultivation of the plant must, along with other access control guarantees, be done indoors and behind security doors accessible through biometrics. The draft also provides that the cultivation can only be done by legal entities that receive special authorisation from ANVISA.'

The second consultation, from the same agency, outlined the specific procedures for registering and monitoring drugs based on cannabis, its derivatives, and its synthetic analogues. Also according to Frizzo:

> 'The draft establishes, among other regulations, that the initial product registration will be valid for three years. Before the drug can then be renewed, companies will have to report the benefits and risks of the drug to ANVISA.'

Next steps

2.31 According to Fernanda Quental, a partner at Daniel Law in Brazil:

> 'Recently, on September 26 2019, the Federal Senate approved the suggestion No. 6/2016 (about The Use of Cannabis for Medicinal Purpose) from Human Rights Committee and Participative Legislation which was converted to a legislative proposal and will follow an analysis by the National Congress. Suggestion No. 6/2016 proposes a comprehensive regulatory standard for medical marijuana and industrial hemp in Brazil.'

President of the Supreme Court of Justice, Justice Dias Toffoli, admitted a 'writ of certiorari' to decide a case that involves the judicial review of the decriminalisation of possession of cannabis, limited to 25g of marijuana for citizens aged over 18.

The judgment session was initially scheduled for 5 June 2019 but was postponed, and the landmark case is expected to have been decided by the time of publication.

CHILE

2.32 Drug reform in Chile has been progressive since 2005, and accelerated under former president Michelle Bachelet, who served between 2014 and 2018.

In 2015, Bachelet signed a decree that removed cannabis from the list of 'hard drugs' as defined under law.[43] The decree also enabled the sale of cannabis-derived medicines at pharmacies. Planting, selling and transporting marijuana remains illegal in Chile and carries prison terms of five to ten years.

The current drug legislation pertaining to recreational use is contained in Law 20.000,[44] which was enacted in February 2005 and later reformed in 2007. It replaced 1995's Law 19.366, which criminalised the illicit trafficking of narcotics and psychotropic substances.

Law 20.000 allows for the personal consumption of any recreational drug, while penalising consumption that occurs in groups. It does not establish a threshold for the permitted quantities, and the distinction between trafficking and consumption is decided by a judge.

Recreational cannabis is in effect decriminalised in Chile, and the drug remains very popular.

In regard to medicinal cannabis, the relevant legislation is contained in Supreme Decrees No 404/1983 (Narcotics Regulation), No 405/1983 (Psychotropic Products Regulation) and No 84/2015 (amends the foregoing decrees).

Under the decrees, the Chilean Ministry of Health authorises the use of cannabis, cannabis resin, extracts and cannabis tinctures, including the manufacture of pharmaceuticals for human use. Additional oversight is carried out by the Chilean Public Health Institute.

According to José Andrés Pascual, a partner in Chilean law firm Prieto:

> 'The laws establish that pharmaceutical specialities containing cannabis, cannabis resin, cannabis extracts and tinctures may be dispensed to the public in pharmacies or laboratories by means of a medical prescription obtained with control of existence.
>
> 'A bill of law related to the legalisation of self-cultivation of cannabis for private consumption is currently under discussion before the Chilean Congress, but there is no urgency attached to it, and it is not likely to attract attention any time soon.'

COLOMBIA

2.33 Colombia is notorious for its standing as one of the world's top producers of illegal drugs,[45] but an attempt to 'go straight' with legalised cannabis cultivation is stumbling due to the opposing stances of successive governments and a restrictive regulatory regime.

In October 2018, Colombia's newly elected right-wing president, Iván Duque attempted to retreat from 25 years of tolerance by signing an executive decree that banned personal cultivation, and gave police power to confiscate and fine for personal possession of medical marijuana.

Duque claimed that it was his 'moral duty' given the 'devastating effects on health and society', but the decree went against several measures the country had drawn up over the past quarter of a century.

A year later, Colombia's Constitutional Court ruled against Duque's Police Code, deeming it unconstitutional as it violated citizens' fundamental rights instead of protecting public and children's safety.

Colombia's ideal climate and expert farming community has made it a target for large Canadian firms who consider it a key strategic export base.

Legal background

2.34 The anti-drug policies of the United States throughout the 20th century had a huge impact on Colombian legislation, as politicians sought favour with Washington DC.

In 1994 the Constitutional Court ruled in favour of decriminalising the personal use of cannabis in Colombia, and for the last 25 years, numerous attempts have been made unsuccessfully to reverse the ruling.

Law 30 of 1986,[46] known as the National Narcotics Statute (Estatuto Nacional de Estupefacientes - ENE), is currently in force. In September 2012, the executive presented a proposal for a new national statute on drugs and psychoactive substances, which would replace Law 30 if approved in parliament.

The law's restrictive stance toward drug use underwent a significant alteration with the pronouncement of Constitutional Court Ruling C-221 on 5 May 1994.[47]

The ruling said articles of Law 30 from 1986 that made it an offence to carry or use minimum permitted doses of drugs were unenforceable. As a result, Colombia was a pioneer in establishing a legal framework that offered an alternative to the total prohibition of drugs.

In 2009, proposals to reform the constitution to prohibit drug use were floated, but without the possibility of imposing punishments or compulsory treatment on drug users.

The Citizen Security Law of 2011[48] updated the Criminal Code to remove the exceptional provision of not punishing the crime of drug possession if the quantity carried was equivalent to a personal dose.

The Public Prosecutor's Office protested, but the waiver of punishment for possession of a minimum dose was upheld.

In its ruling C-491 in 2012, the Constitutional Court clarified that possession of the personal amount remains decriminalised and that drug use should continue to be understood as an activity protected by the right to the free development of personality.[49]

The Citizen Security Law has, however, led to much confusion and uncertainty. Although the 2009 reform only mentions administrative sanctions, police officers on the street may apply repressive measures if they decide to take action against someone found in possession of a minimum amount, especially if that person belongs to a disadvantaged sector of society.

The authorities acknowledged in 2018 that there were still 234 hectares of illicit cannabis crops in the country, which generate more than 900 tonnes of illegal cannabis with more than four harvests every year.

Medicinal cannabis

2.35 In December 2015, Colombian President Juan Manuel Santos signed a decree legalising and regulating medical cannabis. In a nationally televised address, Santos said it would be fully legal to grow, process, import and export cannabis and its derivatives for medical and scientific use.

> 'This decree allows licenses to be granted for the possession of seeds, cannabis plants and marijuana. It places Colombia in the group of countries that are at the forefront ... in the use of natural resources to fight disease.'

He added that the measure 'does not go against our international commitments on drug control.' The law allows for the legal cultivation of up to 40.5 tonnes, 44% of the limit allowed by the International Narcotics Control Board (INCB).

More than 100 companies in the country have applied for licenses issued by the Colombian Ministry of Health and Justice to cultivate marijuana legally for medicinal purposes.[50] As it stands, only a handful have applied for cultivation, and no cannabis currently produced contains THC due to the stringent regulatory procedures for those strains.

As Colombia has not yet defined regulations for the domestic market, producers are focusing on exports. Efforts are ongoing to update the medicinal cannabis laws first laid out in 2015, following complaints that over-regulation and heavy-handed oversight is squeezing farmers.

Legal cannabis growers must obtain permissions from numerous agencies ranging from agriculture and medical authorities to the anti-drug police and drug regulators.[51]

Security regulations are also tough, forcing growers to install cameras, high electric fences around crops and maintain regular communications with the police. The movement of plants to the lab is tracked by satellite and they are occasionally accompanied by bodyguards. Workers at the farm sign in with their fingerprints.[52]

Authorities take between 12 and 18 months to award licenses and growers must then wait between three and six months to get annual permissions that establish the size of their crops and regulate the production of derivatives such as oils and creams.

Next steps

2.36 Colombia has the potential to be a global superpower in medicinal cannabis production, and the market could outstrip Colombian exports of flowers and coffee combined.

The ideal climate and environment have triggered an influx of Canadian business. At least seven companies from Canada have already invested over $100m to set up shop in Colombia, as production is much cheaper given the ability to grow outdoors.[53]

As authorities in Colombia update legislation, North American cannabis companies are likely to enter the cannabis sector in Colombia, which shows massive potential for development.

COSTA RICA

2.37 Costa Rica has long taken a relaxed punitive stance toward drug consumption and personal possession, which has rarely if ever results in prison sentences. Actions such as dealing and trafficking carry a penalty of 8 to 15 years in prison under Law of Narcotics and Psychotropic Substances 8.204,[54] however.

With cannabis decriminalised, there is no appetite for any further relaxing of the rules.

In August 2014, Draft Law 19,256[55] was introduced to regulate cannabis for medicinal and industrial purposes.

A new regulator would be created and grant 42 licenses for cultivation for medicinal purposes, in three categories, depending on their economic capacity.

Under the law, the growers would sell their production to the agency. The measure would also establish licenses for dispensaries and for industrial cannabis, and users would have to register and carry identification.

Despite early momentum, the bill stalled, and in late 2019 Costa Rican legislators, including the bill's main objector, continued meeting with US cannabis activists in California, Denver and Nevada to structure the bill in a way that will best serve the people of Costa Rica.

While the bill struggles to make its way into law, the Health Ministry has previously confirmed:

> 'there currently is no prohibition against registering and commercialising cannabis-based medications, foods and cosmetics, as long as they comply with existing regulations that guarantee their identity, safety, quality and efficiency for the uses for which they are prescribed and used, according to scientific evidence and best manufacturing, agricultural, clinical, medical or other relevant practices.'

ECUADOR

2.38 Under Ecuador's criminal law, possession of up to 10g of cannabis is not considered a crime, however sale and cultivation are. In September 2019, the country's government voted to legalise medicinal cannabis.[56]

The Plenary of the National Assembly approved the reform of the Organic Integral Criminal Code (COIP) that allows the production, commercialisation, distribution, use and consumption of cannabis for medicinal or therapeutic uses in the country.

Possession of up to 10g of marijuana for personal consumption is legal in the South American nation, although its sale is prohibited.

JAMAICA

2.39 Jamaica's laws forbid anyone except Rastafarians from using cannabis recreationally. The Caribbean island is synonymous with cannabis culture, but the strictness of Jamaica's drug laws lies in contrast to the weed-smoking stereotypes it conjures in popular culture.

Cannabis was only decriminalised to any great extent five years ago, after being banned in 1913 under the Ganja Act (Cannabis Sativa is known as 'ganja' in Jamaica).

The Dangerous Drugs (Amendment) Act 2015[57] came into effect on April 15, 2015, updating rules around the possession and smoking of ganja, use of ganja by persons of the Rastafarian faith, and use of ganja for medical, therapeutic and scientific purposes.

Possession of 2oz (approx 56.5g) or less is no longer an offence which can lead to arrest, a charge and time in court, and it will not result in a criminal record. The police may issue a ticket to a person in possession of 2oz (56.5g) or less, and the person would have 30 days to pay the sum of $500 (US$3.7) at any tax office.

Reform of laws to better allow for medicinal cannabis began to emerge in 2014,[58] but the country still has a lot to do to bring it in line with other countries.

National discussions concerning cannabis reform in the Caribbean were brought to a head in August 2018 with the publishing of a report by the influential Caribbean Community (CARICOM) – a regional organisation of fifteen state and dependencies.

The report demanded an end to 'prohibition and draconian criminal penalties' for cannabis possession, and advised countries to consider both decriminalisation and legalisation. It also warned the bloc was at risk of falling behind the rest of the world in regard to medicinal cannabis reform.

Legal background

2.40 Ganja is a way of life in Jamaica. It is used for recreational, religious and medicinal purposes, and has been ever since it was brought to the country in the mid-19th century by labourers from India.

The Ganja Law of 1913 was passed following a convention on opium at The Hague a year earlier that unilaterally included cannabis. In 1948, Jamaica's Dangerous Drugs Act was passed, and this was the main law that outlined the total prohibition of cannabis.

Penalties were tough, and between 1941 and 1972 a sentence of imprisonment for up to a maximum of 18 months was mandatory on conviction for possession.

Things began to shift in 1977 when legislators recommended the decriminalisation of possession of ganja for personal use in small quantities (2oz, 56.5g), and for medical use under prescription.

However, very little happened until 2001 when the National Commission on Ganja, also recommending decriminalisation for possession of small quantities and for use as a sacrament for religious purposes by Rastafarians.

Following a unanimous symbolic vote in the Jamaican House of Representatives last October, the Jamaican government announced in June 2014 that it would decriminalise marijuana possession for personal consumption and religious/medical use by the end of that year.

In January 2015, justice minister Mark Golding introduced the amendments that would eventually lead to decriminalisation of the possession of ganja up to 2oz (56.5g), and establish a cannabis licensing authority to regulate cultivation, sale and distribution for medical, scientific and therapeutic purposes.[59]

Medicinal cannabis

2.41 The Cannabis Licensing Authority (CLA), an agency of the Ministry of Industry, Commerce, Agriculture and Fisheries, was established in 2015 under the Dangerous Drug (Amendment) Act, (DDA) with a specific role to establish and regulate Jamaica's legal ganja and hemp industry.

Its role is to:

- create regulations to guide the development of an orderly legal ganja and hemp industry in Jamaica, for the use of the plant and its by-products for medical, therapeutic and scientific purposes;
- ensure that regulations created and activities within the industry are in keeping with Jamaica's international obligations; and
- issue licences, permits and authorisation for the handling of hemp and ganja.

The regulator has a licensing and application operates division, along with an enforcement and monitoring division. The units vet applications and issue licenses to qualified applicants, ensuring that licensees are held accountable in accordance with the terms and conditions of their license.

In 2017, the CLA implemented the Alternative Development Programme to help cannabis farmers transition to the legal sphere from the black market. The steep licensing fees and expenses involved in meeting the authority's standard have made it difficult for ordinary farmers to enter the legal industry.

Licence applications

2.42 There are five types of licenses that may be applied for; cultivators, transport, processing, retail, and research and development.

Each applicant may apply for more than one licence, and the application process spans two phases: Examination of application information and documents as well as due diligence. Once deemed fit and proper, conditional approval is granted.

The second phase involves the inspection of premises or vehicles for compliance with the regulations. Once all requirements are met, a licence may be granted, then issued upon completion of requisite payments and the execution of tripartite agreements where needed.

Companies applying to operate must be registered with the Companies Office of Jamaica, and must establish their company's 'substantial' ownership and control (over 50%) by a person 'ordinarily resident' in Jamaica.

An ordinarily resident individual for the purposes of the licence applications, is one who has lived in Jamaica for three consecutive years immediately preceding the date of the application and is at least 18 years old.

Personal use

2.43 Anyone who requires cannabis for medicinal purposes can only acquire it if they have obtained a recommendation from a medical doctor certified to recommend ganja preparations and a medical card from the Ministry of Health.

Medical ganja can only be purchased from a retailer licensed by the CLA. Visitors to Jamaica may apply to the Ministry of Health for a permit to legally purchase and possess up to 2oz (approx 56.5g) of medical ganja or ganja products for medical or therapeutic purposes. A fee is payable.

Next steps

2.44 In October 2019, the Minister of State in the Ministry of Industry, Commerce, Agriculture and Fisheries, Hon Floyd Green, said the growing global market for cannabis gave the opportunity for Jamaica to become a first-choice destination for travellers who want to use medical cannabis:

> 'The fact that Jamaica is already a world-renowned hospitality and tourism destination is a guaranteed formula for a successful cannabis industry,' said Green, speaking at the official opening of Apollon Formularies Limited medicinal cannabis plant in Westmoreland. 'We can create more facilities where patients, while being treated, experience the beauty of Jamaica with the most fitting climate, the best people, the best service and, of course, the best cannabis. That is our competitive advantage in the global space.'

PANAMA

2.45 Lawmakers in Panama have been debating the issue of legalising medicinal cannabis for three years. In October 2017, Panama introduced a bill (Bill 595) to set up a regulatory framework, however the proposals are still to become law due to the number of modifications.

The bill passed its first debate in March 2018 but has been subject to multiple updates, and April 2019 was sent back to the preliminary debate stages due to fears over security and access to the marijuana plant, as recreational cannabis consumption is illegal in Panama.

The congressional Commission on Work, Health and Social Development took up the measure in October 2019. It would have to pass through further debates, consultations and votes, and then be signed by President Laurentino Cortizo.

PERU

2.46 Cannabis is also decriminalised in Peru to the extent users can hold up to 8g, under Article 299 of the Criminal Code. Trafficking is punishable by up to 12 years in prison, and growing the crop carries a term of between 8 and 15 years.

In February 2019, regulations governing the use of medicinal cannabis were published in the official gazette, *El Peruano*, 15 months after Law 30681 legalised cannabis medicinal and therapeutic purposes.[60]

The regulations cover guidelines and procedures for research,[61] farming and production limits, importation, and the marketing and sale of medicinal marijuana and its by-products. It also outlines the procedures for medical prescriptions, including a registry of patients/users.

The bill to authorise the use of cannabis for medicinal purposes was introduced to Congress by Alberto de Belaunde, now an independent but at the time a member of the ruling party, and signed into law in November 2017.[62] Since then, some medical prescriptions have been issued but use is limited.

PUERTO RICO

2.47 The Controlled Substances Law of the Free Associated State of Puerto Rico punishes the possession of cannabis with a prison term of up to five years, with a minimum of two depending on circumstances, and a fine of up to US$5,000 for a first offence.

The state's tough drug laws were somewhat relaxed in May 2015 through an executive order by the governor, which also legalised medicinal cannabis.

Cannabis was reclassified, and under the new law, possession of up to 6g of cannabis would not be a priority for prosecution. Whilst still a crime, the authorities would favour treatment or community service for those involved, rather than criminal proceedings.

On announcing the measure, the governor said:

> 'as of December 2014, the Department of Corrections had incurred costs amounting to US$2.28m for incarceration for marijuana users or people caught with marijuana in their possession.'

In early 2016, Reglamento 155/2015[63] took effect, regulating cannabis for the purpose of medicinal and scientific research. The legislation allows physicians to prescribe cannabis for a maximum of 30 days, in amounts that cannot exceed 2.5oz (approx 70g) per day.

It also establishes the cultivation and production of cannabis with a system of licenses granted to private individuals; cultivation for personal use is prohibited. Both doctors and patients must be registered and the latter will have identification showing that they are registered.

In July 2016, this measure was replaced by Reglamento 8766,[64] which cut the amount to 1.5oz (42g) per day and, among other changes, outlines how tourists can acquire the substance.

TRINIDAD AND TOBAGO

2.48 In December 2018, Trinidad and Tobago Prime Minister Keith Rowley announced that cannabis would be decriminalised across the Caribbean nation by mid-2019, but that the government had no plans to legalise the drug.

The government later said it would issue public consultations on the matter, prior to decriminalising the drug for personal use in June 2019.

The date passed with no action taken, and later in the Attorney General went further and said legalisation may be on the cards, as authorities consult with public stakeholders to configure the most appropriate form of cannabis reform.

In August 2019, campaigners expressed anger that the Ministry of Health had not enacted clauses to amendments made to the Dangerous Drugs Act in 2000,[65] that would allow for licenses to grow, import, export, sell and distribute marijuana, and regulates 'the use, purchase, sale or possession of any dangerous drugs for medicinal or scientific purposes.'

URUGUAY

2.49 Uruguay has a long history of unorthodox approaches to tackling the Latin American drug scourge, and in July 2012, President José 'Pepe' Mujica told Parliament 'someone has to be first'[66] as he announced plans for the total legalisation of recreational cannabis.

Five years later in 2017, Uruguay duly became the first country to open a fully legal and regulated cannabis market, albeit one entirely overseen by the government with no commercial interests permitted.

Teething problems have dogged the early years with problems around access to banking services, reputational concerns from the only authorised sellers, and a lack of both supply and availability. The country took the decision as a measure to cut crime, and despite the infrastructure issues, the early signs are that this has been a success.

Legal background

2.50 In December 2013, Law 19172[67] was signed by President Mujica, and the first national cannabis market of its kind anywhere in the world was launched.

Although two US states had created their own domestic cannabis markets in 2012 (Colorado and Washington) following public ballots, no single country had legalised cannabis for medicinal and non-medicinal use at national level, and no government had taken such bold steps alone.

The move contravened international treaties,[68] prompting criticism from the monitors overseeing adherence to the 1961 Single Convention on Narcotic Drugs, the global agreement under which cannabis is controlled.

However, it also drew praise from the likes of Guatemala and Colombia, who are also seeking alternative ways to combat the drug problems that have long blighted their respective countries.

Uruguay's government said the decision was taken for public health reasons, as it hoped to educate users about the harmful effects, and to stamp out black market supply through a cheap supply of home grown product.

Officials felt total prohibition had failed, and controlling the market from seed to point-of-sale was a better way to reduce supply and demand, and steer young people away from drug use.

Law 19172 set out the regulation of production, marketing and consumption of cannabis, and allowed for the formation of a new watchdog, the Institute for the Regulation and Control of Cannabis (IRCC), to oversee efforts to educate cannabis users about the dangers.

The Institute for the Regulation and Control of Cannabis

2.51 Set up purely for the purpose of regulating the marijuana industry, the IRCC was given a mandate to encourage cooperation across separate Uruguayan government agencies in regard to oversight.[69]

The IRCC follows the policy directives of the National Drug Council (JND), and reports to the Ministry of Public Health. Its board includes members of the Ministries of Public Health; Social Development; and Livestock, Agriculture, and Fishing.

Under law, the IRCC has a mandate to maintain anonymous registries of anyone wishing to purchase or grow cannabis, along with club members, requiring documentation for anyone signing up.

It can also inspect any property used in the growing, processing, distribution, or sale of cannabis, however it can only enter the homes of users with a court order. It has powers to analyse commercial strains of cannabis to ascertain whether they meet the legal and regulatory requirements.

General violations of Law 19172 incur warnings, fines, seizure of goods or items, destruction of goods, removing offenders from the pertinent registry, and temporary or permanent disqualification from transacting in cannabis. The IRCC can also partially or entirely close premises.

Law 19172 also amended article 30 of Decree-Law 14294 to state that anyone producing cannabis without authorisation faces a prison sentence of 20 months to 10 years, except when produced for scientific or pharmaceutical research, or for medicinal use.

The production of cannabis by planting, growing, and harvesting cannabis plants with psychoactive effects when meeting legal requirements under the law does not give rise to criminal liability.[70] Unlike many other countries, Uruguay has never criminalised drug possession for personal use.

Recreational cannabis use models

2.52 In 2014, the government issued further guidance[71] which outlined the three methods of access for Uruguayan citizens and residents, and the restrictions that would apply, including limiting the availability of cannabis to domestic citizens.

The three methods are:

1. **Homegrown**: Adults can grow up to six female flowering cannabis plants per household for their own consumption. They must first register their plants with the government. The total annual production of the drug must not exceed 480g, but cultivation of more than six plants is allowed so long as they are either male or not flowering. At time of writing, about 9,000 Uruguayans are registered home-growers.
2. **Cannabis clubs**: Non-profit cooperatives exist where adults can grow cannabis collectively. These 'cannabis clubs' of between 15 and 45 members must also be registered with the IRCCA and other authorities. Up to 99 plants per club can be planted in the same space, but cannot dispense more than 480g of the drug to each of their members per year. Any surplus product must be turned over to authorities. There are approximately 85 clubs in operation.
3. **Commercial purchase**: Individuals can buy up to 40g per month (10g per week, according to updated laws) at sales points. Under law, pharmacies can act as points of sale, however the government may create new, special-purpose outlets to take the strain from pharmacies, which are not required by law to sell cannabis and can opt out. The government intended that a small number of commercial growers could be licensed to produce cannabis for commercial sales, but only 2 of the 22 companies that applied were approved. More than 22,000 Uruguayans have registered as purchasers.

Although Uruguay's model was a world-first, the government was clear the market would be strictly regulated; it is run by the state with almost no commercial or outside business assistance.

Medicinal cannabis

2.53 Uruguay's left-field approach to regulation ensured it permitted recreational cannabis before later addressing medicinal and pharmaceutical use, the reverse of everywhere else on the planet. The first legal sales of medicinal cannabis in Uruguayan pharmacies were recorded in December 2017.

Researchers at Cannabis Monitor Uruguay found that 23% of medicinal marijuana patients bought from abroad. Of those who buy in Uruguay, half do so through self-cultivation (with and without registration in the IRCCA) and the other half through supply by other people (growers, producers of extracts), the academic researchers found.

A 2015 executive order instructed the IRCCA to permit physicians to prescribe cannabis in monthly increments. A single CBD product, Epifractan, at 2% and 5% extracts, is available by prescription. They are imported in 10mm vials.

Cannabinoid oral sprays or synthetic cannabinoids require specialised permission from the Ministry of Public Health to import them under a 'compassionate use' exception.

Prescriptions are valid for 30 days before a new prescription must be filled, during which time patients are forbidden from accessing any other form of legal cannabis.

There are no qualifying illness conditions, however mainly it has been prescribed in limited amounts for pain relief in cases of cancer, seizures, epilepsy, and degenerative neurological diseases.

Teething problems

2.54 On 19 July 2017, the final stages of Law 19172 were enacted and sales began in 16 pharmacies across the country. The response amongst the public was positive at first, according to the researchers at Monitor Cannabis Uruguay.[72]

The number of Uruguayans on the IRCC's purchaser registry increasing more than tripled from 4,900 to more than 13,000 in the first month.[73]

Two varieties of cannabis, Alpha I, an indica, and Beta I, a sativa, were initially available on sale in five-gram containers. In January 2018, the price was increased to 200 Uruguayan pesos (or roughly US$7). At approximately US$1.40 per gram, the figure remains very competitive with the black-market.

Despite the initial optimism, only two companies were able to secure licenses to commercially grow strains with a THC cap of 9%, causing a major supply shortage.

Pharmacy associations reported a low number of businesses registering to sell cannabis due to concerns it would harm their reputations with their regular clients, especially in rural areas that were anti-cannabis.

Almost immediately, banks serving Uruguayan pharmacies began to close accounts linked to cannabis to ensure they could remain compliant with US financial law. Cannabis remains a scheduled drug with recreational sale outlawed almost everywhere else in the world; US banks were risking federal sanctions by taking money from the sale of narcotics.

Pharmacies were forced to sell on a cash-only basis, and many simply pulled out of the cannabis programme altogether. Of more than 1,000 pharmacies in the country, less than 20 now sell cannabis out of an initial 50 who registered.

In 2018, Canada became the second country to launch a fully regulated cannabis market, and subsequently enabled Uruguayan firms to divert business to Canadian banks. Reform of global banking laws to enable sanction-free service of cannabis businesses is probably the most important aspect impacting the sector today, and all roads lead back to the US.

Should Congress eventually approve laws that remove the threat of sanctions for banks dealing in cannabis trade, the knock-on effect would be felt in every country with any connection to the US financial system, be it a business that handles dollars or a firm seeking a loan.

Non-pharmacy sales

2.55 In January 2018, the Uruguayan government (by now under a different but no less cannabis-friendly administration) said it would solve distribution problems by allowing dispensaries, similar to those operational in the US, to sell cannabis on non-pharmaceutical property.

A year later in February 2019, the government issued applications for producers to grow marijuana for commercial purposes, in an effort to increase supply. An annual production quota of 2,000kg, or 4,400lb, of dried flower is permitted. The growers are given around three hectares of government-owned land, and plants must be grown indoors.

World leader

2.56

> 'The government would like to be a world leader in this area, taking advantage of our role to date as a guinea pig - so far with positive results. At the same time, they want to be cautious in approving projects to avoid any negative publicity. If Uruguay can find a way to avoid tying interested parties up in red tape, but still ensuring that criminal ventures or funds are not involved then this could be a very exciting business opportunity for Uruguay, as new markets for medicinal cannabis seem to be opening up almost every day.' (Mark Teuten, Uruguayan lawyer at Teuten Abogados in Montevideo.)

At the end of 2019 the government announced a second tender to increase the amount of cannabis for the local recreational use market, Teuten said: 'I understand that there are a number of projects for medicinal use in the pipeline as well awaiting approval'.

After a stuttering start to the programme, the production of medicinal cannabis appears to be providing the boon the Uruguayan government hoped for. In September 2019, Montevideo firm Fotmer Life Sciences, made the first commercial shipment of medical cannabis from Latin America, 10 kg (22 lb) of dried flowers with high levels of active ingredient THC destined for patients in Australia.

International treaty violation

2.57 Uruguay's decision to legalise cannabis was repeatedly criticised by the International Narcotics Control Board (INCB), whose job it is to monitor and uphold adherence to global drug laws.

In response, Uruguay argued that UN drug control policies have failed to protect the health and welfare of humankind, as intended, and that its own policy was fully in line with these goals.

Uruguay is, by the letter of the law, contravening its obligations under the 1961 Single Convention to limit cannabis exclusively to medical and scientific purposes, but it has sought to reshape the argument by framing its domestic law as a strict adherence to the founding human rights obligations of the UN.

Six years on from its ground-breaking decision to legalise cannabis, Uruguay has shown no intention of rowing back. Indeed, the claim it is doing more to protect the human rights and health of its citizens by creating a safe adult market for cannabis an argument that has been adopted by other countries seeking to do similar.

CARIBBEAN

2.58 In 2014, CARICOM, the Caribbean Community of 20 countries: 15 member states and 5 associate members, set up a Regional Commission on Marijuana to study the social, economic, health and legal issues surrounding cannabis in the Caribbean and to determine whether there should be an adjustment to its current classification as a dangerous drug.

Deep divisions over the issue within CARICOM, and a number of senior Caribbean figures have spoken out about the need for a revision of regional policy on marijuana for both economic and humane reasons.

Eventually, in 2018 the final report appeared,[74] recommending the declassification of cannabis as a dangerous drug in all legislation and the reclassification of the drug as a controlled substance.

> 'The commission believes that the end goal for CARICOM should be the dismantling of prohibition in its totality, to be replaced by a strictly regulated framework akin to that for alcohol and tobacco, which are harmful substances that are not criminalised.
>
> 'The commission is unanimous in its view that the current classification for cannabis/marijuana as a dangerous drug with no value or narcotic, should be changed to a classification of cannabis as a controlled substance.
>
> 'The commission is unanimous in its view that ultimately, legal policy toward marijuana should be informed, not by punitive approaches, but by public health rationales, within a human rights, social justice and developmental perspective. Consequently, there is consensus that all criminal penalties from marijuana laws should be removed.'

As an initial step, the commission recommended the decriminalisation of the drug for personal use in private premises and medical purposes, but stated cannabis should be banned in public spaces.

The commission also recommended that customs law be amended to make provision for the import and export of cannabis and cannabis products, and suggested that commercial cannabis activity be decriminalised or legalised to avoid the implications of anti-money laundering legislation and proceeds of crime legislation.

The report noted that small farmers and small business persons should be included in production and supply arrangements, with appropriate controls limiting large enterprise and foreign involvement, and equitable land use policy for marijuana cultivation should be formulated.

The implementation of 'moderate taxes' was also recommended to ensure that the 'black market is not reinvigorated'.

The commission also noted special provisions to regulate marijuana for medical purposes where access to medical marijuana should be made for qualifying conditions:

> 'After holding national consultations receiving several submissions and a petition from the public, reviewing data from polls and surveys from several countries, it is clear that in the region, attitudes toward cannabis have changed in recent times.
>
> 'There is now overwhelming support for law reform, moving away from the prohibition on cannabis and consequent criminalization.
>
> 'This holds true not only from the data, but the many prominent persons and groups that have lent their voice to this cause from all walks of life, including church leaders, magistrates, judges, social workers, educators, doctors, chief justices, DPPs, members of Parliament and senior members of the bar.'

AMERICAS SETTING GLOBAL AGENDA ON CANNABIS REFORM AMID GROWING REGULATORY ARBITRAGE

2.59 That there is a legal cannabis industry today is almost entirely down to developments in the continent of America over the last decade.

It is no exaggeration to say the future of the sector's medicinal and adult recreational streams elsewhere in the world hinges on the continuation of trends that are accelerating in North America.

North America is likely to continue on its path of opening recreational markets, in contrast to the strong medicinal thread appearing from Europe. This divergence is expected to continue as the European Union pursues.

The first wave of US and Canadian firms attempting to enter Europe's cannabis markets encountered significant problems in regards to misaligned standards.

> 'Some North American firms looking to supply medicinal cannabis were caught flat-footed when they tried to enter the big new European market, because they are prohibited from doing so when they do not meet the Good Manufacturing Practice (GMP) standards.[75] The homegrown medicinal cannabis play is smart, as there is a real barrier to entry for eternal players right now. GMP certification can be a lengthy and expensive process.' (Dylan Kennett, DLA Piper EMEA cannabis lawyer.)

Any manufacturer of medicines intended for the EU market, no matter where in the world it is located, must comply with GMP. This requires medicines are of consistent high quality; are appropriate for their intended use; and meet the requirements of the marketing authorisation or clinical trial authorisation.

Kennett said he expects over the next year to see an increased presence from North American firms once they achieve the GPM certification and/or move into acquiring or opening facilities in Europe to supply the market.

The US domino effect

2.60 When the US states of Washington and Colorado voted in 2012 to legalise cannabis for adult use, the dam was broken. In 2014, Alaska, Oregon and Washington DC did the same, and two years later in 2016 voters in California, Massachusetts, Maine and Nevada also approved ballot measures. Illinois became the latest of the 11 states to do so, with its market due to open 1 January 2020 (more than 30 states have decriminalised cannabis).

More states are expected to follow suit in the coming years. The main stumbling block to more widespread growth is the federal ban. While federal enforcement laws of marijuana remain in place, businesses in those US states cannot expand outside their borders.

Other structural issues exist by virtue of these limitations, including the inability to access large sources of capital and insurance, or other banking services, the over-reliance reliance on cash, and the inability to expand.

US financial services firms are exposed to a variety of heavy federal sanctions when dealing with cannabis businesses, and while it is not impossible to offer services, the risk far outweighs the reward.

SAFE Banking Act

2.61 In an effort to resolve this, the Secure And Fair Enforcement (SAFE) Banking Act,[76] was introduced to Congress in May 2017. The basic intention of the Act is to stop federal banking regulators from limiting the ability of a depository institution from dealing with a legal cannabis business.

The bill would also forbid federal regulators from interfering, or punishing, financial institutions from working with marijuana-based businesses.

Should it become law, the impact would be felt all over the world, and particularly in the markets of Canada and Uruguay. Businesses in these countries would be major beneficiaries, particularly the larger Canadian firms who can tap into greater capital than is available in their own market.

In September, the SAFE Banking Act passed in the House of Representatives by a vote of 321 to 103, and will next go to the Senate. The path to law still has a number of obstacles, however, not least given the vehement and vocal anti-cannabis stance of current Senate Majority Leader Mitch McConnell.

The Act promises to free the vast power of the US banking system to support 'grown in America' firms, and could prove to be truly seismic event, however it does not propose to alter the classification of cannabis as a Schedule I narcotic, and would not alter the current administration's view of cannabis.

According to Daniel Turgel, partner at White & Case in London:

> 'There is potentially a conflict between the Safe Banking Act and other legislative efforts at a federal level to reform cannabis-related laws. However, the general move towards federal clarification regarding the sector is positive. The fact the SAFE Banking Act has got as far as it has may mean that some of the more sophisticated institutions become more comfortable with providing certain banking services to some of these businesses.'

Entering 2020, the US is sandwiched between two countries that have fully legal adult recreational cannabis markets, following events in Mexico. The rest of the world will be watching closely to see how the US responds to the growth of the economies in its neighbouring territories, knowing it will not want to give either too much of a head start.

Mexico and the Canadian model

2.62 Mexican lawmakers are setting rules on which demographics can access both recreational and medicinal products, the strength of the goods, where individuals will be allowed to hold and use, along with laws on advertising and branding.

There are some striking similarities to the Canadian model, most notably the creation of a central regulator, the Cannabis Institute, responsible for oversight, implementing legislation and issuing cultivation and sales licences.

Although Uruguay was the first country to legalise cannabis, Canada's decision to embrace recreational marijuana made it the first industrialised nation to do so, and created a benchmark for other jurisdictions considering a similar move.

According to Zara Snapp, a drug policy reform advocate in Mexico City:[77]

> 'The importance of Canada having regulated is that it broke the taboo on an international level in a way that Uruguay did not. For us, what it taught us is there is a path, and that path is possible without there being any apocalyptic sanctions from international bodies.'

The tiny EU state of Luxembourg announced in 2019 it intends to legalise cannabis in the next two years, and has been studying the Canadian regulatory model closely as it begins to draft its own framework.

New Zealand is holding a referendum on cannabis legalisation in 2021, and in almost all the literature, government briefings and other detail emerging from the country regarding how it would act should the public vote 'yes', the influence of Canada is clear.

Canada's regulated pharmaceutical model is only two years old, however, and has not proved perfect. Government intelligence reports black market sales have not dipped, despite this being the main reason the country decided to pursue full legalisation. There are also currently not enough retailers to meet demand, and the country has struggled with a supply shortage.

Another issue is the domination by a handful of corporations who are controlling production. Local growers have reported being shut out of the market, and this is something that Mexico, Luxembourg, South Africa and a few US states have noted as they consider their own regimes. Mexico has signalled its intent to favour local indigenous growers, and may shape its licensing laws in their favour.

ENDNOTES

1. Health Canada Task Force document on cannabis legalisation and regulation: http://healthycanadians.gc.ca/health-system-systeme-sante/consultations/legalization-marijuana-legalisation/alt/legalization-marijuana-legalisation-eng.pdf.
2. Gross domestic product by industry, July 2019: https://www150.statcan.gc.ca/n1/daily-quotidien/191001/dq191001a-eng.htm?HPA=1.
3. Task Force findings: https://mcmillan.ca/Files/196039_Task_Force_Releases_Report_on_Cannabis.pdf.
4. The Cannabis Act: https://laws-lois.justice.gc.ca/eng/acts/C-24.5/page-1.html.
5. Canada Gazette http://www.gazette.gc.ca/rp-pr/p2/2019/2019-06-26/html/sor-dors206-eng.html.
6. Quebec cannabis regulations: https://encadrementcannabis.gouv.qc.ca/en/loi/loi-encadrant-le-cannabis/.
7. https://laws-lois.justice.gc.ca/eng/regulations/SOR-2018-144/.
8. Industrial Hemp Regulations: https://laws-lois.justice.gc.ca/eng/regulations/SOR-2018-145/.
9. Approved growers 2019: https://www.canada.ca/en/health-canada/services/drugs-medication/cannabis/producing-selling-hemp/commercial-licence/list-approved-cultivars-cannabis-sativa.html.
10. *Why is Canada running out of marijuana?*: https://www.bbc.com/news/world-us-canada-46200873.
11. Canada's supply issues: https://globalnews.ca/news/5463653/canadas-cannabis-supply-feds-denial/.
12. *In Bev enters the cannabis space*: https://www.forbes.com/sites/taranurin/2018/12/19/ab-inbev-enters-the-cannabis-space/.
13. *Canadian medical cannabis exports tripled last year, as race for European market position intensifies*: https://mjbizdaily.com/canadian-medical-cannabis-exports-tripled-in-2018/.
14. *Germany to launch cannabis farming as Canada's Aurora, Aphria win tenders*: https://www.reuters.com/article/us-germany-marijuana/germany-to-launch-cannabis-farming-as-canadas-aurora-aphria-win-tenders-idUSKCN1RT1TL.
15. Statement by the International Narcotics Control Board on the entry into force of Bill C-45 legalising cannabis for non-medical purposes in Canada: https://www.incb.org/incb/en/news/press-releases/2018/statement-by-the-international-narcotics-control-board-on-the-entry-into-force-of-bill-c-45-legalising-cannabis-for-non-medical-purposes-in-canada.html.
16. *Final draft of Mexico's bill to legalize cannabis expected Oct. 17, senator says*: https://mjbizdaily.com/final-draft-of-mexicos-bill-to-legalize-cannabis-expected-oct-17-senator-says/.
17. *The Surprising Link Between U.S. Marijuana Law and the History of Immigration*: https://time.com/5572691/420-marijuana-mexican-immigration/.
18. Council on Foreign Relations backgrounder on the Mexican drug war: https://www.cfr.org/backgrounder/mexicos-drug-war.
19. Ley General de Salud, No. 42-01 (General Health Law Number 42-01): https://www.mindbank.info/item/2784.

20. *Mexico's top court demands regulation on medical marijuana after long delays*: https://www.reuters.com/article/us-mexico-drugs/mexicos-top-court-demands-regulation-on-medical-marijuana-after-long-delays-idUSKCN1V508B.

21. Law Library of Congress: Mexico decriminalisation background: https://www.loc.gov/law/help/decriminalization-of-narcotics/mexico.php.

22. *Mexico's Supreme Court legalizes cannabis for recreational use*: https://www.upi.com/Top_News/World-News/2018/10/31/Mexicos-Supreme-Court-legalizes-cannabis-for-recreational-use/9621541024238/.

23. *Mexican Senate set to pass bill to legalize marijuana in next few days*: https://www.reuters.com/article/us-mexico-drugs/mexican-senate-set-to-pass-bill-to-legalize-marijuana-in-next-few-days-idUSKBN1WU2Q9.

24. *Mexican Committees Unveil Marijuana Legalization Bill Ahead Of Supreme Court Deadline*: https://www.marijuanamoment.net/mexican-committees-unveil-marijuana-legalization-bill-ahead-of-supreme-court-deadline/.

25. Colorado Amendment 64: https://www.fcgov.com/mmj/pdf/amendment64.pdf.

26. *Colorado's legal weed market: $700 million in sales last year, $1 billion by 2016*: https://www.washingtonpost.com/news/wonk/wp/2015/02/12/colorados-legal-weed-market-700-million-in-sales-last-year-1-billion-by-2016/.

27. California cannabis timeline: https://cannabis.ca.gov/cannabis-legislation/.

28. BSA expectations: https://www.fincen.gov/resources/statutes-regulations/guidance/bsa-expectations-regarding-marijuana-related-businesses.

29. Farm Bill 2018: https://www.congress.gov/bill/115th-congress/house-bill/2.

30. Statement on consumer warning to stop using THC vaping products amid ongoing investigation into lung illnesses: https://www.fda.gov/news-events/press-announcements/statement-consumer-warning-stop-using-thc-vaping-products-amid-ongoing-investigation-lung-illnesses.

31. Colorado cannabis inspection procedures update 2019: https://www.colorado.gov/pacific/cdphe/marijuana-sampling-procedures.

32. *Argentina lawmakers approve cannabis oil for medicinal use*: https://www.reuters.com/article/us-argentina-cannabis/argentina-lawmakers-approve-cannabis-oil-for-medicinal-use-idUSKBN170391.

33. Argentina Tiene Su Primera Ley Sobre El Uso Medicinal De La Planta De Cannabis. Historia Y Perspectivas: http://www.medicinabuenosaires.com/PMID/29044015.pdf.

34. *Jujuy cultivará cannabis medicinal*: https://www.eltribuno.com/jujuy/nota/2018-7-30-20-24-0-jujuy-cultivara-cannabis-medicinal.

35. Narcotic Drugs Law 23.737: https://www.unodc.org/res/cld/document/arg/narcotics-drugs-law-23737-mod95_html/argentina-law23737modbylaw24424-95.pdf.

36. The Arriola Ruling: http://sjconsulta.csjn.gov.ar/sjconsulta/%20documentos/verUnicoDocumento.html?idAnalisis=671140.

37. *El Gobierno definirá la cantidad de drogas de tenencia para consume*: http://www.lanacion.com.ar/1892519-el-gobierno-definira-la-cantidad-de-drogas-de-tenencia-para-consumo.

38. *House: cannabis decriminalisation passes*: http://www.royalgazette.com/politics/article/20171209/house-cannabis-decriminalisation-passes.

39. MISUSE OF DRUGS (DECRIMINALISATION OF CANNABIS) AMENDMENT ACT 2017: http://bermudalaws.bm/laws/Annual%20Laws/2017/Acts/Misuse%20of%20Drugs%20(Decriminalisation%20of%20Cannabis)%20Amendment%20Act%202017.pdf.

40. *People can apply for medical cannabis*: http://www.royalgazette.com/news/article/20161125/people-can-apply-for-medical-cannabis.

41. LEI Nº 11.343, DE 23 DE AGOSTO DE 2006: http://www.planalto.gov.br/ccivil_03/_Ato2004-2006/2006/Lei/L11343.htm.

42. Law Library of Congress Brazil background: https://www.loc.gov/law/foreign-news/article/brazil-import-and-use-of-marijuana-based-medicine-products-authorized/.

43. *Chile Marijuana Legalization: Michelle Bachelet Removes Weed From 'Hard Drug' List, Approves Medical Pot:* https://www.latintimes.com/chile-marijuana-legalization-michelle-bachelet-removes-weed-hard-drug-list-approves-357337.

44. LEY-20000: http://druglawreform.info/images/stories/LeyDrogasChileNumero20000.pdf.

45. Colombia's drug trade background, by Colombia Reports: https://colombiareports.com/colombia-drug-trafficking/.

46. Ley 30 1986: http://www.druglawreform.info/images/stories/Ley30-1986.pdf.

47. Constitutional Court Ruling C-221: https://www.alcaldiabogota.gov.co/sisjur/normas/Norma1.jsp?i=6960.

48. Citizen Security Law of 2011: http://wsp.presidencia.gov.co/Normativa/Leyes/Documents/ley145324062011.pdf.

49. Ruling C-491: http://www.corteconstitucional.gov.co/relatoria/2012/c-491-12.htm.

50. *Colombia has 100-plus licensed cannabis firms, but only a handful have registered cultivars*: https://mjbizdaily.com/colombia-has-100-plus-licensed-cannabis-firms-but-only-handful-have-registered-cultivars-necessary-for-commercial-sales/.

51. Regulations For Medicinal Cannabis In Colombia Are Ready: https://www.minsalud.gov.co/English/Paginas/Regulations-For-Medicinal-Cannabis-In-Colombia-Are-Ready.aspx.

52. *Facing stiff competition, will Colombia's marijuana industry go up in smoke?*: https://www.reuters.com/article/us-colombia-marijuana/facing-stiff-competition-will-colombias-marijuana-industry-go-up-in-smoke-idUSKBN1WM1KG.

53. *Cannabis companies from North America and Canada want to establish operations in Colombia*: http://www.vernamagazine.com/2019/10/21/cannabis-companies-from-north-america-and-canada-want-to-establish-operations-in-colombia/.

54. Law No. 8204: Complete Revision of the Law on Narcotics, Psychotropic Substances, Drugs of Unauthorized Use and Related Activities: https://www.unodc.org/res/cld/document/cri/law-no-8204_html/costarica-law_8204-2000.pdf.

55. RESEARCH LAW, REGULATION AND CONTROL OF CANNABIS PLANTS AND HEMP for medical use, DRAFT LAW E INDUSTRIAL FOOD: http://j.b5z.net/i/u/10233704/f/CR_MMJ_Bill_19256_en.pdf.

56. *Cannabis medicinal requiere reglamento para cultivo, producción y distribución*: https://www.eltelegrafo.com.ec/noticias/judicial/12/cannabis-medicinal-ecuador.

57. Jamaica Dangerous Drugs (Amendment) Act 2015: https://www.japarliament.gov.jm/attachments/339_The%20Dangerous%20Drug%20bill%202015.pdf.
58. Transnational Institute Jamaica drug reform background: https://www.tni.org/en/topic/drug-law-reform-in-jamaica.
59. Ministry of Justice Dangerous Drugs Amendment Act 2015 fact sheet: https://moj.gov.jm/news/dangerous-drugs-amendment-act-2015-fact-sheet.
60. Decreto Supremo que aprueba el Reglamento de la Ley N° 30681, Ley que regula el uso medicinal y terapéutico del Cannabis y sus derivados: https://busquedas.elperuano.pe/normaslegales/decreto-supremo-que-aprueba-el-reglamento-de-la-ley-n-30681-decreto-supremo-n-005-2019-sa-1744045-2/.
61. *Peru approves regulations for medicinal marijuana*: https://www.peruviantimes.com/23/peru-approves-regulations-for-medicinal-marijuana/31095/.
62. Peru's medicinal cannabis bill: https://busquedas.elperuano.pe/normaslegales/ley-que-regula-el-uso-medicinal-y-terapeutico-del-cannabis-y-ley-n-30681-1587374-1/.
63. Reglamento 155/2015: http://salud.gov.pr/Estadisticas-Registros-y-Publicaciones/Reglamentos/Reglamento%20155%20I.pdf.
64. Peru medicinal cannabis cultivation and production guidance, Reglamento 8766: http://www.salud.gov.pr/Dept-de-Salud/Pages/Cannabis-Medicinal.aspx.
65. Trinidad & Tobago Dangerous Drugs Act: http://rgd.legalaffairs.gov.tt/Laws2/Alphabetical_List/lawspdfs/11.25.pdf.
66. *Cannabis regulation in Uruguay: "Someone has to be first ..."*: https://www.tni.org/en/article/cannabis-regulation-in-uruguay-someone-has-to-be-first.
67. Institute for the Regulation and Control of Cannabis (IRCC): https://www.ircca.gub.uy/wp-content/uploads/2014/06/Ley_19.172.pdf.
68. Uruguay breaks international conventions: http://www.incb.org/documents/Publications/PressRelease/PR2013/press_release_111213.pdf.
69. About the IRCC https://www.ircca.gub.uy/creacion-del-ircca/.
70. Library of Congress, Decriminalization of Narcotics: Uruguay: https://www.loc.gov/law/help/decriminalization-of-narcotics/uruguay.php.
71. Ley N° 19172. REGULACION Y CONTROL DEL CANNABIS: http://www.impo.com.uy/bases/leyes/19172-2013.
72. Monitor Cannabis Uruguay detail on medicinal cannabis: http://monitorcannabis.uy/cannabis-medicinal-la-revolucion-silenciosa/.
73. *Uruguay's cannabis law: Pioneering a new paradigm*: https://www.brookings.edu/wp-content/uploads/2018/03/gs_032118_uruguaye28099s-cannabis-law_final.pdf.
74. Report of the CARICOM Regional Commission on Marijuana 2018 Waiting to Exhale – Safeguarding our Future through Responsible Socio-Legal Policy on Marijuana: https://caricom.org/document-Library/view-document/report-of-the-caricom-regional-commission-on-marijuana-2018-waiting-to-exhale-safeguarding-our-future-through-responsible-socio-legal-policy-on-marijuana.
75. European Medicines Agency Good Manufacturing Practice guidance: https://www.ema.europa.eu/en/human-regulatory/research-development/compliance/good-manufacturing-practice.
76. The Secure And Fair Enforcement (SAFE) Banking Act: https://www.congress.gov/bill/116th-congress/house-bill/1595/text.
77. *How Canada's legalization is shaping cannabis laws elsewhere*: https://www.apnews.com/ae6205b0a71443afb61b9486adeeef8a.

Chapter 3

Europe

CROATIA

3.01 Croatia's parliament voted to decriminalise personal possession of small amounts of illicit drugs in a December 2012 ruling, with the law coming into effect on 1 January 2013.

Later that same year, Croatia joined the EU, and its drug laws are broadly in line with other member states. Under amendments to the country's penal code, possession of drugs for personal use will no longer be a criminal offence.

'Now youngsters caught in a park with a joint will not go to prison, but pay a fine,' Justice Minister Orsat Miljenic told lawmakers.[1] Anyone found in possession faces a fine of up to €2,680 (US$3,503), can be sent for rehabilitation or ordered to do community service. The judgment on whether the quantity can be classed as 'small' is made by the state prosecutor or court in each case.

Previously, anyone convicted of drug possession could be sentenced to up to three years in jail. Under the new law, however, stricter penalties of up to 15 years in prison can be handed out to anyone convicted of dealing, especially if caught near schools.

Croatia's drug controls concern two legal acts: the Law on Combating Drug Abuse (LCDA) and the Criminal Code. The LCDA, passed in November 2001 and was updated in 2012. It regulates conditions for the manufacture of, possession of and trade in drugs, substances and precursors.

It prohibits unauthorised drug cultivation, possession and trafficking and provides for fines for legal entities that are in breach of drug trading regulations and for individuals who cross the border without declaring psychoactive medicines. More serious offences are prosecuted under the Criminal Code.

Medicinal cannabis

3.02 Croatia is another EU state that has made significant medicinal cannabis announcements in a short timeframe over the last 12 months.

All forms of cannabis production and use were outlawed in Croatia until a 2019 update eased the path for patients to access medicinal marijuana. Healthcare professionals in the country had been making the calls for several years.[2]

On April 25, 2019, amendments to the Act on Combating Drugs Abuse[3] entered into force which allowed for the cultivation and production of low THC cannabis for medicinal purposes in Croatia.

With the new law, companies that have a manufacturing permit for drugs or active substances from the Croatian Agency for Medicinal Products and Medical Devices (HALMED) can cultivate low THC cannabis for medicinal purposes subject to prior approval obtained from the Croatian Ministry of Health.

The same companies will also be able to produce/process low-THC cannabis for medicinal purposes with the prior approval of HALMED. At time of writing, the government is expected to give more detail the requirements and procedure for granting the necessary licenses.

> 'This legislative change is expected to increase the availability and reduce the costs of medicinal products made from cannabis which until now could only be imported to Croatia from abroad. The most important pharma related development introduced by the April 2019 law is the opening up of the possibility for cultivation and production of the medicinal cannabis subject to prior licenses obtained from the Croatian Ministry of Health and the Croatian Agency for Medicinal Products and Medical Devices. However, specific requirements for such activities and the procedure for obtaining the licenses still remain to be determined.' (Luka Tadic-Colic, partner at the Zagreb office of Wolf Theiss.)

A year earlier, Croatia's health minister Milan Kujundžić said the country would not legalise cannabis for recreational use in the manner of Canada, but that it was committed to a full medicinal program.

CZECH REPUBLIC

3.03 The extent of how far the Czech Republic has moved on from the era of Soviet rule is abundantly clear in its liberal approach to drug laws.

The tiny EU state decriminalised the possession of most drugs in 2010, updating its laws to reflect the relaxed approach it has taken since the country was formed in 1993.

Medicinal cannabis has been legal since 2013, although hard to obtain. In 2019, the government announced plans to cover up to 90% of the costs for applicable patients.

Background

3.04 'Fairly tolerant although rather muddy' is how many would describe Czech drugs legislation until the 2010 amendment to the 1961 Criminal Law[4] cleared up the issue and allowed for a possession limit of up to 15g of dried cannabis or up to five plants.

The possession of drugs for personal use in 'small amounts' is not a criminal offense in the Czech Republic, carries a fine of up to 15,000 Czech koruna (approximately US$612). As ever, what constitutes 'small' is at the centre of debates concerning the legal regulation of drug possession.

In 2001, the government adopted Resolution No 1177/01, which categorised drugs according to their social and health risks.

Initially, drugs were grouped into three categories, but the Ministry of Justice subsequently came up with a proposal for two categories, cannabis and other drugs. The provisions of different penalties for cannabis were formalised by virtue of Act No 40/2009 Coll., Criminal Code, which came into effect in January 2010.

Possession of a quantity 'greater than small' of: (a) cannabis or other substances containing THC is punished with up to one year imprisonment, prohibition of business activity, or forfeiture of an item of property or other asset, while possession of; (b) other drugs punishable by up to two years, prohibition of business activity, or forfeiture of an item of property or other assets.

For completion, the Supreme Court decriminalised the possession of 1.5g of methamphetamine, 1.5g of heroin, 1g of cocaine, 10g of cannabis dry matter, 5 units of ecstasy, and 5g of hashish. The court also stated that 'the drug user's possession of only one dose before using it is not illegal possession.'

Medicinal cannabis

3.05 Medicinal cannabis has been legal in the Czech Republic since 2013,[5] but use is limited to individuals over 18 and as a treatment for HIV, cancer, multiple sclerosis and Parkinson's disease. There is an electronic prescription form, and only approved medical professionals are permitted to prescribe cannabis, not general practitioners.

Most medical insurance companies do not cover treatment and it is an expensive product. The Czech Republic imports medical cannabis from the Netherlands, with only producer located in the Czech Republic. The lack of suppliers has resulted in a shortage.[6]

Growing or importing medical cannabis is subject to licensing under Law No 50/2013.

Licensing

3.06 The cultivation of THC cannabis plants for medical purposes is covered by the Czech Act on Dependency Producing Substances. The law states a licence must be granted by the State Institute for Drug Control. Businesses can grow for scientific and research purposes in areas approved by the Ministry of Health to handle the cannabis plants.

The licence is granted in a two-round tender organised by the Czech State Institute for Drug Control. Only applicants who can demonstrate their cultivation meets standard procedures will be considered.

According to Monika Rutland, partner at Czech law firm, Rutland & Partners:

> 'On the other hand, the cultivation of the hemp plants and CBD production from the hemp plants such CBD oil, CBD drops or CBD cosmetics products are less controlled in the Czech Republic, but still are subject to certain regulations which must be observed. A permit issued by the Ministry of Health is almost always required for handling of the hemp plants and CBD production.
>
> 'The special rules also apply for the import or export of cannabis plants and cannabis preparations to and from the Czech Republic, and a special import/export permit issued by the Ministry of Health may be required.'

Government help

3.07 In October 2019, the Czech government announced plans to subsidise the cost of medical cannabis from public health insurance. Patients will be reimbursed for up to 90% of the cost of their prescriptions, according to a bill which went through the country's parliament.

The new rate will apply to up to 30g of medical cannabis per month. There are also plans for the State Institute for Drug Control to regulate the price of the medicine, and for surcharges to be capped.

The government believes that the proposed limit to the proposal will be sufficient to completely cover patients in the country.

DENMARK

3.08 Denmark's approach to drug control has swung back and forth from hard-line to libertarian repeatedly over the last few decades, never quite hitting the sweet spot.

Open-air cannabis markets exist in the Freetown of Christiania, a self-governing commune famed for its anti-authoritarian and hippie-centric approach that has become a marijuana tourist hotspot. The police have cracked down hard on the dealers and gangs, but the government believes this has led to the dispersal of users and a rise in criminal activity across the country.[7]

A model for legalised cannabis in Copenhagen Municipality has since been floated, in part to counter the increasing expenditure on fighting drug trafficking and distribution,[8] and similar steps have been taken in the smaller cities that want to tackle the problem individually.

Two opposing forces are at play in Denmark; there is enormous public support for a modernisation of drug laws for further decriminalisation of recreational use and to allow for medicinal cannabis to be more widely available, but the political will opposing this is currently too great for any real shift to occur.

At the end of 2017, the Danish parliament passed a law permitting selected patient groups to be prescribed cannabis oil by their general practitioners as part of a four-year trial.[9]

Eligible ailments include multiple sclerosis, chronic pain, spinal cord injuries and chemotherapy-induced nausea and vomiting. Doctors were initially reluctant about prescribing the medicine, citing a lack of studies of effectiveness and side-effects.

Around 500 patients were initially expected to make use of the trial, but 12 months on, the Ministry of Health reported 1,400 people had acquired the prescriptions.

The success of this ongoing medicinal cannabis experiment has not caused any weakening of the political resolve to take a hard-line approach to drug enforcement.

Denmark has been identified as a strategically important European market by Canadian producers who have opened bases there following the launch of the trial. The country has a clear legislative framework for medical cannabis, low energy prices, a strong workforce and excellent pharmaceutical talent and experience.

Legal background

3.09 Prior to the medicinal cannabis trial, under Danish law it was legal for doctors to prescribe certain industrially-produced medicinal cannabis products. Sativex was approved by the Lægemiddelstyrelsen and could be prescribed to patients with muscular sclerosis (MS).

However, Denmark had experienced the same kinds of issues prevalent elsewhere; a reticence to prescribe from doctors, prohibitive costs for patients, and a general lack of research data that is inhibiting the market.

It was felt that, alongside helping citizens, the trial would also widen the availability and variety of products which do not have to be approved by the medicines agency or be prepared by a pharmacy.

Such is the demand to enter the market, businesses queued up for licences three years before the trial was due to end. The Laegemiddelstyrelsen medicines agency had issued 12 permits to companies to produce medical cannabis less than two months after the trial began.[10]

The programme is regulated by the Danish Act No 1668/2017 on the Medicinal Cannabis Pilot Programme, as amended.

The products used in the programme take the form of dried cannabis flowers, cannabis oils, capsules, tablets, etc. Doctors must take full responsibility for the product they prescribe and determine the dose for the individual patient.

All conventional treatments must be exhausted before a doctor can prescribe medicinal cannabis. The cannabis used can either be imported or grown in Denmark, and the trial has also opened the market for domestic companies.

All cannabis products must meet established requirements for cultivation of the plant and the manufacturing of the cannabis product, and Denmark is considered to have some of the highest standards in Europe.

Products must be standardised and consistent, meaning that the manufacturer must be able to document the content of the product, so that strength and quality is the same for all packages.

All company activities according to the programme must be authorised by the Danish Medicines Agency, meaning cultivating cannabis, producing and distributing cannabis bulk and cannabis primary products or cannabis intermediate products.

In parallel with the trial, a four-year development scheme was also introduced, under which the Danish Medicines Agency authorises research and development activities in terms of cultivating and handling cannabis, which may form part of the pilot programme at a later stage.

> 'It is expected that the Danish medicinal cannabis industry will grow and evolve. The programme and the development scheme run for four years until December 31, 2021 and is intended to provide a better basis for assessing the use of medicinal cannabis at the end of the trial period. The programme will be evaluated throughout its duration to determine whether it should be extended or made permanent.' (Martin Draebye Gantzhorn, partner at Bech:Bruun law firm in Copenhagen.)

The regulator

3.10 The Danish Medicines Agency is the competent national authority for implementing the programme and the development scheme and is an agency of the Danish Health Ministry.

The authority is responsible for:

- drafting regulations to help implement the programme and the development scheme as decided by the Danish Parliament;
- granting authorisations to companies according to the programme and the development scheme; and
- supervision of companies authorised according to the programme and the development scheme.

Advertising ban

3.11 It is illegal to advertise cannabis products covered by the programme. The legislation in the Medicinal Cannabis Pilot Programme prohibits advertising:

- cannabis end-products;
- cannabis intermediate products included on the published list of cannabis intermediate products; and
- cannabis primary products included on the published list of cannabis primary products.

This also includes any form of door-to-door information, canvassing activity or inducement designed to promote the prescription, supply, sale or consumption of cannabis end-products.

International cooperation

3.12 For trials like Denmark's to have any impact on lives, the standard of research internationally must improve significantly,[11] said the chief executive of non-profit Cannabis Danmark, a cannabis lobby group that connects everyone in the Danish ecosystem.

According to Rikke Jakobsen in an interview with Health Europa:

> 'Everything about cannabis is changing quickly and dependent on the legislation around the world. I don't think that this area can be developed by national states alone. If we want to see a development in the use of cannabis for medicinal purposes, states have to cooperate in the research. At the moment the research is hopelessly behind, and we haven't yet seen anyone who wants to invest in the gold standard of research.'

Jakobsen called on the EU to do more to open up funding for basic research in medicinal cannabis, and to enable medical universities to teach students in the field of the endocannabinoid system.

> 'This is a medical toolbox that can't go away again, and together we have to get it into the promising life science arena where cannabinoids and terpenes can be combined for each individual. That is my hope for the future, and I believe that this is the strategy we have to follow for the sake of the many millions of patients who can benefit from cannabis as a cheap and effective medicine.'

Recreational struggles and next steps

3.13 Possession, production, import/export and buying and selling of cannabis is illegal in Denmark. Cannabis falls under the 1955 Euphoriant Substances Act,[12] which is used for minor offences that can be punished with up to a two-year prison term, and the penal code §191 from 1969, which refers to the organised sale and possession of larger amounts of narcotics.

The Danish judicial framework initially did not distinguish between cannabis and other illegal drugs such as heroin. The penal code §191 from 1969 was, however, amended to allow law enforcement to make the distinction between cannabis and other drugs.

The Freetown Christiania in Copenhagen, Denmark's capital, is at the heart of the debate on policy initiatives relating to cannabis regulation, as smoking cannabis has been central to the social environment of Christiania since it grew from the hippie movement and youth revolts of the 1960s and 1970s.

The Freetown was founded in 1971 by squatters who occupied an abandoned military area in Copenhagen. A street-level cannabis market on Pusher Street has operated at Christiania since its beginning. Pusher Street is now one of the largest street-level cannabis markets in Northern Europe.

Approximately 800 people reside in Christiania, and the commune is a major tourist attraction. These alternative living experiments triggered the birth of several other communes across Denmark.

The police and government have discussed closing the Freetown many times, and this threat often results in locals shutting down cannabis stalls to appease the authorities.

Christiania's cannabis market has traditionally been controlled by the Hells Angels motorcycle gang, along with other factions. As hard drugs have mostly been kept out of Christiania, the cannabis market was tolerated until the early 2000s, when a zero-tolerance crackdown was initiated.

A major flashpoint occurred in September 2016 when a cannabis dealer shot and injured a civilian and two police officers.[13] Residents of Christiania again removed the cannabis stalls, but the sales points soon reappeared.

In response, police began to step up raids and deployed drone surveillance on Pusher Street, resulting in the arrest of 60 buyers and confiscation of 11.7kg of cannabis and 3,478 joints. To this day, stalls are repeatedly shut and then re-opened, with seemingly no end in sight to the cycle.

A majority in Copenhagen Municipality's city council (Borgerrepræsentation) wants to legalise cannabis, but the government remains opposed. Of the 55 city council representatives, 44 support the proposal.

In a written comment, Minister for Health Magnus Heunicke said that the government's position remains opposed to the legalisation of cannabis:

> 'Hash is associated with a long list of detrimental effects which can have serious consequences, particularly for those with mental health risk factors and for children and young people with social problems.
>
> 'Our responsibility is to help them with their education. We won't do that by legalising hash, which worsens the capacity to learn.'

FINLAND

3.14 Finland's drug policy is in line with international treaties on narcotics, and based on specially drafted administrative documents on drug policy, the National Drug Strategy of 1997.[14] Subsequent government resolutions and action plans have built on this.

The country's stance has been one of total prohibition; drug possession and use are illegal and punishable in Finland.

Finland maintains a zero-tolerance approach, but also promotes a policy of harm reduction which emphasises health. To that end, the focus on minimising the harms caused by drug use to individuals means promoting lower-risk ways of using drugs and regulating the safety of certain substances.

Under this policy, the main goal is not to intervene with drug use itself, but to prevent or reduce the most harmful consequences of drug use. Harm reduction was defined as part of Finnish drug policy in the National Drug Strategy of 1997.

The waiving of measures is possible when the punishment is a fine or up to six months' imprisonment. Measures can be waived at all stages of the criminal justice system; by the police, prosecutor, or the judge.

When the offence is minor, the police and the prosecutor can also choose to give a caution instead of bringing charges. Both cautions and waived charges stay in the police register for at least five years.

Legal background

3.15 The central framework for drug legislation in Finland is based on the Narcotics Act.[15] The provisions for drug offences are laid down in Chapter 50 of the Penal Code.

The use of drugs and the possession of small amounts of drugs for personal use constitute drug use offences that are punishable by a fine or a maximum of six months' imprisonment.

Prosecution and punishment can be waived if the offence is considered insignificant, or if the offender has sought treatment specified by the Decree of the Ministry of Social Affairs and Health.

Cannabis is not differentiated from any other drug in the Criminal Code, but according to consistently accepted practice, cannabis incurs the most lenient penalties of the penal range.[16]

Medicinal cannabis

3.16 Limited steps were taken to legalise access to medicinal cannabis in 2008. Medical practitioners were able to apply for a permit from the Finnish Medicines Agency, Fimea, in order to be able to prescribe medical cannabis for a specific patient. The permit must be renewed every year. Only a few hundred patients have prescriptions for medical cannabis in Finland.

Since 2012, Finland's medical marijuana program has undergone multiple updates. The approval of Sativex eliminated the application process for both pharmacies and patients, though traditional medical cannabis, which is supplied by Bedrocan, requires a special permission permit. Prescriptions are valid for a 30-day supply and are covered by health insurance.

Outlook

3.17 A survey by the Finnish National Institute for Health and Welfare (which is carried out every four years) found the proportion of people who said they have at least experimented with cannabis has quadrupled.

In 1992, some 6% of respondents said they'd tried cannabis once in their lives, while in 2018 that figure jumped to 24%. The use of cannabis appears rose, and was the most commonly-used illegal drug according to the survey. The use of prescription medication for non-medicinal purposes was the second-most commonly used group of drugs.

The survey found that Finnish residents have become more liberal in their views on the use of cannabis as medication and on questions regarding the legal penalties for drug use in general.

Some 42% of respondents said that criminal punishment for cannabis use should be eliminated, while 20% said Finland should consider decriminalising all recreational drugs.

Around 72% of respondents said they approve of the use of medicinal cannabis. About 18% of respondents said that cannabis should be legally obtainable for any purpose, while 54% said that cannabis should only be obtainable for medicinal purposes.

The THL's substance abuse survey reached out to 3,229 Finnish residents between the ages of 15 and 69 in 2018.

FRANCE

3.18 France regularly tops Europe's cannabis consumption polls despite having some of the continent's toughest anti-drug laws. According to Statista, between 2015 and 2017 11% of the population admitted they are regular smokers,[17] more than anywhere else in Europe.[18]

A year-long prison sentence and fines upwards of €3,400 (US$3,776) await individuals caught with relatively small amounts.

Despite updating laws in 2013, medicinal cannabis has proved almost impossible for patients to access, user groups report, and this is where the government is keen to focus efforts. According to patient groups, somewhere between 300,000 and 1m patients could be eligible to its use.

In May 2019, the government announced plans for a large 'medical marijuana experiment'.[19]

'There will be about two years of experimentation with therapeutic cannabis, beginning as soon as the health ministry gives the green light,' Professor Nicolas Authier, the head of pharmacology at Clermont-Ferrand University Hospital Centre's pain clinic, told FRANCE 24.

Campaigners believe the time is right for a rethink of both recreational and medicinal cannabis laws, however, given the amount of resources France expends on drug control and the tough punishments that are out of step with other large European economies.

In June 2019, the think tank set up to advise the government on policy, le Conseil d'analyse économique, estimated that there are 700,000 daily cannabis users in France, while 1.4m use it on a regular basis.[20]

It has argued that cannabis should be completely legalised for both medicinal purposes and adult recreational use in order to cut crime and create an income stream for the government. Such an industry would create up to 80,000 jobs, while bringing in up to €2.8bn (US$3.2bn), the think tank concluded.

Legal background

3.19 In France, use and possession of illicit drugs are criminal offences, and the law does not distinguish between possession for personal use or for trafficking, nor by type of substance.

The charges depend on how the prosecutor views the case, based on quantities of the drug found and the context.

In 2012, a directive establishing a criminal policy strategy for drug-related crimes reiterated that, when sentencing, courts should take into account simple drug use or drug dependence. New psychoactive substances are controlled under the Criminal Code, which lists them as drugs based on a decision of the Ministry of Social Affairs and Health.

A parliamentary report in January 2018[21] recommended introducing a fixed fine of €150 to €200 (US$166 to $222) for cannabis possession, instead of the harsher criminal penalties.

France's cannabis laws have not seen any significant revision since they were introduced in 1970. The current French President, Emmanuel Macron has given lukewarm backing to drug reform, but given France's volatile political environment and other priorities, the matter is not of major importance to his administration.

An IPSOS survey in October 2016 revealed 52% of French citizens backed legislation to cut crime,[22] and 43% support the decriminalisation of cannabis.

Medicinal cannabis

3.20 Medical cannabis has technically been legal in France since 2013, but there have been few, if any, recorded sales in the country. A decree which updated the Code of Public Health permitted the production, transformation and distribution of cannabis flowers and derivatives, by way of registration with the ANSM (Authorité National de Sécurité du Médicament).

Similar to the situation in the UK, specialists must recommend medical cannabis before doctors can prescribe it. For Bedrocan, Bediol and Bedica prescriptions, patients must have a 'special permission for compassionate use' permit.

The decree was meant to bring France in line with the rest of Europe in regard to Sativex availability in pharmacies. A dispute over the sale price of Sativex broke out between the manufacturer and the health authority, ensuring a ban on sales from 2014.

Bedrocan, Bediol and Bedica prescriptions are not restricted to specific conditions, but Sativex can only be prescribed for MS and a limited number of other conditions. National health insurance partly covers the cost of the Sativex or Bedrocan purchases.

Many French patients travel to other countries to obtain medicinal cannabis after being prescribed by a French doctor, with the Netherlands the most popular destination.

The situation became such a mess, a specialised committee on cannabis (CSST) was set up in the French parliament, and in 2019 it presented its final recommendations for the implementation of a two-year medical cannabis pilot programme to the French National Agency for Medicines and Health Products Safety (ANSM).

The experiment will officially launch in early 2020, running until 2022, before a final report containing all the clinical data will be presented to the committee. Any change in the law will only happen post-2022 when the report has been fully digested by all relevant parties.

French patients who have been unable to cure their pain with other medicines are eligible, and the committee has sought individuals in palliative care, epilepsy patients, and those suffering from the side effects of chemotherapy to take part.

Patients with muscle spasms related to multiple sclerosis will also be part of the tests.

Ingestion is to occur via oils, drops and capsules, at participating pain centres, multiple sclerosis clinics, and other medical centres across the country.

It is likely that in 2021 France will update its laws to legalise medicinal cannabis again, having technically legalised it in 2013.

Recreational movement

3.21 Life sciences partner at Allen & Overy LLP Eveline Van Keymeulen noted that during a French senate hearing, Republican politicians warned the authorisation of medical cannabis 'should not be a Trojan horse for the legalisation of recreational cannabis'.

Meanwhile, other senators and stakeholders drew attention to the fact that France will additionally have to consider adequately regulating so-called well-being cannabis (CBD food supplements, cosmetics with very low levels of THC etc).

An investigation into other uses of cannabis in France is likely, but regulatory amendments with respect to well-being cannabis is unlikely to take place before the Court of Justice of the European Union takes a decision in the pending referral (Case C-663/18), and the French Supreme Court stayed proceedings pending the judgment of the CJEU in this respect.[23]

France is the world's sixth largest economy and the third largest in Europe; therefore any moves to liberalise and create a cannabis industry would immediately make it a major global player.

> 'Stakeholders have repeatedly underlined that France is the leading country in Europe for industrial hemp production, and the third largest producer of hemp in the world. It has the necessary skills and expertise to ensure proper and sufficient production of cannabis for medical purposes as well.' (Van Keymeulen.)

GEORGIA

3.22 Georgia grows most of its own illicit cannabis and, due to its strategically important location between two continents, serves as a well-established smuggling route for drugs into Europe and Russia from Central Asia.

Cannabis in Georgia is legal in terms of its possession and consumption following a ruling by the Constitutional Court of Georgia on 30 July 2018.[24]

It thus became the first former Soviet state to completely decriminalise cannabis consumption. The decision marked another instance of a high court ruling cannabis prohibition was unconstitutional, as has occurred in South Africa and Mexico in recent years.

Georgia's highest court ruled that punishing an individual for using cannabis restricts an individual's freedom as the plant can only potentially cause harm to the individual. The court ruled that punishing a person for using cannabis will only be allowed if their actions put a third party at risk. Cultivation and selling remains an offence, however.

In accordance with this ruling, the court announced that respective norms of Georgia's Criminal Code[25] and Code of Administrative Offenses were now null and void.

Reform had been on the cards for a number of years. In 2015, the same court delivered a verdict stating the rule of imprisonment for personal use of marijuana was 'too strict' and needed to be relaxed, and a year later declared the rule invalid.[26]

Despite this, the norms envisaging imprisonment for this offence still remained in other legislative documents of Georgia, in particular in the Criminal Code and Administrative Offenses Code. The details were removed following the 2018 ruling.

Medicinal cannabis

3.23 The court's decision also had an impact on how medicinal cannabis would be industrialised within the country. Georgian Prime Minister Mamuka Bakhtadze stated that an Interior Ministry initiative concerning marijuana export from Georgia for medical and cosmetic purposes would be strongly regulated.[27]

He tasked officials with drawing up 'tough regulations' to control the cultivation and export domestically, 'to avoid chaotic and illegal processes'.

Licensees are to be determined on a competitive basis, and criteria will include geographical area, the amount of marijuana produced, and others.

As of October 2019, the bill was deadlocked with no further movement.

GERMANY

3.24 Germany's 83m population makes it the largest European market for medicinal cannabis, and the largest cannabis market in the world outside of North America.

Medicinal cannabis was legalised in March 2017, but in a very un-German manner the process was fraught with delays, regulatory mix-ups, court cases and bureaucratic inefficiencies.[28]

Patient demand surprised government officials and led to frequent shortages in pharmacies, as the country had no domestic production operations. Every ounce of medical marijuana had to be imported, at great expense.

A tender process to anoint domestic cultivators eventually yielded three victors, all with Canadian roots, and now production in Germany is underway. Legal experts say the amounts to be grown will come in significantly below demand as the government feels its way into the new regime.

There are no immediate plans to open a recreational cannabis market in Germany, but the matter has been openly discussed by Angela Merkel's ruling coalition party.

Legal background

3.25 A partial decriminalisation by the German Supreme Court for holding small amounts of personal cannabis for recreational purposes in 1994 was the most notable aspect of reform until 2016. During this period, medicinal cannabis in Germany was only available for critically ill individuals who received special permission to use it.

Medicinal cannabis was legalised in 2017 under an update to the Narcotic Drugs Act, which reaffirmed that recreational use and home-growing were not permitted.[29]

The amendment allowed doctors to on a case-by-case basis, prescribe medical marijuana to seriously ill patients either if there is no generally accepted medical standard for the treatment of the disease or symptoms. They could also prescribe it if alternative treatments are available but the physician concludes that they should not be applied in this particular case after considering the risks and the condition of the patient.

In addition, for both options, there needs to be the likelihood that the treatment will have a noticeable positive effect on the illness or on certain symptoms.

The definition of 'serious illness' is not given in the Act, however the non-binding Regulation on Medicinal Products from the German Federal Joint Committee, composed of physicians, dentists, hospitals and health insurance funds, defines it as 'an illness that is either life-threatening or that will affect the quality of life permanently because of the severity of the resulting health problems.' The Federal Joint Committee is the supreme self-regulatory body in the German health sector.

The Parliament also amended the Social Security Code n 5 on Statutory Health Care Insurance (Sozialgesetzbuch V – gesetzliche Krankenversicherung, SGB V) and introduced Sec 31 para 6 SGB V, which dictates the legal requirements for physicians to prescribe cannabis for medical use. In the context of the amendment, the Parliament created within the Federal Authority for Medicine and Medical Devices (Bundesanstalt für Arzneimittel und Medizinprodukte, BfArM) the sub-unit Cannabis Agency (Cannabisagentur).[30]

The Cannabis Agency regulates the domestic cultivation and production of pharmaceutical-grade cannabis, the sub-unit Federal Opium Authority (Bundesopiumstelle) remains competent to approve the import and trade of narcotic drugs in general, including pharmaceutical-grade cannabis.

Germany offers full medical aid coverage for cannabis-based medicines, and it was the first country in the world to cover the cost of medicinal cannabis, when approved by physicians, through its national health insurance system.

Outcomes

3.26 In 2017, as they drew up the bill to enable more individuals to use medicinal cannabis, German lawmakers estimated that about 700 patients per year would want the prescriptions.

The government was stunned when inside the first 10 months, more than 13,000 applications were made. By November 2018, 40,000 patients had been prescribed marijuana in Germany.

With no domestic production, the government had been forced to rely on expensive imports from the Netherlands and Canada, which resulted in a shortage.

An initial tender process for domestic growers was launched by the regulator, BfArM, in March 2017. It was an extremely lucrative contract for the production and delivery of up to 6.6 metric tons of cannabis per year, with the cultivation to take place within Germany.

To qualify, applicants had to meet a number of requirements, one being experience of growing cannabis. Unfortunately, as this was against the law in Germany, no domestic firms could progress to the next stage of the tender process, which had been set up to serve them specifically.

The tender was halted, the rules updated, and it was restarted only for a second legal challenge in a Dusseldorf court to halt it again in March 2018.

In April 2018, Germany's Federal Agency for Medicines and Medicinal Products (BfArM), published an 18-page tender document, for which 118 companies applied. It envisaged the growing of up to 6,600kg (14,550lb) by the year 2022, with the first harvest in 2019.

Eventually, after more legal wrangling, three companies were awarded domestic cultivation licences in April 2019. The three were selected from a field of 79 entrants, and were graded on domestic cultivation, based on a points system focused on infrastructure, quality standard, security plans and price.

Aurora Produktions GmbH, the German arm of Canadian giant Aurora were handed five lots, as were Aphria Deutschland GmbH, another German office of a Canadian cannabis titan. Demecan GmbH was handed three lots. Demecan is a joint venture partner of Canadian firm Wayland Group. Trading of Wayland's stock was halted on the Canadian Securities Exchange pending the news.

Demecan was contracted to grow 600kg (1,320lb) a year for a period of four years[31] and subsidiaries of Aurora and Aphria were contracted to grow 1,000kg each annually.[32]

The three companies have until September 2020 to deliver the first harvest, which must meet Good Agricultural and Collection Practices (GACP) and Good Manufacturing Practice (GMP) quality standards.

They are not expected to meet demand by the time the first harvests are available; during the first half of 2019, about 2,500kg of cannabis flower was imported from the Netherlands and Canada.

Growers in Germany must have indoor facilities with 'bunker style' security measures. The contracted production for the 13 lots totals 10,400kg (22,928lb) over a period of four years, with each lot representing 200kg per year.

A clause that could allow production to increase by 10% during that period is included in the contracts.

To comply with the Single Convention on Narcotic Drugs of 1961, all the production will be bought by BfArM and resold to medical marijuana manufacturers, wholesalers or pharmacies. The price at which the BfArM will buy the flowers from the producers is not publicly released.

Next steps

3.27 Germany is the top destination for cannabis businesses wanting to crack Europe, but there are still uncertainties within the regulation, and the path for companies is not entirely clear either.

> 'Everyone wants to enter the German market. But it's tough for companies to do so because you cannot advertise for medical cannabis, as that is prohibited. To put on a round-table event is a big thing, you may just want to do some simple promotion, but it is very difficult and will take a long time [for the market to open]. I think longer than four or five years.' (Kai-Friedrich Niermann, Rechtsanwalt lawyer.)

Clarification in certain regulatory areas that have not yet been addressed would definitely be helpful, according to Peter Homberg, head of the life sciences practice at Dentons in Berlin:

> 'Today, it is clear that you need to obtain a specific import permit from the BfArM in order to export irradiated cannabis plants to Germany, but that had not previously been addressed in the legislation and so existed in a kind of grey area.'

He said this is one of a number of issues that have to be clarified, including laws around CBD products:

> 'Part of the problem is perhaps that the legislation was made relatively quickly. We also need better guidance for doctors so that they are able to compliantly prescribe cannabis products.'

Under the current legislation, it is not clear what the preconditions for prescribing are, or whether there are any indications besides chronic pain and multiple sclerosis, for example, where cannabis can be helpful.

> Much more information and education is needed, for businesses, patients and in the medical sector. The patients affiliated to medicinal cannabis are being catered for, everyone else has to fight,' he said. 'Doctors and physicians are reluctant to prescribe; they don't know much about medicinal cannabis. The patients who are suitable don't know much about it either. We have a lot of education work to do to broaden the market.' (Niermann.)

CBD products are increasingly popular, and there are legal options besides the licensing as a regular medicine in order to get them to market.

> 'But they both cost money, and you have to be prepared to spend to get a licensed CBD product which allows you to make health claims.

Once again, the quirks of German laws around advertising have stymied progress. As Niermann points out: 'What's the sense in developing products and brands when you can't tell the consumer what the product is good for?'

GREECE

3.28 Greece is pushing hard to become a major player in the European cannabis market, and is hoping to steal a march on other Mediterranean countries as an export-friendly cultivation hub with its fast-tracked reforms.

The country legalised industrial cannabis production in 2016 after a joint ministerial decision between the ministries of Health and Finance, and ban on growing was lifted in 2018.

Former deputy economy minister Stergios Pitsiorlas told reporters in 2018 that 'the impact that medical cannabis could have on Greece's struggling economy could be substantial.'

Greece's climate and environment, along with its welcoming regulatory approach, have made it a more desirable location than northern European for international cannabis firms seeking a base.

Bioprocann SA was the first recipient of a Greek licence, and Biomecann was the second. The companies pledged to invest a combined $25m and hire over 100 people. All cultivation licenses are for a five-year period and are reviewed annually.

In total, firms must acquire three licences; cultivation, installation, and medical. As of October 2019, no business had negotiated the entire process, however optimism in Greece is high that 2020 will see the first harvests.

While Greece's liberalisation of its cannabis sector began under the previous administration, the momentum has continued under the new regime. In the first year, 26 cultivation licences were approved.

The pro-business framework in the cannabis sector continues as Greece joins the ranks of European states moving away from a state-monopoly model on cultivation.

Recreational cannabis in Greece remains outlawed. Greek Law No 4139/2013[33] stipulates that those who obtain, process, or cultivate cannabis plants may still be sentenced to prison, although for no more than five months.

Law No 4523: 'Provisions on the production of medical final cannabis products and other provisions' was published in the *Official Gazette* on 7 March 2018.[34]

According to the legislation, cannabis producers are required to obtain pre-authorisation before they plant, and must also obtain and use cannabis seeds which meet certain criteria.

Costas Vamvakas, managing director of Greek business consultancy VK Premium and former chairman of the country's chamber of commerce, has been at the centre of the burgeoning sector since 2016, coordinating business, healthcare and government networks.

'The Greek legislative regime is in my opinion one of the most favourable anywhere in the world for the investors,' Vamvakas said, laying out the steps:

1. Establish a business entity in Greece.
2. Identify an appropriate land plot that meets the legal requirements for growing.
3. Complete the form for an installation license, which is actually a questionnaire. The requested info refers to the selected land plot, the products to be made and high-level technical specifications such as type of facilities and processing methods.
4. On gaining the installation licence, the investor may build the facilities.
5. In parallel, they can prepare the file to receive the EU GMP standards certificate.
6. Upon completion of construction and machinery installation, the investor will request for the operation licence.
7. The investor may start testing his cultivation and processing facilities producing relevant products, but cannot sell.
8. Finally, the marketing licence must be issued by the Greek Organization of Drugs following the acceptance of the EU GMP standards certificate.
9. Acquire all of the above and products can be sold to the markets.

As per the law, the facilities must be vertically-integrated, including cultivation and processing units on the same plot of land.

'I have been involved in business for many years and this is the first time I have seen things move so quickly, it's amazing,' said Vamvakas.

Patient information

3.29 Stergios Pitsiorlas, the deputy economy minister, said the first medicinal cannabis products were expected to hit the market in 2020, and that initially the industry would be mainly export-oriented.

Thousands of patients in Greece are thought to use cannabis for a range of serious medical conditions, however there are no figures presently.

Under Greece's licensing system, medicinal cannabis products would be available on prescription from chemists. Health minister Andreas Xanthos explained that it would not be subsidised through state health insurance schemes.

IRELAND

3.30 After years of delays, in June 2019 Ireland published legislation to allow for a five-year medical cannabis trial.[35] France and Switzerland are running similar experiments through 2020.

Under the Medical Cannabis Access Programme (MCAP), Irish specialists can prescribe pre-approved medicinal cannabis to patients who have failed to respond to standard treatments for specific conditions.

These include spasticity associated with multiple sclerosis, intractable nausea and vomiting that comes with chemotherapy, severe refractory epilepsy.

Under the new law, commercial operators whose cannabis products meet the specified requirements can supply products to the Irish market. Suppliers apply to have their medical cannabis products assessed for suitability in the first stage of the process.

Canadian giant Tilray, as an example, had certain cannabis oils approved, having lobbied the Irish government successfully throughout 2018 and 2019.

The Access Programme makes products available for prescription once it is satisfied that they meet the criteria. Medical consultants must prove the patient has failed to respond to other treatments, as cannabis will still be defined as a 'specified controlled drug'.

According to the Health Service Executive (HSE), authorisation will be on a named-patient arrangement and subject to the following conditions:

- treatment is consultant-initiated;
- online reimbursement approval is required for each patient;
- all standard approved treatments have been exhausted for that patient; and
- new patients are initiated on Irish pharmacy-supplied products.

The Medical Cannabis Access Programme will operate on a pilot basis for five years before a review in 2024.

Legal background

3.31 Under Ireland's Misuse of Drugs Act 1977, cannabis, cannabis resin, cannabinol and its derivatives are Schedule 1 drugs. In 1998,[36] an update to the regulations expressed that the manufacture, production, preparation, sale, supply, distribution and possession of cannabis was unlawful for any purpose, except under licence from the Minister for Health.

British company GW Pharmaceuticals acquired licences in 2002 and 2003 to allow medical trials of the cannabis extract nabiximols (Sativex). In 2014, the 1998 regulations were amended further to allow nabiximols to be prescribed.

The first licence for medical use of cannabis oil was issued in December 2016 to allow Tristan Forde, a two-year-old boy with Dravet syndrome, to continue treatment begun in Colorado.[37]

Similar to the experiences of individuals in other EU states, Irish citizens have been forced to travel to areas such as Canada and the Netherlands to access cannabis-based medicines they believe will help ease their symptoms.

In 2017, the Irish government visited several countries searching for an appropriate cannabis supplier, meeting with government and business figures eventually an agreement was struck with Denmark.

Canadian firms had been lobbying Ireland vociferously,[38] with Aurora aggressive in its assertion that Irish government was missing an opportunity to have cannabis grown locally.

Aurora plant scientist Shane Morris told the Irish Times:

> 'If they want domestic production [versus importation], it is more likely that there would be a tender process, which we would be happy to engage in. Our cannabis isn't grown by guys in dreadlocks. It is grown at full pharmaceutical facilities with all the scrutiny and requirements that go with that.'

Next steps

3.32 Several (Irish) commentators have concluded that as the psychological barrier of medicinal cannabis has been breached, a full-scale recreational market will follow inside five years.[39]

ITALY

3.33 Italy has a tightly regulated medicinal cannabis market; domestic cultivation is quite literally a military operation, as the army has the sole licence to grow.

With a pro-cannabis population of 60m people, a faltering economy, and ideal growing conditions, the country's immense potential has been identified by Canadian producers and distributors who consider it a strategically important market.

Italy was the second largest global producer of hemp until manufacturers under US pressure turned to cotton following the Second World War, and the market collapsed.[40]

In December 2016, the government attempted to jump-start the dormant industry by enacting Law 242[41] to regulate hemp cultivation and production. Although the consequences were not clear until later, lawmakers neglected to address cultivation of trace amounts of THC in hemp flowers.

A loophole allowing cannabis flower to be sold if the level of THC was under 0.2% created a 'cannabis light' market as quick-thinking entrepreneurs took advantage of the regulatory grey area.

Stores selling 'cannabis light' opened across the country and the product proved enormously popular. Eventually in May 2019, Italy's Court of Cassation, the country's highest court, ruled that the sale of 'cannabis light' is against the law.[42]

The fight by campaigners is ongoing, and Italy has a new government. This has given hope to the many businesses angry at the Court of Cassation's judgment.

Medicinal marijuana has been legal in Italy since 2006, but demand has always greatly exceeded supply.

In August 2018, Italy's health minister announced plans to widen the domestic market for cultivation. In July 2019, then-minister Giulia Grillo announced on a Facebook post Italy was willing to increase production through licensing public-private partnerships.

Lobbyists believe the promise of more jobs and taxable revenue will be enough to sway the country in favour of outsourcing medicinal cannabis production to the private sector.

There is almost no chance of a recreational market opening in Italy, despite multiple campaigns, and petitions, and an unsuccessful push by 218 elected politicians to railroad through change in 2015.

Numerous Italian governments have been presented with historic evidence that legalising a recreational market would break the stranglehold the Mafia has on Italy's drug supply and black market, but the appetite does not exist at the highest level yet to facilitate the necessary adjustments.

In December 2019, Italy's Supreme Court handed down a surprise ruling that growing cannabis at home for private usage is legal. The court stipulated the product must be for 'the exclusive use of the grower'.

The case was brought by a citizen and concerned two plants he had grown at home.

The court has not issued any further guidance and much of the ruling, including the limits on the amount grown, or whether it concerns hemp or marijuana, is unclear. The court is expected to further outline its decision, but there is currently no date as to when.

Legal background

3.34 The Italian Ministry of Defence (MOD) has the only licence to grow cannabis domestically, and it controls the country's production. The arrangement has led to a bottleneck where demand is significantly outstripping supply, and the government must import the remaining amount to cover the shortfall.

Canada's Aurora Cannabis Inc announced in July 2019 it had won a two-year contract to supply 400kg of medical cannabis, still felt by many to be insufficient to deal with demand. The supply contract was signed in September.

Aurora has EU GMP certified facilities, and imports the product into Italy through Aurora Deutschland, its wholly-owned European unit.

Until 2019, Italy also relied on imports of Bedrocan from the Netherlands, and in 2018 this concerned around 450kg in 2018, covering two-thirds of Italy's supply.

The medicinal product in question is dried cannabis flower, whole or milled, and the most recent tender won by Aurora is spread over three lots: 320kg of high THC content, 40kg of a CBD/THC split product, and 40kg of high CBD content.

The MOD wants the supply to be delivered every four months with the target price on the contract set at €3 or €4 per gram (US$3.3–$4.4) depending on the strain, with the contract worth around $1.2m.

Canadian influx

3.35 The 2019 tender was only open for two weeks and caught the market by surprise,[43] but any concerns over the MOD's activities has not stopped a slew of Canadian firms increasing their presence in Italy over the last 12 months.

On December 6, 2018, Toronto cannabis investment vehicle Canopy Rivers pumped $17m into CanapaR Italy, an Italy-based organic hemp production and processing platform, taking its total shareholding to 49.9% as part of a $25m investment.

Canopy Rivers is planning to spend more than €100m ($115m) on greater production in the EU over the next two years.

In late November 2018, Toronto-based investment firm LGC Capital snapped up almost half of EasyJoint, Italy's 'cannabis light' originators for €4.8m ($US5.3m) in cash and stock.

EasyJoint was the first firm to successfully scale hemp flower production after the 'cannabis light' legislative tweak in December 2016.

Vancouver's CROP also announced its large Italian CBD greenhouse facility had been upgraded ready for the start of the 2019 growing season, and that it had identified six new retail locations to sell products on the high street.

CROP and partner XHemplar are currently working with Italian agencies to import new CBD genetics to populate its upgraded facility that are expected to command premium prices. Discussions are also continuing with an Italy-based pharmaceutical company to secure off-take agreements for the 2019 harvests.

CROP is also planned to build a state-of-the-art extraction facility allowing for in-house processing of hemp biomass.

> 'Italy is our bridgehead into Europe. Our Italian partners are making significant progress on multiple fronts to ensure that the European operations are running at full capacity to take full advantage of the rapidly growing demand there.' (CROP Infrastructure CEO, Michael Yorke.)

LUXEMBOURG

3.36 The Grand Duchy of Luxembourg began briefing in August 2018 it wanted to become the first European Union state to make recreational cannabis legal, and it wants the market open by 2021.[44]

The legislative proposals are underway, and the Luxembourg government has approached Canadian and European drug policy researchers to provide data on Canada's regulatory model.

Should it enact full legalisation, Luxembourg will join Canada, Uruguay, South Africa, and 11 US states (along with Mexico, which is likely to be up and running by 2021) in diverging from international agreements to outlaw non-medical use of cannabis.

Luxembourg's neighbours within the EU have already voiced concerns over the impact of drug smuggling on their borders and the potential for a recreational domino effect, just as the single market begins to open to medicinal use.

The EU has repeated its stance that its member states must remain in adherence to the 1961 Single Convention on Narcotic Drugs.

Legal background

3.37 The state of Luxembourg is one of the more liberal EU jurisdictions in regard to cannabis, and in 2001 decriminalised possession for personal use. A fine is the most common outcome, however prison sentences are possible if there are aggravating circumstances (eg use in schools or in the presence of minors).

The basic national drug law *Loi concernant la vente de substances médicamenteuses et la lutte contre la toxicomanie*[45] regulates both the selling of controlled medicines and the fight against drug addiction. It dates back to 19 February 1973 and was amended to decriminalise cannabis on 27 April 2001.

Use of cannabis or cannabis resin, without aggravating circumstances such as in presence of minors, is punishable by a fine of €251 to €2,500 (US$278–$2,774) in the Correctional Court (article 7B). Use of other drugs (not cannabis) without aggravating circumstances is punished by the same bracket of fine and/or a prison sentence between eight days to six months in prison (7A).

Luxembourg officials made a research trip to Canada in 2017, and were optimistic they could create a similar model and run a regulated legal cannabis market, in the hopes of reducing harm, cutting the crime rate, and better educating citizens about the dangers of drugs.

Luxembourg's current National Drug Strategy and Action Plan 2015–19 explicitly refers to such research as an integrated part of the transversal axes of demand and supply reduction, supporting evidence-based drug policies. A new National Strategy and Action Plan on Drugs and Addictions 2020–24 is nearing publication, at the time of writing.

In early 2018, a public petition regarding the legalisation of recreational use of cannabis gained the critical number of signatures to allow for a public debate in the Parliament. This led each political party to state a position on the legalisation of cannabis for recreational purposes before the elections that took place in October 2018.

Under the new proposals, Luxembourg will permit adults aged 18 and over to possess up to 30g of cannabis while in public. Minors aged between 12 and 17 will not be criminalised for possessing up to 5g of the drug, but the consequences they may face have not been finalised.

The government also intends to introduce strict regulations on the sale of cannabis. The THC content of cannabis will have an upper limit, which has yet to be fixed, and people who break the new rules will face harsh punishments 'even harsher penalties than now', according to the government.

Authorities are yet to decide if residents will be permitted to cultivate cannabis for their personal use.

The bulk of national funding for research is provided by the Ministry of Health, the National Research Fund, the National Fund against Certain Forms of Criminality and the Grand-Duchesse Charlotte National Welfare Organisation (the Oeuvre Nationale de Secours Grand-Duchesse Charlotte). The national focal point is a reference centre for drug-related research and manages most of these funds. Other relevant actors include the National Prevention Centre for Drug Addiction and research departments at the University of Luxembourg.

Medicinal cannabis

3.38 Luxembourg's politicians unanimously passed a bill in 2018 to legalise medicinal cannabis. In the pilot scheme that followed, the government said applications for the drug had 'exceeded expectations', resulting in a shortage.[46]

Following the success of the trials, Deputy Prime Minister and health minister Étienne Schneider said that the potential for cannabis farms in Luxembourg would be examined when drawing up the recreational bill.

Specially trained practitioners can prescribe medicinal cannabis in the event of an advanced or terminal illness causing chronic pain, for cancer patients who suffer nausea as a result of chemotherapy, or for multiple sclerosis to help control muscle spasms.

Luxembourg signed an agreement with Canadian firm Canopy Growth Germany, which began supplying from September 2019, in the hopes of avoiding a future shortage.

Government thinking

3.39 Speaking to Luxembourg media outlet *Paperjam* in August 2019, Deputy Prime Minister Étienne Schneider revealed a little more about the government's cannabis thinking:[47]

Updating the laws had been a long-term government objective and the state planned to invest 'a lot of money' in the years to come, acknowledging that the subject of cannabis legalisation was of interest all over the world.

The country is wary of attracting cannabis tourists, which is why the limits on sales only to residents will apply, and an ID system will be created.

> 'In practice it will be complicated, with the confidentiality of personal data, we have to see how we manage all that. We want to prevent Luxembourg from becoming Amsterdam and everyone coming here to buy cannabis. It will be forbidden to consume in public, in bars or in the street.'

Schneider also said the country would also try to limit the proliferation of border controls by its French, German or Belgian neighbours. Ultimately, the aim is not to reduce consumption, he said, but to fight against drug trafficking and to stop potentially dangerous products entering the country.

> 'For decades we have been running a drug policy that has no result. 'People, especially young people, get their supplies of cannabis from the black market and what they sell is shit. And then there is always the risk, when you start with cannabis, to switch to other more dangerous products. As you are always in contact with your dealers, they always end up trying to sell you things that have a bigger profit margin for them. That's why we thought that by removing cannabis from the black market, we would not only control the quality and therefore the harmfulness, but in addition, we would get consumers out of this environment.'

MALTA

3.40 Malta has never been slow to catch on to populist trends that can bring in quick investments, and it has opened arms to remote gambling operators, bitcoin and blockchain entrepreneurs (and tax refugees) in recent years. Now Malta is positioning itself as the European medicinal cannabis jurisdiction of choice for scientists and researchers.

The country updated its drug laws in 2018, and has since put on a spread of events and conferences aimed at attracting healthcare professionals and cannabis investors.

Malta officially legalised medicinal cannabis in March 2018, and under the law, family doctors can prescribe it to patients. Patients can access non-smoking forms of medicine at pharmacies with a doctor's prescription after a control card has been approved by the Superintendent of Public Health.

Three conditions are eligible to be treated by medicinal cannabis: chronic pain, spasticity in multiple sclerosis and side effects of chemotherapy, with more expected to be approved in time.

Almost immediately on the bill being enacted, Malta Enterprise, the government's inward investment agency, announced agreements with five foreign companies to produce medicinal cannabis; three Canadian firms and one each from Australia and Israel.[48]

The government said the initiative would create 185 jobs, and the combined investment was worth €30m. In total, more than 40 international companies applied to start investing in the Maltese cannabis sector, out of which Malta Enterprise accepted 20 projects.

MGC Pharma, Supreme, Aurora, Aphria, Columbia Care, MPXI, Wayland, Alvit, Nuuvera and Panaxia have all been awarded Malta Enterprise's Letter of Intent, the first step towards a licence.

Background

3.41 In 2018, Malta enacted the Production of Cannabis for Medicinal and Research Purposes Act[49] which provides the legislative measures to permit the production of cannabis for medicinal and research purposes.

This law followed the amendment of the Drug Dependence Act[50] with respect to prescribing of medicinal preparations of cannabis.

The Production of Cannabis for Medicinal and Research Purposes (Fees) Regulations, 2018 is available here: http://justiceservices.gov.mt/DownloadDocument.aspx?app=lp&itemid=29382&l=1.

Companies producing medicinal cannabis in Malta are subject to annual fees amounting to a maximum of €63,000 (US$70,000) if all related activities are undertaken, and an initial application fee of a maximum of €100,000 ($110,000), according to the government.[51]

Regulatory Framework

3.42 The Medicines Authority provides guidance and consultation on scientific matters to support research and development as well as accessibility of quality medicinal cannabis.

The regulator reviews applications for the importation and wholesale distribution of cannabis-based products for medicinal use.

Activities related to the production of cannabis for medicinal and research purposes are regulated through comprehensive evaluation of scientific and technical documentation, security considerations, and good practices.

Importation and wholesale distribution of medicinal cannabis

3.43 A licensed importer or wholesale distributor may source to Malta cannabis-based products or synthetic cannabinoid products licensed under the Medicines Act (Chapter 458 of the Laws of Malta) or manufactured under EU Good Manufacturing Practice (GMP), subject to the necessary approvals and permits, granted by the Superintendence of Public Health.

The application for the importation and/or wholesale distribution of cannabis-based products or synthetic cannabinoid products in accordance with the Medicines Act and the Drug Dependence (Treatment not Imprisonment, Act) form is available at: https://eforms.gov.mt/pdfforms.aspx?fid=HCC075e.

Production of cannabis for medicinal and research purposes

3.44 Operations related to medicinal cannabis production, analysis and research require a Letter of Intent (LoI) from Malta Enterprise, followed by assessment through the regulatory authority. Inspections of facilities are carried out in accordance with the principles and guidance of EU good practices.

The Medicines Authority considers applications for EU-GMP certification, both for local and international facilities. The application for a licence in accordance with the Production of Cannabis for Medicinal and Research Purposes Act (Cap. 578 of the Laws of Malta) is available at: https://servizz.gov.mt/en/Pages/Health-and-Community-Care/Health/Medicines/WEB2427/default.aspx.

The application for a variation to a licence issued in accordance with the Production of Cannabis for Medicinal and Research Purposes Act (Cap. 578 of the Laws of Malta) is available at: https://servizz.gov.mt/en/Pages/Health-and-Community-Care/Health/Medicines/WEB2426/default.aspx.

Recreational use

3.45 The government has no timeframe for the full legalisation of cannabis, according to a response from the Office of the Prime Minister (OPM) to the Malta Independent newspaper, but it has refused to completely rule it out.

In 2015, the government partially decriminalised cannabis for small amounts (3.5g) for personal consumption. The updates to the medicinal laws sparked fresh interest from pro-cannabis groups who sense the government may be considering a fully-regulated adult market.

Cynicism

3.46 As a benefit of being a European Union state, international businesses setting up shop in Malta can easily obtain a licence that allows them to passport that service across the single market without having to gain the necessary approvals in each area.

Malta's success as an online gambling hub has been down to its willingness to take on smaller operators attracted to Malta's tax breaks who can then target areas such as the UK.

However, many of gambling's problem operators either banned from serving the UK (and elsewhere), or fined for anti-money laundering failures[52] in recent years, are Maltese-licensed, prompting questions over the robustness of Malta's licensing system. Some observers are cynical of the speed at which Malta has made itself open for cannabis business, effectively accusing it of passing laws first and thinking second.[53]

During a tour of North America in October 2019, Malta's Prime Minister Joseph Muscat said cannabis companies based in the country are set to produce and export around €1bn (US$1.1bn) worth of products over the next three years.

'Exportation will begin in the first quarter of next year,' Muscat said in comments to TVM. 'We are estimating that exports by Year 3 of these companies will reach more than €1bn and that 900 jobs will be made available; however, we can attract even more players in this respect.'[54]

NETHERLANDS

3.47 When debating the issue of cannabis legalisation, politicians will often declare they do not wish their town and city to become 'the next Amsterdam'. Notwithstanding Quentin Tarantino's bid to educate us in his movie *Pulp Fiction*, many misconceptions remain about Netherlands drug laws and particularly cannabis consumption in public.

Selling drugs is illegal, however, some city councils allow the sale of soft drugs in so-called 'coffeeshops'.[55] The coffeeshop owners are not prosecuted if their establishment meets strict requirements. This situation has led to something known as the 'back-door problem'.

Since 1976, the Dutch government has regulated the 'front-door' of Dutch coffeeshops; the sale and consumption of cannabis, primarily through the country's Opium Act.

In the 1990s the government introduced the AHOJ-G criteria in 1991, and enacted later in 1994, (the G was introduced in 1995). The letters refer to conditions:

A No advertising
H No hard-drugs
O No disturbance
J No sales to minors under 18
G No sales of more than 5g in one transaction

Also introduced were enforcement tools for tax office and law enforcement officials.

The 'back-door problem' refers to the production and cultivation of cannabis, which remains completely unregulated. Supplying coffeeshops with their product, therefore, is illegal, and coffeeshops buying the product are also on uncertain ground.

Coffeeshops usually require an operating permit for a catering establishment, but different municipalities have different rules with regard to the sale of cannabis, many city councils do not allow coffeeshops at all. At present, it is illegal to grow cannabis plants intended for making soft drugs. This also applies to acts of preparation with regard to illegal hemp production.

The front door/back door paradox has caused a split in the Netherlands government as to how they should proceed, and two options were discussed.

The first was to scrap the coffeeshop system that has made the Netherlands internationally renowned as a liberal jurisdiction for drug regulation. The second, which eventually won out, was to create a regulatory framework for supply and production, put in place adequate safeguards and protect against the black market.

Coffeeshop trial

3.48 A small-scale trial for the supply of cannabis was due to begin on 1 December 2019[56] to find out whether it is possible to create a closed supply system for supplying and selling cannabis in coffeeshops.

In the trial, growers with a special licence would be allowed to supply coffeeshops legally. The cannabis will be subject to quality controls. The closed system will exclude criminal activity from the supply chain.

A number of rules would apply:

- all coffeeshops in the participating municipalities must take part;
- the administration of these coffeeshops and their suppliers would be transparent and watertight;
- market forces would determine the price and range of products available;
- the amount of active substances (THC and CBD) must be clearly indicated on the packaging; and
- the coffeeshops must sell these pre-packaged products as supplied by the growers.

Almost every major city, including the capital and most famous cannabis tourist hotspot, Amsterdam, rejected the proposals. Amsterdam officials believed the legitimately acquired cannabis would cost more than the black-market supply, putting pressure on businesses to raise prices. There was also concern customers would simply go straight to the illegal suppliers if prices were too high.

Eventually an agreement was struck and a trial will take place at 79 coffee shops in 10 towns, which will be supplied by legal cultivators between 2021 and 2025. If the trial proves successful, the Dutch government will expand it nationally.

The 10 towns taking part are Arnhem, Almere, Breda, Groningen, Heerlen, Hellevoetsluis, Maastricht, Nijmegen, Tilburg and Zaanstad.

The four largest Dutch cities; Amsterdam, Rotterdam, The Hague and Utrecht, will not take part. The government eventually agreed it would be a logistical nightmare and potentially dangerous if all cafes in major cities abandoned their suppliers simultaneously.

The 79 coffee shops taking part represent 14% of the cannabis cafes in the Netherlands.

Netherlands Opium Act

3.49 The Netherlands Opium Act[57] is the basis for the country's current drug legislation. It defines drug trafficking, cultivation and production and dealing in and possession of drugs as criminal acts. The Act and its amendments confirm the distinction between Schedule I drugs such as heroin, cocaine, MDMA/ecstasy, amphetamines, and Schedule II drugs such as cannabis, and hallucinogenic mushrooms.

The Opium Act is implemented by the national Opium Act Directive to prosecutors, which is periodically revised. From 2018, prosecutors have been asked, when appropriate, to consider replacing community service and prison sentences with a fine. New psychoactive substances are regulated through amendments to relevant schedules of the Opium Act.

Individuals found in possession of a small amount of drugs for personal use will generally not be prosecuted, though the police will confiscate the drugs. The threshold amount for cannabis is set at 5g. Since 2012, the Opium Act Directive has left open the possibility of arresting and prosecuting individuals in possession of less than 5g of cannabis in certain circumstances.

Medicinal cannabis

3.50 In 2003, the Netherlands launched one of the first medicinal cannabis programs anywhere in the world, where patients are provided with pharmaceutical-grade cannabis of standardised cannabinoid composition.[58]

The program is overseen by the Office of Medicinal Cannabis (OMC), which is part of the Ministry of Health. The OMC launched on 1 January 2001, and is the government agency responsible for implementing the 1961 Single Convention on Narcotic Drugs. It is also responsible for overseeing the production of cannabis for medicinal and scientific purposes.

The OMC has a monopoly on supplying medicinal cannabis to pharmacies, and on its import and export. The OMC also processes applications for exemptions from the Opium Act relating to cannabis and cannabis resin.

The quality of the medicinal cannabis is guaranteed by a constant supervision of the grower and the distributor.

Medicinal cannabis is available on prescription only and can be dispensed by all Dutch pharmacies. Currently, five different cannabis strains are offered, including THC and CBD dominant varieties, as well as indica and sativa types.

Medicinal cannabis is recommended in the Netherlands mainly for treatment of chronic neuropathic pain, spasms and pain related to multiple sclerosis (MS), lack of appetite/nausea/vomiting related to cancer or HIV/AIDS, therapy-resistant glaucoma, and Tourette's syndrome.

Production

3.51 Contrary to popular opinion and the frequency of Netherlands-produced Bedrocan in medicinal cannabis markets around the world, exportation pales in comparison to the larger producers.

A UN report in 2016[59] revealed the United Kingdom was the main producer of legal cannabis, with 95t (44.9 per cent of the total), followed by Canada, with 80.7 tonnes, mostly intended for domestic consumption. They were followed by Portugal (21 tonnes), Israel (9.2 tonnes), the Netherlands and Chile (both 1.4 tonnes).

Foreign patients

3.52 The progressive healthcare system of the Netherlands has made it the top destination in Europe for individuals in other countries to travel in which to obtain medicinal cannabis. A European non-Dutch patient can, in principle, obtain medicinal cannabis in the Netherlands using a prescription from their own doctor. The patient has to cover the cost of the application fee for an export licence and contract and transport costs, making it an expensive ask for anyone who undertakes it.

Information for doctors

3.53 The OMC has several detailed information brochures (written in English) for doctors and pharmacists explaining every aspect of medicinal cannabis that is relevant to them and prescribing it to patients. They can be found on the OMC website https://english.cannabisbureau.nl/.

The future of medicinal cannabis

3.54 As of October 2019, the Netherlands was planning to issue a second licence for the production of medicinal cannabis to meet growing demand patients.[60] The only company authorised to produce cannabis for medical use, Bedrocan in Emmeloord, has increased its output fivefold in the last five years to 2,604kg.

Bedrocan received its licence 16 years ago from the OMC, which buys the entire stock and distributes it to hospitals and pharmacies.

Around half of it is sold abroad to countries including Germany, Italy and Poland. The OMC is expected to start the European tendering process for a second licence in early June 2020.

An earlier attempt to issue a second licence for medical cannabis was abandoned after an objection was made to the procedure.

Bedrocan produces five types of cannabis with different levels of THC and CBD. The main advantage of medicinal cannabis is that the strength and quality of the drug is much more consistent than the varieties grown for commercial use.

NORWAY

3.55 Cannabis consumption was at one time considered so serious an offence in Norway it carried the threat of jail time for smokers, with life sentences for dealers in possession of large amounts.

At the height of the American drug war in 1984, Norway's right-wing government implemented the maximum prison sentence for drug offences, putting them on a par with murder.[61] From the mid-1980s, Norway began to relax policies and implemented harm reduction measures.

The tide began to shift throughout the 2010s as crime grew along with public resistance to the punishments handed out for smoking small amounts of cannabis. According to statistics, almost a quarter of Norwegian citizens aged between 16 and 84 have tried cannabis.[62]

In 2017, the right-leaning government announced it would decriminalise possession for personal use, making it the first Scandinavian state to do so.

In late 2019, the proposal still had not been presented. Today, possession for personal use of less than 15g of cannabis is usually resolved with a fine, but can also leave the individual with a criminal record.

In 2019, the non-profit drug-policy organisation Normal Norge (Norwegian Organization for Reform of Marihuana Legislation) received funding from the Norwegian Directorate of Health to produce a human rights complaint to the United Nations Office of the High Commissioner for Human Rights on the basis of the negative consequences of control from the enforcement of the Norwegian ban on cannabis.

Legal background

3.56 The current Medicinal Products Act was introduced in 1964 following the UN Single Convention on Narcotic Drugs in 1961, to which Norway signed up.

In the decades that followed, cannabis use rose consistently, and eventually the police created their own narcotics section. The maximum penal sanction was raised, and all procedures on illegal substances apart from possession for personal use were moved from the Medicinal Products Act to the Criminal Code.

Policy approaches began to shift throughout the 2000s, and in 2011 a Norwegian government committee proposed alternative sanctions for minor drug crimes and a focus on motivational treatment forms and consent-based interventions.

Although the socialist democrat government of 2012 rejected the notion that easing drug laws could benefit Norwegian society and reduce harm, proposals made their way back to Parliament in 2017.

> 'The Parliament decided to move the responsibility for sanctions for use and personal possession of illicit drugs from the justice sector to the health sector,' The thinking behind this is that drug use is primarily a health issue, and a concern for heavy users who are burdened with fines that they cannot pay for behaviour that is closely linked to their drug addiction.' (Stig Erik Sørheim from Actis, the Norwegian Policy Network on Alcohol and Drugs.[63])

The Minister of Health has appointed a commission to look into how this can be implemented. The commission had until 31 December 2019, to submit its report, and the final details will be negotiated in the parliament in 2020.

> 'Since the health sector cannot punish people, this essentially means that drug use and possession will be decriminalised. Drug use will remain illegal, but the sanctions will be administrative rather than judicial.' (Sorheim.)

The appointed commission must agree on how this will be implemented and what sanctions will be available, but few details have been made public.

Similar to legislative direction in Israel, the commission was asked to look specifically at the Portuguese model. Portugal decriminalised drug use in response to enormous public health problems, soaring addiction and AIDS rates, and overcrowded prisons; those caught in possession are sent to a 'dissuasion commission', and the results have been overwhelmingly positive.

Such dissuasion commissions have a wide variety of tools available, from treatment to administrative fines to travel restrictions, although most cases are dismissed after an initial interview.

Cannabis is regulated in the Medicinal Products Act § 24 cf. § 31 and in the Criminal Code § 231 and 232.

Originally, illegal substances were regulated in the Medicinal Products Act, but in the late 1960s, all procedures on drugs apart from use and possession for personal use were moved to the Criminal Code. Criminal Code § 231 (common drug offence) or § 232 (aggravated drug offence) apply in more serious cases, such as distribution, production, import, export, storage (possession of larger quantities), or purchases.

Use and possession of doping substances is regulated in the Medicinal Products Act, whereas doping violations or aggravated doping violations are regulated in Criminal Code § 234 and 235.

If the violation concerns very large quantities, a maximum penalty of 15 years applies. A sanction of 21 years can be imposed in certain aggravating circumstances. The penalty scales can be doubled (more or less) for repeated, similar violations of the Code.

Medicinal cannabis

3.57 Medical cannabis was sold legally in Norwegian pharmacies until the ban in 1965 following the country's decision to join the 1961 Single Convention on Narcotic Drugs.

At the turn of the millennium, an underground network of cannabis growers called Dyrkeklubben began to deliver free medical cannabis to Norwegian patients in need. By 2004, the network had gained so much attention that health minister Bjarne Hakon Hanssen ordered the Norwegian Drug Agency to review the country's laws.

In 2010, a Norwegian was stopped in at Oslo airport customs with medical cannabis obtained from Netherlands producer Bedrocan. The individual was arrested on suspicion of drug smuggling, despite having official approval from the Norwegian Drug Agency and all relevant documents, and having acquired a legally prescribed by a Netherlands doctor.

Eventually the case was dismissed and all charges were dropped, but the controversy forced the government to grant special permission for Norwegians to bring medicinal cannabis back from other Schengen Area countries.

In 2012, the spray Sativex was approved by the Norwegian Drug Agency for individuals with MS, and in June 2013 the first cancer patient was prescribed Bediol at Sørlandet Hospital.

There are two legal routes open for patients; the first is to travel to another Schengen country where medical cannabis is available. The products must be legal and have approval from the local health regulator or government department, and the drug must be prescribed by a doctor and acquired from a pharmacy.

The second option, considered slower and more difficult, is to apply through a Norwegian specialist. The application must be sent to the Norwegian Drug Agency and the Health Ministry for approval. Sativex, Dronabinol, Marinol and Bedrocan products are available via a special import licence.

PORTUGAL

3.58 In 2001, Portugal rewrote its drugs policy to allow for a system based on treatment rather than punitive penalties. The results over the next 19 years have been extraordinary as drug-related crime, hard-drug use, addiction, deaths and infections plummeted.

Norway, Israel, New Zealand and a clutch of other countries looking to reform their drug laws have gone on record stating they admire the Portuguese approach and would consider emulating it.

The subject of drugs still divides Portugal, despite the clear benefits the country has observed since the turn of the millennium.

Possession of personal quantities of all drugs, including cannabis, is no longer a criminal offence, but contrary to some media reports, the liberalisation stopped with decriminalisation. In February 2019, the Portuguese parliament rejected two proposals to legalise recreational cannabis.

In July 2018, Law no. 33/2018[64] was published in Portugal, legalising the use of cannabis for medicinal purposes, but it took until January 2019, for the Decree-Law no. 8/2019[65] to be released. Qualifying patients in Portugal are still struggling to access medicinal cannabis despite these detailed regulations.

Legal background

3.59 The main drug law in Portugal is Decree Law 15/93 of 22 January 1993, which defines the legal regime applicable to the trafficking and consumption of narcotic drugs and psychoactive substances.

Law 30/2000,[66] adopted in November 2000 but in force since July 2001, decriminalised consumption, acquisition and possession of drugs for personal consumption.

A regulation sets out maximum amounts of drugs in grams, these amounts being estimates of the average required for 10 days' consumption. A person caught using or possessing less than the maximum amount of a drug for personal use, where there is no suspicion of involvement in drug trafficking, will be evaluated by the local Commission for Dissuasion of Drug Addiction, composed of three members; two being medical doctors, psychologists, sociologists or social workers and the third being a legal expert.

Punitive sanctions can be applied, but the main objectives are to explore the need for treatment and to promote healthy recovery.

Epidemic

3.60 During the 1990s, 1% of Portugal's population reported heroin abuse problems. It was one of the worst epidemics in the developed world, and in 2001 it prompted the government to take a fresh approach by decriminalising all drugs.[67]

Drug dealers are still jailed, but anyone caught with less than a 10-day supply of any drug, including heroin, is given mandatory medical treatment. No judge, no courtroom, no jail.

Fourteen years later, Portugal's drug-induced death rate had dropped to five times lower than the European Union average.[68] Drug-related HIV infections in Portugal also dropped 95%.

Uncertainty

3.61 INFARMED (the National Institute of Pharmacy and Medications) is the Portuguese Government agency, accountable to the Health Ministry, that oversees the supervision and regulation of medicinal cannabis.

It regulates the industry's licensing, and approves and conducts studies into the industry, determining the list of approved conditions and medical cannabis therapies. Any cannabis-based medications must be approved by INFARMED, and personal cultivation of the plant remains illegal, even for people with relevant medical conditions.

Until now, only one cannabis-based medication has been legal in Portugal; Sativex, produced by GW Pharmaceuticals. Despite being available since 2012, Sativex uptake has been minimal due to the stigma associated with cannabinoids, cannabis's opaque legal status, and due to the high costs not covered by national health insurance.

Cannativa, the Association of Cannabis Studies, brings together a range of Portuguese stakeholders, among them activists, health professionals, politicians, farmers, lawyers and patients, to study cannabis. It believes INFARMED is hindering the advancement of medicinal cannabis in Portugal.[69]

Cannativa's Maria Álvares told Health Europa:

> 'The regulatory entity has been analysing dozens of applications, but few licences have been approved and all of them still according to previous rules, targeted at exportation. Even before the new regulation was in place, in what looks like a response to the growing interest in the Cannabis market, INFARMED aggravated the checklist of prerequisites for the granting of licences and licences granted are dominated by already established players, and international pharma companies. Production is still in its first steps, and companies are now establishing their sites of production, with only [Canada's] Tilray hoping to produce in the immediate future.'

The lobby group said the regulator was 'not willing or able' to implement the law.

> 'Holders of marketing authorisations need to supply the market with the medicines for which the licence was granted. This is not happening with GW Pharmaceuticals, who holds a marketing authorisation for Sativex. Despite the medical need and the existence of a licence it is not commercially available in Portugal. Under the approved law no co-payments were defined; hence, cost could limit access to patients. In addition to cost, the availability of medical cannabis in pharmacies is another key concern.'

Export boom

3.62 There are signs Portugal may soon improve its cannabis production infrastructure, as it is becoming more attractive to Canadian exporters. Portugal's ideal climatic, and top tier local cultivation talent make it a perfect location.

In 2019, Portuguese company Holigen teamed up with Canadian firm Flowr to create one of the largest legal cannabis cultivation facilities in the world. Holigen will be able to initially produce about 500,000kg of cannabis per year on the 72-hectare site in the Alentejo region. According to estimates, the annual figure could rise to more than 630,000kg.

Holigen is said to have invested €40m (US$44m) in the project and sold a 19.8% stake to Flowr for a cash payment of nearly €4m ($4.4m).

In April 2019, Edmonton's Aurora Cannabis Inc, signed an agreement to acquire a 51% ownership stake in Gaia Pharma, a Portuguese-based company with plans to develop a local facility to produce medical cannabis and derivative products.

Aurora said it had advanced its strategy 'to attain early mover advantage in countries with nascent medical marijuana markets'.

SPAIN

3.63 Spain's underground cannabis culture is flourishing through the popularity of underground 'cannabis social clubs'.[70] The groups are private, non-profit organisations in which marijuana is collectively grown and distributed to registered members. They are also entirely illegal and subject to frequent police raids.

The social club scene developed in the 1990s as a political movement designed to fight for the constitutional rights of cannabis smokers. Today it has an echo of the US prohibition-era speakeasies, engaged in a game of 'whack-a-mole' with the courts and governments who shut them down only to see replacements emerge almost immediately.

Spanish authorities are concerned about the 'cannabis tourism' aspect of having hundreds of such clubs operating in major cities. Barcelona has been dubbed 'the next Amsterdam', a phrase you will read multiple times in this book deployed whenever a country does not want to encourage recreational open-air marijuana usage.

In 2015, the Spanish Supreme Court stated that 'organised, institutionalised and persistent cultivation and distribution of cannabis among an association open to new members is considered drug trafficking.'

Regional attempts to regulate these clubs have been declared unconstitutional. Numerous legal battles have waged since the early 1990s over their status,[71] and their owners, who have on occasion been categorised as drug traffickers by police.

The Transnational Institute country report on Spain from March 2019 is a fascinating dive into the legal labyrinth that is the battle between the social clubs and the Spanish authorities.[72] Ultimately, cannabis is illegal in Spain, despite its overwhelming popularity and the inability of the ruling politicians to stamp it out.

There are also no medicinal marijuana regulations. Spain is extremely unwelcoming from both a legitimate business and pro-cannabis healthcare perspective, despite having a very strong cannabis research reputation and high usage rate amongst adults.

Legal background

3.64 Spain's legislation on drugs predates the 1961 Single Convention on Narcotic Drugs. Today, consumption or minor personal possession in public places is deemed a non-criminal order offence, punishable by fines of €601 to €30,000 (US$667 to $27,000) under the 2015 Law on the Protection of Citizens' Security 2015, Article 36. For minors, the fine can be suspended if the offender voluntarily attends treatment, rehabilitation or counselling activities.

Members only

3.65 A set of guidelines laid out by the Catalonian Federation of Cannabis Associations (CatFac) is the closest thing the social clubs have to a set of formal rules.[73]

Members can receive up to three grams per day from a single club, and up to 25g per week. Putting a limit on the quantity of cannabis a user can acquire eliminates the risk of members selling club produce to a third party. The clubs operate as non-profit organisations, with earnings used to cover running costs and maintain low prices.

The social club model is not limited to Spain; Uruguay has made such co-ops part of its regulated recreational market.

Informal clubs have been accommodated within domestic drug laws in Argentina, Colombia and Chile. Belgium has a handful of clubs, and the local government of Utrecht in the Netherlands has considered establishing a club as a means of solving the issue of illegal, unregulated supply to the city's cannabis coffee shops. The Swiss canton of Geneva has also researched the possibility of setting up cannabis user associations.

Medicinal cannabis

3.66 Spain has no specific regulations governing medicinal cannabis. Multiple cancer associations have stated their desire to see access to therapeutic cannabis increase, and members of Spain's national government have lent their support.

There has been no political appetite to move the issue forward, however, and it is not uncommon for groups of people diagnosed with diseases for which the therapeutic benefits of cannabis have been demonstrated to join the social clubs.[74]

In 2010, Sativex was approved to be sold in Spain, and since then its use has been legal, but in practice its use is restricted solely for alleviating symptoms in patients with multiple sclerosis who have not responded well to other medications.

Next steps

3.67 The current government of Socialist Party (PSOE) Prime Minister Pedro Sánchez has no intention of regulating cannabis. There have been very few debates on the matter from any party, to that end.

A parliamentary commission for the drug's legal status supported by the anti-austerity party Podemos and centre-right Cuidadanos was never considered a serious proposal.

SWITZERLAND

3.68 Switzerland has taken a unique approach to regulatory reform of cannabis by allowing a fixed number of residents to 'legally' receive a small amount every month, including edibles, as part of a five-year trial.

The government felt that, with 200,000 Swiss people regularly using cannabis, and no sign of a decline despite numerous efforts and a partial decriminalisation in 2013, a different approach was necessary.

The black market for the drug is advanced, and the government estimates efforts to shut down illicit cannabis use costs the country around $1bn each year. It estimates a fully regulated market would bring in around $600m in tax.

Medical cannabis is currently too expensive for many patients to acquire, and so the government is also committing to a review of access, having been lobbied heavily by Switzerland's pharmacies.

Switzerland is a founding member of the European Free Trade Association, but it is not part of the EU or the European Economic Area. It participates in the Schengen Area and the European Single Market through bilateral treaties.

Should Switzerland fast-track a cannabis support scheme, or a CBD market, and look to export, it will not be bound by EU laws and restrictions domestically, and will not have to answer to Brussels should the EU decide to develop an overarching regulatory framework. It will have to abide by the EU laws and standards on selling into that market, however.

The country is famed for its advances in medicine, it has a supportive government and a rigid, healthy financial services network and is a major international banking centre.

As one of the most developed countries on earth, Switzerland has all the potential to become a key player in the global cannabis market in the coming years, especially in regard to services and R&D.

Legal background

3.69 In 2013, Switzerland decriminalised possession of small amounts of cannabis, 10g or less. Rather than jail individuals and waste time and resources, police issue a US $100 on-the-spot penalty. Officials felt there was very little quality control of the drug entering the country, and that if it did not step in to regulate, some of the stronger strains could have a detrimental impact on citizens.

It is estimated about 500,000 of Switzerland's 8.45m population regularly consume cannabis, and around 40% of men and 33% of Swiss women have tried it at least at least once in their lives, according to domestic statistics.[75]

Forms of cannabis that contain negligible amounts of THC are not banned under Swiss narcotics legislation, provided they contain less than 1% THC.[76] 10g or less of cannabis or a narcotic with the same effect is regarded by law as a negligible quantity. This is a greater amount permitted than anywhere else in Europe.

Persons under the age of 18 caught with cannabis are dealt with under the criminal law applicable to juveniles, the Federal Act on Narcotics and Psychotropic Substances: Article 19.[77]

CBD in Switzerland

3.70 CBD, unlike THC, is not subject to Switzerland's Narcotics Act (NarcA, CC 812.121) as it does not produce a comparable psychoactive effect. However, this does not mean that CBD can simply be added to random preparations at will or advertised arbitrarily.

In order to be marketed, products must comply with the legislation of the country where it originates. Depending on the classification, the corresponding Swiss legislation is applied.

There are several regulations that must be complied with in order to produce and sell CBD products legally. The Federal Office of Public Health, Federal Office for Agriculture, Federal Food Safety and Veterinary Office and Swissmedic have put together a factsheet, which can be accessed here: https://www.swissmedic.ch/swissmedic/en/home/news/mitteilungen/products-containing-cannabidiol--cbd---overview.html.

The range of CBD products includes raw materials such as cannabis buds or powder with a high CBD-content; extracts in the form of oils or pastes; and ready-to-use products such as capsules, food supplements, liquids for e-cigarettes, tobacco substitutes, scented oils, chewing gums and ointments, some of which are offered as personal care products.

Once a product has been assigned to a particular product category, the corresponding Swiss legislation is applied. If the legal requirements in relation to a specific intended purpose are not satisfied, a product may not be distributed in Switzerland and therefore cannot be sold.

The end products are classified on a case-by-case basis, taking account of all the relevant factors, including composition, intended use, dosage, etc. Differing enforcement authorities are responsible for control, depending on the products' classification. In cases of doubt, the enforcement authority assigns a product to particular legislation and takes the necessary measures.

There is no clear assignment, particularly for offerings involving pure raw materials. Products for which there is no specific applicable law (eg Therapeutic Products Act [FTPA, CC 812.21], Foodstuffs Act [FSA, CC 817.0]) are covered by the Federal Act on Product Safety [CC 930.11] a catch-all legislation.

Medicinal cannabis

3.71 Medicines containing the active substances in cannabis require authorisation. Currently only Sativix, a mouth spray intended to alleviate neuropathic pain, spasticity, and other symptoms of multiple sclerosis, is licensed for sale in Switzerland.[78] Sativex was developed in the UK by GW Pharmaceuticals.

The Federal Office of Public Health (FOPH) grants special authorisation for the medical use of prohibited narcotics, however only the doctor overseeing the case can apply, and the patient must consent.

Next steps

3.72 In February 2019, Switzerland's government said it will allow 5,000 citizens to use cannabis legally, as part of a five-year clinical trial.

Lawmakers conducted multiple scientific studies regarding the impact of cannabis on public health and safety. Any update is unlikely to occur in the next decade unless fast-tracked.

Those who sign up to the trial receive a small amount of cannabis each month, to smoke or eat. The studies are strictly controlled; trialists must be over 18, be residents in the city where the tests are being carried out, and already be using the drug.

To avoid the obvious consequences of handing out free cannabis to members of the public, trialists are given a 'cannabis ID' when they sign up, and are forbidden from passing on the drug or reselling it for the five years of the study.

Multiple Swiss cities and institutions announced their support for the plan, but required approval from the hard-line Swiss parliament before they could take part.

One previous attempt to launch a cannabis trial was torpedoed by the parliament as politicians believed it would lead to full-scale recreational laws being approved. The plans eventually made their way back with tighter controls around the trial environment.

Pharmacy involvement

3.73 In January 2019, Switzerland's pharmacies backed legalisation of a recreational market, and began lobbying to sell both medicinal and non-medicinal recreational products.[79]

Currently about 3,000 patients currently have the medical exemption necessary to obtain higher THC versions of the plant or drugs. However, the process is considered arduous and time-consuming for patients and their carers, which led to the calls for a rethink.

The Pharmacy Association issued a position paper[80] stating its argument for decriminalising marijuana, which it says would deter black market trade and provide safer products for the market.

The group said it would not support the 'unrestricted liberalisation' policy implemented in some US states, and did not want to copy the coffee shop approach of Amsterdam.

Cannabis should be classified as a medicinal product, the association said, and therefore all active ingredients would be displayed on the packaging.

The proposals limit recreational use to over 18s, and users could be given advice in pharmacies on how best to consume marijuana and a 'cannabis helpline' could be set up.

Switzerland's former drug commissioner and current university lecturer, Michael Herzig gave his backing and said pharmacies were best suited to running the market.

Herzig said pharmacies would provide a quality control mechanism the black market cannot, and would also reduce the potentially dangerous commercialisation of the drug and avoid products like cannabis lollipops and gummy bears being sold or advertised.

Herzig said a tax could be levied on the drug and that Swiss farmers could be brought on board as potential producers.

Pushback came from Pharma-Suisse, the national umbrella organisation for pharmacies in Switzerland, followed Dora's announcement; it said it is 'not convinced' that public pharmacies are suitable locations for sale, despite giving backing to the legalisation plan.

Instead, it says that scientific pilot trials like those approved by the Swiss Federal Council in July 2018 would be preferable.

TURKEY

3.74 Turkey legalised cannabis production for medicinal and scientific use in 19 provinces in 2016 in a government push to cut illegal production. Three years later, in a single operation, Turkish security forces confiscated a domestic record 5.5m cannabis plants after targeting the PKK terrorist group. In addition to the cannabis plants, 63kg of hashish were also seized.[81]

In Europe, the Kurdistan Workers' Party (PKK) controls 80% of the cannabis drug trade, reaping some $1.5bn a year, according to Turkey's Interior Minister Suleyman Soylu. The country has a major problem with illegal cannabis cultivation, and the government issues frequent updates stating it has uncovered and burned new black market grow-ops.

Turkey's relationship with cannabis has been a long and strange journey. The cannabis plant is known as 'kendir', and has been grown in the region for hundreds of years, booming during the period of the Ottoman Empire.

In January 2019, President Recep Tayyip Erdogan said he intends to restart Turkey's hemp trade for industrial use. The populist president blamed 'Western imperialists' namely US President Franklin Roosevelt, for killing off what was once a lucrative Turkish market with the Marijuana Tax Act.

Hemp was estimated to be cultivated on about 42,000 acres of land back in 1989, but that declined to just 66 acres by 2009. The amount has since increased slightly, reaching 200 acres last year for harvesting the plants seeds and fibres.[82]

For now, the government only aims to produce cannabis with low levels (about 0.2 to 0.3%) of THC, in line with international guidance from the INCB. The cultivation will primarily focus on industrial use and research purposes. However, some Islamists are also pushing for more, as they want to the plant to be used in medicines again.

Agriculture Minister Berat Pakdemirli unveiled the project in January following Erdogan's address.[83] He recalled the 2016 effort to permit cannabis production in 19 provinces, and said there were plans to increase the number of farms depending on the demand:

> 'Samsun Black Sea Agricultural Institute and Ondokuz Mayis University are conducting a research project on cannabis. We will approve new locations that will produce organic cannabis,' he said. 'There are 2.5m cannabis plants naturally grown in our city. We won't burn them anymore. We will contribute to the economy with them.'

There has been no movement since that announcement.

Legal background

3.75 Regulations by The Ministry of Food, Agriculture and Livestock,[84] published in the Official Gazette in September 2016 – the Hemp Cultivation and Control of Regulations – allow highly-controlled and ministry-sanctioned cannabis production in selected provinces for medical and scientific purposes.

Under the regulations, growers must obtain permission from the government allowing them to grow the plant for a three-year-period.[85] Potential growers must produce a warrant proving they have not been involved in any illegal cannabis production activity or narcotic production or use in the past.

The regulations stipulate that authorised growers must dispose of all parts of the cannabis plant after the harvest period to prevent any being sold on as a psychoactive drug.

The selected provinces include: Amasya, Antalya, Bartın, Burdur, Çorum, İzmir, Karabük, Kastamonu, Kayseri, Kütahya, Malatya, Ordu, Rize, Samsun, Sinop, Tokat, Uşak, Yozgat and Zonguldak.

Ministry officials check the fields each month before the start of harvest season, and growers must discard all parts of the cannabis plant after the harvest period in an effort to avoid it being sold illegally for consumption.

The regulations do not legalise cannabis in Turkey. The possession and purchase of the drug continues to be illegal and punishable by up to two years in prison. The sale or supply of cannabis is punishable by up to ten years, while the unlicensed production or trafficking of marijuana is susceptible to a minimum jail term of ten years.

There is also the option of treatment and/or probation of up to three years. If drug users refuse treatment or do not comply with their probation requirements, the courts can impose a prison sentence. No punishment will apply if treatment is requested before an investigation; in such cases, healthcare professionals are not obliged to report the offence.

The Turkish government still strictly condemns recreational use of marijuana.

Medicinal cannabis

3.76 The Turkish medical cannabis program has been slow to develop and the tough penalties in place for any kind of use is often given as a reason for the poor uptake. The only treatments approved within the country are oromucosal sprays (taken by mouth) containing CBD and THC (Sativex).

Turkish doctors can prescribe patients, and should an individual qualify, they will be issued with a 'red prescription'.

Although cannabis production is legal in 19 regions, this is for scientific and medical testing, and is not for domestic use. Cannabis medications are imported from other nations for patient use.

THE UK

3.77 Patients are unable to access medicinal cannabis, only a handful of prescriptions have ever been handed out, recreational marijuana is illegal, and yet the UK is the world's largest cultivator of legal cannabis, accounting for almost half of global production.[86]

Ninety-five tonnes of marijuana was produced in the UK in 2016 for medicinal and scientific use, totalling 44.9% of the world total, according to the International Narcotics Control Board (INCB).[87]

This was more than double the 2015 total of 42 tonnes, and made the UK the largest exporter, overtaking Canada. Much of this can be attributed to one company; GW Pharmaceuticals, based in Cambridge, which is one of the world's largest cannabis firms.

The firm was founded in 1998, and successfully developed the world's first prescription medicine derived from the cannabis plant, called Sativex (delta-9-tetrahydrocannibinol and cannabidiol in the EU; nabiximols in the US), which is approved in over 25 countries outside of the US for the treatment of spasticity due to multiple sclerosis.

In November 2018, following a string of media campaigns from affected families, the Home Office announced a tweak to UK laws that moved cannabis into a less tightly-controlled category in order for specialists to be able to prescribe it in certain circumstances.

This was hailed as a historic shift that would allow for cannabis to be prescribed to sick children and individuals with debilitating illnesses in the UK for the first time. However, a year on, only a handful of prescriptions have been written, and the process has been roundly criticised.

In November 2019, two cannabis-based medicines used to treat epilepsy and multiple sclerosis in adults were approved for use by the NHS in England. Epidiolex was approved to treat two rare forms of epilepsy; Lennox-Gastaut and Dravet syndromes.

Oral spray Sativex was approved to treat muscle spasms stemming from multiple sclerosis.

In the same month, a project was launched by the Royal College of Psychiatrists to trial medicinal cannabis in 20,000 patients. The two-year study would be the largest of its kind in Europe, collating more information than previously gathered in a single project, with the aim of putting more evidence in front of the NHS to support cannabis-based medicines.

With Brexit on the horizon, and the ramifications for business that will occur once the UK is out of the EU single market and split from the European Medicines Agency, it is an uncertain time for UK cannabis businesses, as with every other sector.

However, there seems little sign of a slowdown, especially given the numerous CBD offerings that are launched every week. Numerous cannabis consultancies and think tanks have sprung up in London and the number of events launched has increased dramatically since 2017.

As one of the world's top financial centres, second only to New York, London has access to the levels of capital and liquidity that cannabis businesses need for growth, and is in no danger of losing that spot any time soon. It has the infrastructure and business environment necessary to service the global cannabis sector, which will remain a selling point for firms looking to set up shop.

GW Pharmaceuticals

3.78 One of the world's leading and most influential medicinal cannabis companies is British, and yet not a household name in the UK. Listed on the USA's Nasdaq Stock Exchange Market, the bio-pharmaceutical company GW Pharmaceuticals makes no secret of its desire to become the worldwide leader in medical marijuana treatments.

The firm was co-founded in 1998 by Dr Geoffrey Guy and Dr Brian Whittle, two well-known entrepreneurs in the UK biotech sector.

In 1999, GW commenced its first clinical trials evaluating different cannabinoid formulations as potential therapeutics with an initial focus on the development of an oral mucosal spray with two principal cannabinoid components, CBD and THC.

The firm's first product was Sativex, a mouth spray intended to ease symptoms of multiple sclerosis, licenced as a prescription-only medicine in the UK in 2010.

When launched, Sativex became the world's first prescription medicine derived from the cannabis plant. It contains combination of CBD at 2.5mg and the psychoactive component THC at 2.7mg. Sativex aims to treat spasticity, neuropathic pain, overactive bladder and other features associated with multiple sclerosis.

GW's lead product is a liquid formulation of highly purified CBD. In June 2018, the FDA approved this product as Epidiolex for the treatment of seizures associated with Lennox-Gastaut syndrome (LGS) or Dravet syndrome, two rare and particularly difficult to treat forms of epilepsy, in patients two years and older. The product was launched in November 2018 and is now available by prescription in the US.

GW's growth has not been without some controversy, and it is fighting multiple legal battles over IP and patent trademarks on cannabinoid-based treatments around the world.

In May 2019, it emerged GW has already filed at least 14 patents in New Zealand that would give them sole use of CBD to treat a wide range of diseases and disorders, to the anger of local patient groups.

Legal background

3.79 Recreational cannabis is illegal under the Misuse of Drugs Act 1971,[88] and the Misuse of Drugs Regulations 2001[89] account for the licensing of production, possession and supply of substances classified under the act.

The Misuse of Drugs Act 1971 is little more than a list of categorised substances.

The government classifies cannabis as a Class B substance ranked alongside ketamine, codeine, and amphetamines.

In 2004, cannabis was briefly reclassified to the lesser status of Class C, but then-Prime Minister Gordon Brown reinstated its Class B classification in 2008. His actions went against the advice of the Advisory Council on the Misuse of Drugs.

In November 2018, the UK amended the Misuse of Drugs Regulations to move cannabis from Schedule 1, under which it had no therapeutic value and researchers needed a Home Office licence[90] to obtain and store it, to Schedule 2, a category for drugs which are still tightly controlled, but have a recognised medical use and can be prescribed in certain circumstances.

Cannabis remains a controlled Class B drug, meaning it is illegal to possess without a legal prescription or licence. Possession carries a penalty of up to five years in jail, while supplying it can be punished with a 14-year jail sentence or an unlimited fine.

Media pressure

3.80 The 2018 legislative amendment was driven mainly by the stories of Billy Caldwell[91] and Alfie Dingley,[92] two young boys with severe and treatment-resistant epilepsies. Their parents' unsuccessful attempts to get cannabis medication into the UK for their children featured regularly on newspaper front pages.

The two boys had been treated with cannabis-based medicines containing THC and CBD abroad and showed significant clinical improvements in seizure control and quality of life. The mothers of both boys had campaigned tirelessly for several years, and eventually the law was updated to ensure they could be prescribed medicine containing both THC and CBD on the NHS.

They remain the only two NHS prescriptions of this type that campaign group Epilepsy Action says it aware of.

Campaigners said cannabis-based medicines were as inaccessible in December 2019 as they were before November 2018.

Patient access problems

3.81 Initial interim clinical guidance for both paediatric and adult epilepsies recommend against prescribing products containing THC and CBD in almost every circumstance. This status is unlikely to alter given the draft guidance from the National Institute for Health and Care Excellence (NICE) published in August 2019[93] which will ultimately supersede the interim guidance.

Neurologist and Rehabilitation Physician Professor Mike Barnes, director of education at the UK Academy of Medical Cannabis, said technically it is possible for a person to walk into a specialist consulting room and come out with a prescription:

> 'It's just that no one has on the National Health Service since the law change. GPs can't prescribe yet. There have been 29 prescriptions written in the private sector (as of October 2019). Why so slow? Probably lack of education, poor and misleading guidelines by the Royal College of Physicians, and British Paediatric Neurology Association (BPNA) and now NICE. The fact it is an unlicensed medicine which means more responsibility for the doctor and some say not enough evidence, but I don't agree.'

Former teacher Carly Barton has also been at the forefront of the right for patients to access medicinal cannabis in the UK. Barton developed the neurological condition fibromyalgia after suffering a stroke aged 24. The condition left her in constant pain, and after becoming fed up of opiates she tried cannabis and found it was the only way to make the 'constant burning pain' stop.[94]

In December 2018, it emerged Barton was the first UK adult to get a private prescription for cannabis, however later she revealed given the legal hoops she had to negotiate it would cost £1,400 (US$1,811) a month.[95]

She has launched a 'safe access to cannabis' campaign for patients who live with medical conditions listed under the guidelines, are unable to afford a private prescription and would consider growing their own supply of medical cannabis.

She told the author that even a year on she is still being told how hard it is for patients to access products they are entitled to, and how she is attempting to transform the prescription-acquiring process by personally testing it:

> 'At the moment, in order to prescribe, doctors look at the clinical interim guidelines written by the Royal colleges and the draft NICE guidelines, which stipulate that they advise not to prescribe for any of the indications outlined by the government last year. We have tested this, in that my NHS doctor wrote a script against this advice, it was then blocked at Clinical Commissioning Groups level.'

NICE guidance

3.82 The NICE processes for developing the clinical guideline on cannabis-based medicinal products and the technology appraisal guidance on specific cannabis-based medicinal products can be found at https://www.nice.org.uk/process/pmg20/chapter/introduction-and-overview and https://www.nice.org.uk/Media/Default/About/what-we-do/NICE-guidance/NICE-technology-appraisals/technology-appraisal-processes-guide-apr-2018.pdf respectively.

NICE told the author it has not yet made any final recommendations to the NHS in England about the use of cannabis-based medicinal products:

> 'Details of our clinical guideline in development on cannabis-based medicinal products is available on our website. You will see that full details of the evidence considered is included. Details of our technology appraisal guidance in development on cannabidiol for the adjuvant treatment of seizures associated with Dravet syndrome are available online, and for our technology appraisal guidance in development on cannabidiol for the adjuvant treatment of seizures associated with Lennox-Gastaut syndrome are available.'

Next steps

3.83 Britain's uneven political landscape has made fools of most individuals making policy predictions, however there is no sign of any liberalisation in terms of recreational cannabis use. The UK is a world leader in R&D and is likely to remain part of the medicinal cannabis advancements in Europe regardless of the outcome of Brexit.

SIR NORMAN LAMB: THE UK PATH TO LEGALISATION OF CANNABIS

3.84 Ask any UK cannabis industry observer to put a number on it and most believe marijuana will be legalised within ten years, as public opinion continues to shift.

Sir Norman Lamb, former UK government health minister and one of the most prominent pro-cannabis voices in British political history, believes it will happen in five.

The plight of two epileptic boys, Billy Caldwell and Alfie Dingley, whose fight to access the cannabis-based medicines that had helped their conditions was the breakthrough, Lamb believes, as Billy and Alfie's struggle gained traction in the traditionally right-leaning British media.

The cases gained so much attention that Britain updated its laws in November 2018 to move medicinal cannabis into a category that would allow doctors to prescribe it under certain circumstances.

> 'We crossed quite a significant psychological barrier. The old resistance to anything other than prohibition was suddenly breached at that moment. The government made a huge judgment call under enormous pressure from campaign groups and parents of children with epilepsy.'

The former Liberal Democrat MP, who was appointed health spokesman in 2006, said this he felt it brought forward the day cannabis would be legalised for recreational purposes in the UK.

> 'Legalisation may happen in the UK within five years, as the pace of change is accelerating enormously. Attitudes have shifted dramatically.'

It remains a psychological barrier, as on the ground the update has not filtered through to doctors, and 'only a handful' of prescriptions for medical cannabis were written 12 months on.

> 'In the journey we are on, which inevitably leads to legalisation, it's quite a significant staging post.'

The next step is for the government to further set out guidance for doctor, clinicians and physicians, he said. In 2018, Lamb introduced a Ten-Minute Rule Bill to the UK House of Commons that would fully legalise cannabis. However, the motion was voted down.

> 'The problem is the regulatory framework, and the incentives and threats that clinicians face. 'The rules say that clinicians can prescribe, but because the cannabis products are not licensed drugs, the clinicians think they face personal responsibility if anything goes wrong. They feel they are taking a huge risk by prescribing cannabis in those circumstances.'

It was one of his final acts before announcing his decision to stand down as an MP in 2019, and upon the announcement of the general election in December, Lamb left Parliament with a vow to continue campaigning for marijuana access.

Home-grown cannabis is not permitted in the UK, and only specialist clinicians can prescribe when they feel all other possibilities have been exhausted. General Practitioners still do not have the legal power to write a prescription for a cannabis medicine.

The Home Office, which updated the UK law, cannot make the clinicians prescribe either. Guidelines produced by the National Institute for Health and Care Excellence (NICE) advise the National Health Service on structuring its services and treatments. It believes cannabis medicines do not present value for money, and it feels there is not enough research available to show they help sick children in particular.

As a result, the drugs are not being purchased by the NHS to be made available for prescription by GPs. The individual must make the case that they are in effect an exemption to the rules, and then the specialist may consent to writing a prescription.

The inability to access cannabis medication at home has caused parents and other individuals to spend huge sums of money travelling to the Netherlands and Canada where it can be prescribed, and invariably having the drugs seized by the Home Office on returning to the UK.

> 'For all intents and purposes, it's a completely failed initiative, as it has not led to prescriptions for anyone in need. It's a dreadful situation.'

He said the UK is stuck in a hiatus, while other countries are 'falling over themselves to change the law', with the European market particularly active.

However, he is confident the situation will move quickly, especially given the amount of money and interest the sector is generating: 'It's the biggest job creator in Canada at the moment, a big deal. There are very serious investments, and an explosion of activity is just around the corner.'

That presents risks too, said Lamb, as the industry has a very large financial stake:

> 'If we are to take the public with us and remain focussed on harm reduction, we have to be careful it's not seen as a capitalist rush. On the spectrum, at one end we have enforced and total prohibition, at the other end is free-for-all. At either of those extremes there is a significant risk of harm.'

He said overly-tough regulation will not undercut the black market, and any legal product must be attractive and sensible enough:

> 'Reining it in becomes difficult, if you don't start fairly strict, however, as we have seen with cigarettes and alcohol. My preference is to start with tough regulation and then review, loosen the controls if appropriate, based on an evidence-led review. It is easier to loosen than it is to tighten, as you then have massive economic interests influencing government and getting in the way of reform.'

Lamb feels Britain might even need its own cannabis regulator, similar to the authority setup in Uruguay:

> 'A domestic regulator feels proportionate given the scale of the industry that would suddenly be created on a legal basis.'

For Lamb, the legalisation of cannabis would be the start, however, and he envisioned such a regulator morphing into a wider harm reduction authority:

> 'If you had a body that built up expertise on cannabis, then any other change to the framework to other drugs could be given to that body,' he said. 'As a liberal I do not see value in taking people through the criminal justice system for using a substance.'

EUROPE BEGINS TO UNPICK CANNABIS REGULATION PATCHWORK

3.85 Throughout 2020 the EU will seek to create a stable framework for medicinal cannabis research and development only; talk of recreational breakthroughs is somewhat premature. The regulatory framework across the continent is not as volatile or subject to violent swings as other areas of the globe, given the control exerted by Brussels. Despite the apparent slow pace of municipal change, the legal landscape for medicinal cannabis at least, could look very different in 12 months' time.

According to Dylan Kennett, M&A lawyer at DLA Piper:

> 'In 2019 there was a real move from talking to actually doing. The capital is available in Europe, but it may take a nudge for people working in different sectors to team up, similar to what we saw with the financial technology boom in the UK.'

Europe is lacking a critical mass of strong cannabis companies, Kennett said, but this could quickly alter in the coming years if restrictions on the abilities of funds to invest are eased:

> 'There is a concern perhaps in the market that the underlying fund documentation may prohibit them from investing in the first place. Over time, I'm hopeful that people will see the use case, and the money will follow into genuinely investable companies.'

By the end of 2020, Kennett said for the European market to be in good shape it requires a combination of more money, a reduced risk profile of investing following the entrance of good characters, and strong clear uses cases for the products as a result of strong research and development (R&D).

Northern European territories such as the UK and Germany are likely to continue on their path of strong R&D and providing capital and other professional services to the sector, while southern areas appeal to cultivators:

'I think we can also expect to see more specialisation across Europe, less in terms of vertically integrated companies. The production and extraction facilities may continue to trend towards Mediterranean, Iberian Peninsula, and other low-cost jurisdictions.'

Medicinal cannabis and EU law

3.86 Through 2020, the EU is creating a harmonised set of rules for medicinal cannabis that will apply across each of its member states, following a pledge to fund research projects and make access to cannabis research easier.

Wildly different definitions and standards apply in every EU state, and the first step for lawmakers is to agree on a legal definition of 'medicinal cannabis' for each member country to transpose into their domestic laws.[96]

A non-binding resolution drawn up members of the Environment, Public Health and Food Safety Committee of the European Parliament, the bloc's directly elected legislative, requesting formal guidance to be drawn up on medicinal cannabis research was approved in February 2019.[97]

It called for the European Commission (the bloc's executive) and each Member State to formally address the issue of cannabis as used in medicine, and how the catch-all term 'medicinal cannabis' refers to a wide variety of products and preparations with different active ingredients that can be administered differently.

The divergent regulatory regimes within the EU creates a further complexity, and a harmonised set of rules would in theory stem the regulatory arbitrage and splintering that is occurring as countries proceed at different speeds.

Members noted that: 'the policy landscape for medical cannabis is still evolving, with the different Member States taking different approaches'.

The existing patchwork of rules has led to a situation where individuals wishing to use medicinal cannabis to ease symptoms such as multiple sclerosis or cancer-related sickness, or to reduce the seizures associated with epilepsy, often have to travel to other bloc states as their home jurisdiction makes access to medicinal cannabis almost impossible.

The agreement secured promises action from the Commission, the EU states and the research community to make dedicated efforts to support research for cannabis-derived therapies.

It will also aim to ease the path to medical cannabis for those in need, and the establishment of unified standards for cannabis used for medicinal purposes. Finally, it bids to improve knowledge of cannabis-based therapies among the public and healthcare professionals.

The Commission responded in late 2019 with a statement on the follow-up work it had undertaken, and clarifying some of the existing laws:

> 'Cannabis-derived medicinal products already fall under the existing definition of a medicinal product laid down in the legislation. However, the classification of 'medical cannabis' is out of the scope of the pharmaceutical framework. It is a Member State's competence to decide whether medical cannabis use is legal or not on its territory.'

For a medicinal product to appear on the market, authorisation must be granted by the appropriate regulator of a member state, or by the Commission for the entire EU.

In both cases, a marketing authorisation is granted to a medicinal product only after its quality, safety and efficacy have been evaluated and a positive benefit-risk balance related to its use has been established:

> 'It would be great to see European harmonisation of medicinal cannabis occur in the medium to longer term, so there is a pan-European framework. With that said, I do not see this happening by the end of 2020, as that would be extremely ambitious.' He said he feels Europe is much stronger both from a consumer safety and business efficacy point of view when there are such rules in place.
>
> 'It definitely makes the frictional cost of capital far less for companies, especially given the capital-intensive nature of the business – they do not need to be spending money on significant legal fees to understand the playing field.' (Kennet)

Research call

3.87 There will be further opportunities to support this field of scientific research in the upcoming 'Horizon 2020 call for proposals for 2020', including the New therapies for Non Communicable Diseases call.[98]

Throughout 2020, Horizon Europe, which identifies key areas of research for the European Commission will continue with its approach to fund impactful research through competitive, open calls for proposals that benefits our society, including areas of novel therapeutic interventions.

In recent years, the EU has funded a number of relevant projects and fellowships in Europe and worldwide with over €40m dedicated to research on cannabis and cannabinoid-based compounds.

The NeuroPain project ran a clinical trial on the analgesic use of the specific cannabinoid, cannabidivarin (CBDV), in patients with HIV-associated painful neuropathy.[99]

The EU's CORDIS database lists additional projects in relation to the medicinal use of cannabis, including a project regarding the use of standardised extracts of cannabis in the treatment of migraine and rheumatoid arthritis, and a separate investigation into the effects of cannabinoids on neural activity and their potential to reduce epileptic seizures.

The Commission also reminded member states that recreational cannabis 'remains clearly prohibited'.

In 2019, Luxembourg signalled its intent to legalise recreational cannabis by 2021, and the Dutch government has also taken steps to regulate the marijuana sold and consumed in cafes throughout the country.

The EU drugs agency

3.88 The Commission said it also expects a more active role in the drafting of a regulatory framework for medicinal cannabis to be played by the European Monitoring Centre for Drugs and Drug Addiction (EMCDDA), which is the EU's drugs agency.

The Lisbon-headquartered agency was established in 1993, and exists to provide the EU and its Member States with a factual overview of European drug problems and an evidence base to support the drugs debate.

It has about 100 staff, a handful of researchers, and an annual budget of approximately €15m, of which most is spent on rent for its headquarters and staffing.

The EMCDDA has published two large papers on cannabis since 2018, the first in April 2018 was its very first look at medicinal cannabis, in response to growing interest.[100]

Although it plays a central role in EU drug policy thinking, and can influence individual member states with the evidence it presents, the EMCDDA does not carry out any research itself.

The EMCDDA collates information from its networks and compiles reports on that basis; it reports on work created by other agencies, usually the main national health authority in a given state.

The agency rarely deals with business, and the focus of its reports are policymakers. It is understood Luxembourg's lawmakers have requested information from the agency relating to Canada and Uruguay's experiences of legalising recreational cannabis.

Luxembourg would be the first EU Member State to fully legalise cannabis, going against EU advice, should it follow through with proposals announced in 2019.

The agency tracks, but does not take a view on, cannabis market projections provided by consultancies and private information providers that have entered the space in the last three years. Privately, the agency questions the accuracy of the data and numbers attached to current cannabis market sizing.

> 'We try to gather what information there is and translate into simple useful products, primarily for policymakers:
>
> Until now we have only dealt with illicit drugs, where it is simple to say 'this is bad. In future that will not be the case. We are working on a report about low-THC cannabis, and we must be very careful to represent both sides of the story, not just one. Policymakers who do not like cannabis do not like that there are legitimate interests now, but we have to recognise today there are two sides rather than one.' (Brendan Hughes, lead researcher at the EMCDDA).'

CBD AND THE EU NOVEL FOOD REGULATION WRANGLE

3.89 In January 2019, the European Commission updated its Novel Food Catalogue to state that extracts of Cannabis sativa L. and derived products containing cannabinoids, namely CBD, are considered as novel foods, as a history of consumption has not been demonstrated.

The law set out in Novel Food procedure (Regulation (EU) 2015/2283), applies across all member states, means any product deemed as 'novel' must be approved by food authorities before it can be sold as a foodstuff within the EU.

A food is considered 'novel' if it was not consumed in the EU to any significant degree before May 1997, and the ruling applies to all foodstuffs, including food supplements, food ingredients, and substances intended to be incorporated into food.

As a result, all extracts of hemp and derived products containing cannabinoids, including CBD, are regarded by Brussels as novel foods. This categorisation applies to the extracts themselves and also any products to which they are added as an ingredient (for example, hemp seed oil). Synthetically obtained cannabinoids are also considered to be novel.

The decision upset the CBD market, said Keller and Heckman LLP partner Katia Merten-Lentz, which has burst onto the world stage in recent years, with the EU being no exception.

> 'While CBD can be incorporated into cosmetics and used for medical uses, it is quickly gaining traction in the food and drink market, with CBD found in supplements, infused into teas and coffees, cocktails, confectionary and a variety of other edible items.'

CBD is generally made from the Cannabis sativa L. plant; a variety of industrial hemp. The cannabis plant contains nearly 500 different compounds and of these, there are more than 100 cannabinoids which, depending on the compound, have either psychoactive or non-psychoactive effects. CBD is a non-psychotic compound, and has become prevalent in a new wave of food products such as dietary supplements.

The novel foods list is not legally binding, but is used as a reference by many watchdogs in the EU for the purposes of the Novel Food Regulation ((EU) 2015/2283). The upshot is EU member states can refuse to permit supply of foods and food supplements containing CBD, pending formal approval by the European Food Standards Agency (EFSA) under the Novel Food Regulation.

Austria was one of the first countries to do so, and Germany has also followed suit. In the UK, the Food Standards Agency and Trading Standards have informally stated they intend to pursue enforcement activity from January 2020 and will remove food products from shelves while applications to authorise use are reviewed.

> 'As part of this process, food or drink producers will be required to present a case that evidences CBD as a safe, albeit novel ingredient in food and beverages if consumed in certain amounts.' (Merten-Lentz.)

Pro-cannabis and hemp groups have lobbied Brussels on the matter, worried that their members and clients are unwittingly breaking a regulation that should not apply – supporters say hemp flower products such as hempseed and hempseed oil (extract) are already authorised, and the ban is unlawful.

It is expected that further guidance from the EU's food regulator will be issued at some time in the first half of 2020.

> 'Simply put, any food which is not expressly approved by the EU is considered as 'unsafe' – given the EU's last ruling on the topic, CBD food and drinks currently fall into this categorisation. As a result, any CBD food or drink product on the market in the EU, is not compliant with EU Novel Food laws.' (Merten-Lentz.)

ENDNOTES

1. International Drug Policy Consortium note on Croatia drug reform: https://idpc.net/alerts/2012/12/croatia-decriminalizes-drug-use.
2. *Croatia Medics Back Legalizing Medical Marijuana*: https://balkaninsight.com/2015/01/21/croatia-moves-towards-legalizing-medical-marijuana/.
3. Government of the Republic of Croatia: Legal and institutional framework of combating drugs abuse in the Republic of Croatia: https://drogeiovisnosti.gov.hr/UserDocsImages/nijdarhiva/2012/10/EXASS_OCDA.pdf.
4. Government of the Czech Republic, Government Council for Drug Policy Coordination detail: https://www.vlada.cz/en/ppov/protidrogova-politika/government-council-for-drug-policy-coordination-72748/.
5. Zákon č. 50/2013 Sb. (Czech law): https://www.zakonyprolidi.cz/cs/2013-50.
6. *The Policy of the Czech Republic in regards to Cannabis*: http://www.conbiz.eu/information/articles/cannabis-in-czech-republic.
7. Transnational Institute paper, New Approaches on Harm Reduction Policies and Practices: https://www.tni.org/en/page/new-approaches-on-harm-reduction-policies-and-practices.
8. *Copenhagen city council supports cannabis legalization trial*: https://www.thelocal.dk/20190912/copenhagen-city-council-supports-cannabis-legalization-trial.
9. Danish Medicines Agency – Medicinal cannabis pilot programme detail: https://laegemiddelstyrelsen.dk/en/special/medicinal-cannabis/citizens/medicinal-cannabis-pilot-programme/.
10. *Denmark's high hopes to become Europe's biggest medical cannabis producer*: http://cphpost.dk/news/denmarks-high-hopes-to-become-europes-biggest-medical-cannabis-producer.html.
11. *The changing face of medicinal cannabis in Denmark*: https://www.healtheuropa.eu/medical-cannabis-denmark/88367/.
12. Danish Medicines Agency, lists of euphoriant substances: https://laegemiddelstyrelsen.dk/en/licensing/company-authorisations-and-registrations/euphoriant-substances/lists-of-substances/.
13. *Two police officers, one civilian shot in Christiania*: https://www.thelocal.dk/20160901/two-police-officers-one-civilian-shot-in-christiania.
14. Ministry of Health and Social Affairs background: https://stm.fi.
15. Finland narcotics legislation, narcotics control: https://www.fimea.fi/web/en/supervision/narcotics_control.
16. *Cannabis policy and legislation in the Nordic countries*: https://nordicwelfare.org/wp-content/uploads/2019/04/Cannabis-policy-and-legislation-in-the-Nordic-countries_FINAL.pdf.
17. Drogues, Chiffres *clés rassemble les indicateurs chiffrés les plus récents et les plus pertinents pour quantifier et décrire le phénomène des substances psychoactives*: http://www.ofdt.fr/BDD/publications/docs/DCC2017.pdf.
18. Statista, *Prevalence of cannabis use in the last year in Europe as of 2018, by country*: https://www.statista.com/statistics/597692/cannabis-use-europe-by-country/.
19. *France to launch medical cannabis experiment in coming weeks*: https://www.france24.com/en/20190602-france-launch-medical-cannabis-experiment-authier.
20. *Légaliser le cannabis récréatif: la proposition choc du Conseil d'analyse économique*: https://www.lefigaro.fr/actualite-france/legaliser-le-cannabis-recreatif-la-proposition-choc-du-conseil-d-analyse-economique-20190619.
21. *France looks to soften laws against cannabis use*: https://www.france24.com/en/20180122-france-laws-against-smoking-pot-cannabis-marijuana-drugs-legislation-Poulliat.
22. (Ipsos) *La légalisation du cannabis: le débat doit-il s'ouvrir?* https://www.ipsos.com/fr-fr/la-legalisation-du-cannabis-le-debat-doit-il-souvrir.
23. (Case C-663/18): Request for a preliminary ruling from the Cour d'appel d'Aix-En-Provence (France) lodged on 23 October 2018: http://curia.europa.eu/juris/document/document.jsf?text=&docid=209505&pageIndex=0&doclang=en&mode=lst&dir=&occ=first&part=1&cid=8836965.
24. *Smoking Marijuana Legalized in Georgia*: http://georgiatoday.ge/news/11592/Smoking-Marijuana-Legalized-in-Georgia.
25. Law of Georgia, Criminal Code of Georgia: https://matsne.gov.ge/en/document/download/16426/157/en/pdf.
26. *Norms envisaging imprisonment for marijuana use now null and void in Georgia*: https://agenda.ge/en/news/2016/3159.
27. *Georgian PM: Marijuana cultivation for medical purposes will be strongly regulated*: https://agenda.ge/en/news/2018/1895.
28. *Why can't Germany get its medical marijuana industry going?*: https://www.handelsblatt.com/today/companies/cannabis-why-cant-germany-get-its-medical-marijuana-industry-going/23811676.html?ticket=ST-26204115-yZ30r6Bw7ca6dnbyfbqS-ap6.
29. Germany Narcotic Drugs Act: http://www.bgbl.de/xaver/bgbl/start.xav?startbk=Bundesanzeiger_BGBl&jumpTo=bgbl117s0403.pdf.
30. *GERMAN LEGAL REGIME CONCERNING CANNABIS FOR MEDICAL USE*: https://www.mwe.com/insights/overview-german-legal-regime-concerning-cannabis-for-medical-use/.
31. *German cannabis firm Demecan secures 7 million euros in financing*: https://mjbizdaily.com/german-cannabis-firm-demecan-secures-7-million-euros-in-financing/.
32. *Germany confirms marijuana licenses for domestic cultivation after challenges fail*: https://mjbizdaily.com/germany-confirms-cannabis-licenses-domestic-cultivation/.
33. Terms and conditions for the manufacture and marketing of final pharmaceutical cannabis products: http://www.minagric.gr/images/stories/en_docs/CANNABIS/EOF_REGULATION__FINAL310119.pdf.
34. *The legal framework on the cultivation of medical cannabis in Greece*: https://www.vdilawfirm.com/the-legal-framework-on-the-cultivation-of-medical-cannabis-in-greece/.

35. Medical Cannabis Access Programme launch enables compassionate access to cannabis for medical reasons: https://www.gov.ie/en/press-release/ad78dc-medical-cannabis-access-programme-launch-enables-compassionate-acces/.
36. S.I. No. 69/1998 – Misuse of Drugs (Designation) Order, 1998.: http://www.irishstatutebook.ie/eli/1998/si/69/made/en/print.
37. *Cork toddler, 2, gets cannabis oil permit for epilepsy treatment*: http://www.rte.ie/news/2016/1223/841009-tristan-forde-cannabis/.
38. *Canadian cannabis giant lobbies State to supply Irish medical* market: https://www.irishtimes.com/business/health-pharma/canadian-cannabis-giant-lobbies-state-to-supply-irish-medical-market-1.3860236.
39. *Roll up, roll up: capitalism will drive cannabis legalisation in Ireland*: https://www.irishtimes.com/business/agribusiness-and-food/roll-up-roll-up-capitalism-will-drive-cannabis-legalisation-in-ireland-1.3994192.
40. *Italy Publishes New Regulation on Hemp Production and Sale*: https://www.liberties.eu/en/news/boosting-new-capana-economy-italian-government-publishes-new-regulation-to-enhance-production-and-commercialisation-of-legal-marijuana/15231.
41. LEGGE 2 dicembre 2016, n. 242: https://www.gazzettaufficiale.it/eli/id/2016/12/30/16G00258/sg.
42. Sezioni Unite Penali: sentenza in materia di cannabis sativa L: http://www.cortedicassazione.it/cassazione-resources/resources/cms/documents/cannabis.pdf.
43. *Italy announces new medical cannabis tender*: https://prohibitionpartners.com/2019/06/18/italy-announces-new-medical-cannabis-tender/.
44. *Pass the Duchy: Luxembourg's grand plan to legalize cannabis*: https://www.politico.eu/article/luxembourg-legalize-cannabis/.
45. Luxembourg Official Gazette: A 1973, p.319.
46. Question écrite n. 961 – Sujet : Pénurie du cannabis medical: https://chd.lu/wps/portal/public/Accueil/TravailALaChambre/Recherche/RoleDesAffaires?action=doQuestpaDetails&id=17692.
47. *"J'espère bien qu'un jour on aura un astronaute luxembourgeois"*: https://msan.gouvernement.lu/fr/support/recherche.gouvernement%2Bfr%2Bactualites%2Btoutes_actualites%2Binterviews%2B2019%2B09-septembre%2B27-int-schneider.html.
48. *Malta Enterprise approves 4,000 sq.m medical cannabis facility*: https://www.maltatoday.com.mt/business/business_news/86065/malta_enterprise_approves_4000_sqm_medical_cannabis_facility#.Xg9Xwi2ZPxh.
49. Production of Cannabis for Medicinal and Research Purposes Act: http://justiceservices.gov.mt/DownloadDocument.aspx?app=lom&itemid=12821&l=1.
50. Drug Dependence Act: http://www.justiceservices.gov.mt/DownloadDocument.aspx?app=lom&itemid=12289&l=1.
51. http://www.justiceservices.gov.mt/DownloadDocument.aspx?app=lom&itemid=12928&l=1.
52. *More anti-money laundering fines for Malta-based gaming firms*: https://timesofmalta.com/articles/view/more-anti-money-laundering-fines-for-malta-based-gaming-firms.710114.
53. *Merrily manufacturing marijuana in Malta?*: https://timesofmalta.com/articles/view/merrily-manufacturing-marijuana-in-malta.690965.
54. *Substantial investment in Malta by Canadian companies in medical cannabis sector – 900 new jobs to be created*: https://www.tvm.com.mt/en/news/substantial-investment-in-malta-by-canadian-companies-in-medical-cannabis-sector-900-new-jobs-to-be-created/.
55. Netherlands Government, Sale of cannabis in coffeeshops: https://business.gov.nl/regulation/cannabis-sale-coffeeshop/.
56. Netherlands Enterprise Agency, RVO, budget day 2018 info: https://business.gov.nl/prinsjesdag-2018--budget-day/.
57. Netherlands Opium Act: https://www.belastingdienst.nl/wps/wcm/connect/bldcontenten/belastingdienst/customs/safety_health_economy_and_environment/safety/opium_act_drugs/.
58. Medicinal Cannabis on Prescription in The Netherlands: Statistics for 2003–2016: https://www.researchgate.net/publication/324072084_Medicinal_Cannabis_on_Prescription_in_The_Netherlands_Statistics_for_2003-2016.
59. INCB, COMMENTS ON THE REPORTED STATISTICS ON NARCOTIC DRUGS: http://www.incb.org/documents/Narcotic-Drugs/Technical-Publications/2017/7_Part_2_comments_E.pdf.
60. *Government to issue second licence for medicinal cannabis as demand grows*: https://www.dutchnews.nl/news/2019/05/government-to-issue-second-licence-for-medicinal-cannabis-as-demand-grows/.
61. *NORML Norway: Cannabis law reform in Norway*: https://www.normalnorge.no/english.
62. *Negative consequences of control in the enforcement of current Norwegian law regarding cannabis*: https://www.normal-norge.no/negative-consequences-of-control.
63. *What Norway actually changed in its drug policy*: https://nordan.org/sorheim-decriminalisation-will-send-a-signal-to-young-people-that-drug-use-is-relatively-safe/.
64. *Use of the Cannabis Plant for Medicinal Purposes*: https://www.plmj.com/en/knowledge/informative-notes/Use-of-the-Cannabis-Plant-for-Medicinal-Purposes/19027/.
65. Decree-Law 8/2019: https://dre.pt/application/conteudo/117821806.
66. Decree-Law 30/2000: https://www.unodc.org/res/cld/document/prt/law30_html/portugal_law_30_2000.pdf.
67. *Drug Decriminalization in Portugal: Lessons for Creating Fair and Successful Drug Policies*: https://www.cato.org/publications/white-paper/drug-decriminalization-portugal-lessons-creating-fair-successful-drug-policies.
68. EMCDDA European Drug Report 2015: http://www.emcdda.europa.eu/attachements.cfm/att_239505_EN_TDAT15001ENN.pdf.
69. *After legalisation, what next for medical cannabis in Portugal?*: https://www.healtheuropa.eu/medical-cannabis-in-portugal/90986/.
70. *Cannabis social clubs in Spain: legalisation without commercialisation*: https://transformdrugs.org/cannabis-social-clubs-in-spain-legalisation-without-commercialisation/.
71. *El cannabis pelea por un espacio legal*: https://elpais.com/diario/2008/12/09/sociedad/1228777201_850215.html.
72. *Cannabis Regulation in Europe: Country Report Spain*: https://www.tni.org/files/publication-downloads/cr_spain_final.pdf.

73. Código de Buenas Prácticas para las Asociaciones Cannábicas: http://catfac.org/wp-content/uploads/2014/10/Código-Buena-Pràcticas-CatFAC-Castellano.pdf.

74. *Introducing the battle to regulate therapeutic medical cannabis in Spain*: https://www.healtheuropa.eu/therapeutic-medical-cannabis-spain/90880/.

75. *Swiss teens among Europe's top pot smokers*: https://www.swissinfo.ch/eng/high-ranking-_swiss-teens-among-europe-s-top-pot-smokers/42023308.

76. Switzerland cannabis laws and regulations: https://www.bag.admin.ch/bag/de/home/gesund-leben/sucht-und-gesundheit/cannabis.html.

77. Federal Act on Narcotics and Psychotropic Substances: Article 19: https://www.admin.ch/opc/en/classified-compilation/19981989/.

78. Sativex®, Spray zur Anwendung in der Mundhöhle (cannabis sativae folii cum flore extractum spissum): https://www.swissmedic.ch/swissmedic/de/home/humanarzneimittel/authorisations/new-medicines/sativex---spray-zur-anwendung-in-der-mundhoehle--cannabis-sativa.html.

79. *Swiss pharmacies want to sell medical and recreational marijuana*: https://www.thelocal.ch/20190111/swiss-pharmacies-want-to-sell-marijuana-in-the-future-valeria-dora-cannabis.

80. *Immer mehr Menschen konsumieren Cannabis. Deshalb wollen die Zürcher Apotheken künftig Marihuana verkaufen*: https://www.nzz.ch/zuerich/apotheken-in-zuerich-wollen-cannabis-verkaufen-ld.1450593.

81. *Turkey seizes 5.5M cannabis plants*: https://www.trtworld.com/turkey/turkey-seizes-5-5m-cannabis-plants-27965.

82. *TURKEY'S ISLAMIST GOVERNMENT PUSHES FOR RAPID INCREASE IN NATION'S HISTORIC CANNABIS PRODUCTION*: https://www.newsweek.com/turkey-islamist-government-increase-cannabis-production-1294290.

83. *Tarım Bakanı Pakdemirli: Kenevir üretimini artıracağız*: https://www.gazeteduvar.com.tr/ekonomi/2019/01/10/tarim-bakani-pakdemirli-kenevir-uretimini-artiracagiz/.

84. Cannabis related searches and relevant info: http://www.hukukturk.com/en/Sonuc.aspx?q=kenevir.

85. *Turkey permits controlled cannabis production in 19 provinces*: http://www.hurriyetdailynews.com/turkey-permits-controlled-cannabis-production-in-19-provinces-.aspx?PageID=238&NID=104974&NewsCatID=345.

86. United Nations office on Drugs and Crime, Analysis of drug markets 2018: https://www.unodc.org/wdr2018/prelaunch/WDR18_Booklet_3_DRUG_MARKETS.pdf.

87. INCB statistics: http://www.incb.org/documents/Narcotic-Drugs/Technical-Publications/2017/7_Part_2_comments_E.pdf.

88. Misuse of Drugs Act 197:1 http://www.legislation.gov.uk/ukpga/1971/38/contents.

89. Misuse of Drugs Regulations 2001: http://www.legislation.gov.uk/uksi/2001/3998/contents/made.

90. Home Office drugs licensing info: https://www.gov.uk/government/collections/drugs-licensing.

91. *Epilepsy Society Welcomes Government Response To Billy Caldwell Case*: https://www.epilepsysociety.org.uk/news/epilepsy-society-welcomes-government-response-billy-caldwell-case-16-06-2018#.Xa3QdC2ZPx4.

92. *Why I campaign for children like my son Alfie Dingley to be able to get medical cannabis*: https://www.bmj.com/content/365/bmj.l1921.

93. *NICE draft guidance and NHS England review highlight need for more research on cannabis-based medicinal products*: https://www.nice.org.uk/news/article/nice-draft-guidance-and-nhs-england-review-highlight-need-for-more-research-on-cannabis-based-medicinal-products.

94. *'I shouldn't have to look over my shoulder': Carly Barton's fight for medicinal cannabis*: https://www.theguardian.com/society/2019/apr/25/i-shouldnt-have-to-look-over-my-shoulder-carly-bartons-fight-for-medicinal-cannabis.

95. https://www.carlysamnesty.org/.

96. Procedure file: 2018/2775(RSP) Use of cannabis for medicinal purposes.

97. As above. Adopted text: http://www.europarl.europa.eu/doceo/document/TA-8-2019-0113_EN.html.

98. European Commission health work programme 2018–2020: http://ec.europa.eu/research/participants/data/ref/h2020/wp/2018-2020/main/h2020-wp1820-health_en.pdf.

99. Neuropathic pain: biomarkers and druggable targets within the endogenous analgesia system: https://cordis.europa.eu/project/rcn/111184/factsheet/en.

100. *EU drugs agency publishes its first report on the medical use of cannabis*: http://www.emcdda.europa.eu/news/2018/9/emcdda-publishes-first-report-medical-use-of-cannabis_en.

Chapter 4

Africa

LESOTHO

4.01 The tiny enclaved Kingdom of Lesotho made history in 2017 by becoming the first African nation to legalise the cultivation and export of cannabis for medicinal purposes.

Lesotho is responsible for the majority of black-market cannabis supplied in South Africa, the country that surrounds it. Criminal gangs have long taken advantage of Lesotho's perfect growing climate and environment and its poor economy.

The illicit cash crop is also a significant livelihood strategy for smallholder farmers and vulnerable households in the kingdom, and it is hoped the new laws will give farmers a financial incentive to turn away from selling their crop to drug traffickers.

In May 2017, Medi Kingdom, founded in the UK, was awarded the first legal cannabis operators cultivation licence in the Kingdom of Lesotho.

Nomadic tribes

4.02 In his book, A Short History of Lesotho,[1] author Stephen Gill sketches the importance of cannabis to the settlers who are responsible for present day Lesotho; the crop was used in bargaining over land for the early tribes.

There is evidence that cannabis cultivation and trade networks have been evident for the past two or three centuries at least, and that the crop's value encouraged other nomadic tribes to settle.

Over time, large-scale dams and hydro-electric generators were built in Lesotho for various projects, and illicit cannabis cultivation became a major source of income for hundreds of farmers.

The main areas of production in Lesotho are the high mountain zones in the centre and east of the country, and the western foothills region and in the Senqu River valley.[2]

Within one small community in the foothills, a 2009 field survey and household income analysis found that up to 39% of the total field area in the village was planted with cannabis and 28% of the village's income came from the sale of cannabis.

Cannabis was previously regulated under the Dangerous Medicines Act of 1973 (Government of Lesotho, 1978), which was superseded by the Drugs of Abuse Act 2008.

This allowed the government to provide access to specific drugs for medical and scientific purposes.

The International Narcotics Control Board in 2007 noted the efforts made by the Government of Lesotho to control drug cultivation and comply with the international drug control treaties.[3]

A decade later, Lesotho made history by becoming the first African nation to decriminalise and legalise cannabis cultivation for medicinal use.

Lawmakers began updating the legislation in 2016, and the new laws came into effect in May 2018 through the Drug of Abuse (Cannabis) Regulations Act of 2018. This Act was updated in 2019 to add additional standards for international firms.

In May 2017, Medi Kingdom was awarded the first full cannabis operator's licence (No.18/08/01/2017), and the company began exporting following the passing of the 2018 legislation.

Under each licence, which is for ten years, the Lesotho Ministry of Health approves firms to cultivate, manufacture, supply, hold, import, export and transit cannabis.

Licences cost approximately €30,000 (US$33,000) and are issued by the Lesotho Narcotics Board. Although Lesotho legalised cultivation in an effort to help domestic firms, the cost has prohibited local farmers, and a number of foreign companies have entered the market.

In March 2018, Medi Kingdom became the first company to successfully export cannabis flower from Africa to Canada since 1961, and throughout 2019 the company exported to Australia and Europe.

Lesotho's Prime Minister, Dr Motsoahae Thomas Thabane officially marked the occasion in December 2018 with a ribbon-cutting ceremony at the Medi Kingdom site, which the firm runs in partnership with local firm Agri-Go.

In May 2019, Toronto-headquartered cannabis producer White Sheep announced that it had broken ground on a facility in Lesotho, having purchased 9.7 hectares of real estate in Masianokeng, along a road just outside the capital city of Maseru. The company planned to build a 300,000 sq ft cannabis production facility to grow medical marijuana and process it into high concentration oils.

It chose Lesotho, it said:

> 'because it is known for benevolent mountainous conditions that are ideally suited for controlled greenhouse operations: high altitude, low humidity, and sunny climate. [Lesotho is a] politically stable constitutional monarchy led by a pro-medical cannabis government with favourable corporate tax rates'.

Licence controversy

4.03 As of December 2019, Lesotho has handed out around 60 licences, but the project was put on hold amid fierce criticism of the government's methods.

In July 2019, *Marijuana Business Daily* reported Lesotho was updating its laws to effectively erect barriers for prospective industry entrants.[4] Industry sources told the publication it would focus regulatory resources on the more serious players.

According to the proposal, some of the new factors the government would consider before granting a licence include:

- a public interest argument;
- the proximity of villages, towns, schools, parks, churches or 'public institutions' to the proposed cannabis business if within 5k (3.1 miles);
- whether the number of licenses already awarded is adequate to meet demand;
- access to roads, clean water and electric power, or whether supplying those is part of the business plan;
- the risk of diversion to the illicit market; and
- the potential for economic decentralisation.

Many of the problems stemmed from Lesotho updating its laws to allow cannabis businesses to operate without diverting enough regulatory resources to handle the influx of business.

The country's future success as a medical cannabis producer will also hinge on how South Africa proceeds, given its government has until September 2020 to update laws reflecting a court judgment to declare the continued criminalisation recreational cannabis use unjust.

Dr Julian Bloomer wrote, in his detailed analysis of the cannabis trade in Lesotho through history:

> 'Whether Lesotho remains a key producer of medical cannabis in the region, must surely depend on whether South Africa decides to embark on a similar route, and indeed recent legislation appears to be moving exactly in this direction. If this transpires, the competitive advantages that Lesotho's neighbour maintains over the land-locked mountain kingdom would surely also mean that South Africa can dominate in this area of trade as well.'

MOROCCO

4.04 Morocco is the world's largest producer of cannabis resin (hashish). The country's black market has thrived despite multiple attempts to eradicate production and has even evolved to meet the shifting demands of users.

Moroccan authorities have stepped up efforts to tackle the illicit drug trade following a 2018 announcement, but the strategy seems to be one of containment, forbidding new areas of cultivation to appear whilst allowing the existing farms to continue operating.

Proposals to regulate cannabis have been on the table since 2014, when an opposition party in the Moroccan parliament submitted a bill to legalise production for medical and industrial use. That bill failed, and the movement has been stuck ever since.

Legal background

4.05 Morocco grandfathered its anti-drug laws from France following independence in 1954, including the Dahir prohibiting kif hemp. The legislation remained untouched for almost 20 years, and the Criminal Code of Morocco, adopted in 1962, was the first post-independence legislation.

Moroccan law refers to the concept of 'poisonous substances', drawing on the classification contained in the 1961 Single Convention on Narcotic Drugs and the 1971 Vienna Convention. The Order of the Minister of Public Health lists all licit and illicit drugs, and was last updated in 1997.

The main legislative instrument is the Dahir law on the suppression of drug addiction (No. 1-73-282 of May 21, 1974).

Drug use is a criminal offence in Morocco, and the Code details the punishment for drug-related offences with up to 30 years' imprisonment and a fine of up to €60,000 (US$51,000). Drug traffickers are on average sentenced to imprisonment of between eight and ten years.

Article 8 of the Law on the Suppression of Drug Addiction sets out the possibility for criminal proceedings to be cancelled in cases where an offender submits to drug treatment.

The unregulated cannabis market in Morocco is enormous, and currently some 48,000 growers have arrest warrants hanging over their heads.

Next steps

4.06 Morocco is known for cannabis tourism and an increasing influx of foreign 'hippies' into the country in the late 20th century is often blamed for the growing demand for kif (a mixture of tobacco and chopped pieces of marijuana).

It is trying (unsuccessfully) to shake the tag of the world's illegal drug supplier, and most attempts at bringing regulatory proposals to the table have died in parliament.

A United Nations Office on Drugs and Crime (UNODC) report that Morocco remains the world's largest producer of cannabis resin, producing over three times more than the next highest contender, the European country Moldova.[5] The EMCDDA report that most of the hash in Europe originates from Morocco.

Moroccan cannabis production in 2017 was over 36,000 tons, dwarfing all other countries output. The majority of this is processed into cannabis resin. As a comparison, the same report estimates Mexico produced a little over 5,000 tons in the same year.

The EMCDDA said, in its annual drug report:[6]

> '[European cannabis] Resin potency has shown a continuous increase since 2009. Drivers of this increasing average potency in resin likely include the introduction of high-potency plants and new production techniques in Morocco, and, to a lesser extent, the greater use within Europe of resin extraction techniques that provide higher potency products.'

In July 2019, Moroccan police seized a record 27.3 tonnes in one haul.[7]

The UN's International Narcotics Control Board said 400t of cannabis was seized in 2017, the largest of all African nations and almost as high as all resin seizures in the whole of Europe, which according to EMCCA was 466t.

There are several active campaigns to legalise cannabis for both recreational and medicinal use, but most proposals have been knocked back in parliament.

SOUTH AFRICA

4.07 On 18 September 2018, South Africa's Constitutional Court, the highest in the Republic, decriminalised cannabis growing, use and possession in private spaces,[8] making it the first country in the continent of Africa to do so.

In a unanimous ruling,[9] the court sided with three users facing prosecution for using the drug, which is known as 'Dagga' in Afrikaans. The trio argued prohibition 'intrudes unjustifiably into their private spheres', and the court agreed.

Constitutional courts in Mexico and the tiny former Soviet state of Georgia have made similar rulings that international treaty agreements on cannabis control infringe on the rights of citizens. Their decisions may trigger wider ramifications, particularly in areas where cannabis was part of the social fabric for thousands of years until the early 20th century when imperial powers stepped in.

South Africa's job judge gave the government a two-year deadline to enact the new laws, which come into force on 18 September 2020. The ruling, which is binding, sent shockwaves through South Africa, and dealt a huge blow to the government, which has long opposed any form of cannabis legalisation.

Nobody can safely predict what the legislation will look like in September 2020, despite the limited guidance that has been published. Experts believe an overly-complex licensing scheme with high barriers to entry is one likely outcome.

As it is, with near perfect conditions for growing, a large domestic market, well-established trade routes into nearby countries, and now regulatory freedom to proceed, South Africa may unwittingly become an important, if reluctant, force in the global cannabis world.

Legal background

4.08 On 18 September 2018, South Africa's Constitutional Court handed down a judgment which declared legislation criminalising the use, possession, purchase and cultivation of cannabis unconstitutional.

The matter arose from three different court proceedings in 2017 instituted in the High Court of South Africa, Western Cape Division, Cape Town (High Court) which were consolidated and heard as one matter, as they were all premised on the same basis.

This was that certain sections of the Drugs and Drug Trafficking Act 140 of 1992 (Drugs Act)[10] and the Medicines and Related Substances Control Act 101 of 1965 (Medicines Act)[11] were constitutionally invalid.

Section 4(b) of the Drugs Act prohibits the use or possession of any dangerous dependence-producing substance or any undesirable dependence-producing substance unless exceptions listed in the provision apply.

Section 5(b) of the Drugs Act prohibits dealing in any dangerous dependence-producing substance or any undesirable dependence-producing substance unless exceptions listed in the provision apply.

Section 22A(9)(a)(i) of the Medicines Act, read with Schedule 7 to the Medicines Act, prohibits the acquisition, use, possession, manufacture or supply of cannabis, and section 22A(10) of the Medicines Act read with Schedule 7 prohibits the sale or administration of cannabis other than for medicinal purposes.

The High Court declared sections 4(b) and 5(b) of the Drugs Act, read with Part III of Schedule 2 to the Drugs Act, and sections 22A(9)(a)(i) and 22A(10) of the Medicines Act read with Schedule 7 to the Medicines Act, inconsistent with the right to privacy guaranteed by section 14 of the Constitution.

The High Court suspended the order of invalidity for a period of 24 months from 31 March 2017, to give Parliament the opportunity to resolve the constitutional defects in the statutory provisions concerned, and the matter went to the Constitutional Court.

In a unanimous judgment written by Deputy Chief Justice Raymond Zondo ACJ, as he then was, the Constitutional Court declared that:

1 Section 4(b) of the Drugs Act was unconstitutional and, therefore, invalid to the extent that it prohibits the use or possession of cannabis by an adult in private for that adult's personal consumption in private;
2 Section 5(b) of the Drugs Act was constitutionally invalid to the extent that it prohibits the cultivation of cannabis by an adult in a private place for that adult's personal consumption in private; and
3 Section 22A(9)(a)(i) of the Medicines Act was constitutionally invalid to the extent that it renders the use or possession of cannabis by an adult in private for that adult's personal consumption in private a criminal offence.

The Constitutional Court held these statutory provisions to be constitutionally invalid to the extent indicated, because they infringed the right to privacy entrenched in section 14 of the Constitution.

Zondo ACJ also went further than the High Court's limitation of its order to the use, cultivation or possession of cannabis 'at home or in a private dwelling'. He held that the right to privacy extends beyond the boundaries of a home.

The effect of the judgment is two-fold: (a) it decriminalises the use or possession of cannabis by an adult in private for that adult person's personal consumption in private; and (b) it decriminalises the cultivation of cannabis by an adult in a private place for that adult's personal consumption in private. However, the use or possession of cannabis by a child anywhere, or by an adult in public, is not decriminalised.

The Constitutional Court suspended its order of invalidity for a period of 24 months to give Parliament an opportunity to correct the constitutional defects in the two Acts.

However, in order to ensure that people who fall into the same category as the trio who brought the case received effective relief, Zondo ACJ granted interim relief by way of a reading-in of the two Acts to ensure that, during the period of suspension of invalidity, it would not be a criminal offence for an adult person:

(a) to use or be in possession of cannabis in private for his or her personal consumption in private; and
(b) to cultivate cannabis in a private place for his or her personal consumption in private.

Zondo ACJ took the view that it should be left to Parliament to decide on the quantity of cannabis that an adult person may use, possess or cultivate in order for it to amount to 'personal use'. He was of the view that the court would infringe the doctrine of separation of powers if it determined the amount itself.

As to how a police officer would know whether the amount of cannabis in the possession of an adult is or is not for that person's personal consumption, the court held that a police officer would have to consider all the circumstances, including the quantity of cannabis found in that person's possession. Police can make arrests if they suspect someone of dealing, but it will be up to a court to decide on the outcome.

In the end the appeal by the state was dismissed and the Constitutional Court confirmed the order of the High Court in so far as is reflected above.

Regulation and monitoring

4.09 Such was the unexpected nature of the court ruling, the entire country was caught off guard, and a flood of CBD and low THC products began to appear on sale throughout South Africa.

Current laws only allow growing cannabis for medicinal purposes with a valid licence from the health ministry, and in February 2019, the South African Health Products Regulatory Authority (Sahpra) released a statement reaffirming that the Constitutional Court ruling did not mean people could use, manufacture and sell their own cannabis medicines.

While it is no longer an offence to use or be in possession of cannabis in private, or to grow the plant in a private place for personal consumption, the regulator said a number of outlets and individuals selling cannabis-containing products, including oils, for medicinal use, were breaking the Medicines and Related Substances Act.

Regulations allowing sale of regulated cannabis 'health products' were later updated, and the country's Health Products Regulatory Authority (SAHPRA) intends to approve a wider range of products in line with the new laws before the end of 2020.

Cannabis products considered to be health supplements are those containing a daily dose of less than 20mg cannabidiol (CBD), as well as those containing less than 0.001% of THC, or less than 0.0075% CBD.

These products may be bought and sold relatively freely as a result of the exemption published in the South African *Government Gazette* on 23 May 2019.

'It is anticipated that in the near future more legislation and guidelines will be passed, weeding out the old laws,' said Ferosa-Fae Hassan of Africa's largest law firm ENSafrica. 'This will ensure adherence to legal standards and the general regulation of the cannabis industry.'

In August 2019, the South African Trade Marks Office published updated Guidelines on the Examination of Trademark Applications. Per these guidelines, cannabis-related trade mark applications will now be accepted on condition that the Applicant undertakes that the products comply with the standards set by the Minister of Health. Non-compliance with these standards would render the sale of the product and its trade mark application(s) contrary to law.[12]

It is certain that this newly tapped CBD and hemp market in South Africa will result in more cannabis-related trade mark applications being filed. Of the other agencies involved, the Central Drug Authority of South Africa backs decriminalisation but not full legalisation, as it does not believe sales would benefit the public.[13] South Africa's Medical Research Council has also issued research backing the use of cannabis for medical purposes.[14]

Exportation

4.10 South African companies obtaining licences to supply medicinal cannabis to the export market must have a contract in place with an overseas buyer of the product prior to gaining approval from the Medicine Control Council of SA (MCC).

This covers producers involved in the cultivation, drying and packaging of cannabis, as well as extracting cannabis oil.

An application must be submitted to the MCC, which will then inspect the plans for a facility, including security measures and the positioning of tunnels, said Nico Kriek, managing director at the Cannabis Compliance Bureau.

The physical structure of a facility must be approved, along with a quality-control procedure, to include:

- recruitment forms for job applications;
- document management system;
- fully-functional legal compliance system;
- details on cultivation systems;
- manufacturing standards; and
- systems for handling cannabis.

As part of the application process, businesses are allotted a quantity to be grown that is determined by the contract with the foreign buyer and the size of the facility.

Medicinal cannabis

4.11 Patients seeking cannabis-containing medicines were advised by the regulator to apply for an exemption to section 21 of the Medicines Act, which enables the importation of medicines that have been registered in other countries, such as Canada and the Netherlands.

To date, 56 such applications have been approved by Sahpra, based on motivation for use in specific patients by an authorised prescriber. The two key compounds of interest in cannabis are THC (delta-9-tetrahydrocannabinol), which has psychoactive properties, and cannabidiol.

In 2017, the regulator eased some of the restrictions on medicinal cannabis, to make it easier for patients to access. It reclassified it from a tightly restricted Schedule 7 product, to a permitted Schedule 6 (containing THC) or Schedule 4 product (without THC).

It also created the legal framework for legalising the cultivation of cannabis for medicinal use or research, in conjunction with the Department of Health and the Department of Agriculture, Forestry & Fisheries.[15]

Red tape

4.12 The court's decision has caused confusion and surprise amongst consumers and businesses, but the reaction from the public has been 'overwhelmingly positive' said Paul-Michael Keichel, partner at Schindlers Attorneys in Johannesburg who leads the firm's M&R cannabis law department:

> 'So many people are 'coming out of the cannabis closet' and reinforcing that prohibition has never been and never will be a good idea.'

Cannabis beverages, oils, soaps, creams and foods infused with cannabidiol (CBD) oils have appeared on sale, as they have across the rest of the world, and a series of cannabis events, exhibitions and festivals have also been held.

Only the private use of cannabis is permitted, and there are still unanswered questions about production, supply and sale of recreational cannabis, all of which are technically still criminal activities.

> 'It's impossible to say how supportive the government is. They fought us tooth and nail when we were forced to sue them for reform. They have a year now to pass reactive laws, but there's no saying (yet) what those laws will be. Certainly, at this stage, they still take a hard line with enforcing prohibition.' (Keichel)

The red tape is still strong enough as to handbrake anything pro-cannabis:

> 'The licensing scheme is incredibly tough, and not geared towards cannabis. Enough so to put off most people who're interested. The multinationals, or local elites, are seemingly the only ones with sufficient impetus and deep enough pockets to run the gauntlet. This is a major pity, as we really could, through conscious liberalisation of our laws, grab at the opportunity to create a viable industry for the poorest in our population.'

CBD legislation

4.13 On 23 May 2019 Notice No. R.756 of the *Government Gazette* No. 42477 (the Notice) came into effect in which the Minister of Health, in terms of section 36(1) of the Medicines and Related Substance Act 1965 (Act No. 101 of 1965) and on the recommendation of the South African Health Products Regulatory Authority (SAHPRA), excluded from the operation of the Schedules Act 1965, preparations containing cannabidiol (CBD) that:

- Contain a maximum daily dose of 20mg cannabidiol (CBD) with an accepted low-risk claim or health claim which only refer to:
  1 General health enhancement without any reference to specific diseases;
  2 Health maintenance; or
  3 Relief of minor symptoms (not related to a disease or disorder);

or;

- Consist of processed products made from cannabis raw plant material and processed products, where only the naturally occurring quality of cannabinoids found in the source material are contained in the product, and which contained not more than 0,001% of tetrahydrocannabinol (THC) and not more than 0,0075% total cannabidiol (CBD).

Keichel and his team explained that before the notice came into effect, section 22A(5) of the Medicines and Related Substances Act 101 of 1965 (the Medicines Act) would only cater for a defined list of persons, pharmacists being among them, to sell Schedule 4 substances.

Despite the fact that this section would also allow for other persons (such as manufacturers and wholesalers of pharmaceutical products and medical practitioners) to sell Schedule 4 substances, save for where the Medicines and/or the Pharmacy Acts expressly provided otherwise, a pharmacist was effectively placed at every juncture at which a scheduled substance was to be dispensed.

> 'This brings us to the conclusion that CBD products, which adhere to the requirements set out in the Notice, have been de-scheduled and may now be freely traded in South Africa. However, these CBD products may not contain more than 0.001% of tetrahydrocannabinol (THC) and not more than 0.0075% total CBD.'

The exclusions detailed expire on 15 May 2020, until such time as the exceptions are renewed by the Minister of Health.

CBD, when intended for therapeutic purposes, is listed as a Schedule 4 substance in terms of the Medicines Act. CBD is not recognised by South African law as a medicine in and of itself, but rather, as an active pharmaceutical ingredient (API) to be used, in different concentrations, as part of a medicine.

> 'At the time of writing, there are no registered medicines in South Africa which contain CBD. Although the relevant legislation would appear to suggest otherwise, the Pharmacy Council and SAHPRA confirm that APIs may not be sold to the general public. We have been advised by SAHPRA that the 'pain management' class of substances, which includes CBD, has been called up for registration.' (Keichel.)

Notwithstanding the fact that the activity of importing scheduled substances is quoted in regulation 3 of the Practice Regulations especially pertaining to the profession of a pharmacist, it does not fall within the scope of the activities which may be conducted by any category of pharmacy defined in the Licensing Regulations.

> 'In fact, the issue of importing scheduled substances, such as CBD, is not dealt with anywhere in the Pharmacy Act.'(Keichel.)

The importation of scheduled substances is specifically dealt with in section 22C(1)(b) of the Medicines Act which provides that the SAHPRA may, on application, issue licences which allow for specific groups of people, including, inter alia, distributors of scheduled substances, to import and distribute same.

> 'Overall, it is apparent that South Africa's cannabis industry remains extremely limited in that, despite the availability of the licence and permits set out above, the market to which such cannabis may be supplied is severely limited.' (Keichel.)

ZIMBABWE

4.14 Zimbabwe updated its regulations in 2018 to allow for the legal production of medicinal cannabis, in hopes it can replace tobacco as the country's largest export earning crop.

The African country has significant agricultural expertise and an ideal growing climate for cannabis, but long-standing corruption concerns, a potential shortage of the volumes of water needed for industrial operations and other structural issues stand in the way of progress.

Initially, the laws allowed for cannabis to be produced for medicinal or scientific purposes, and in September 2018, the regulations were further updated to repeal a ban on the growing of industrial hemp for export.

Legal background

4.15 The production of cannabis for medicinal or scientific purposes was legalised in Zimbabwe in 2018 by virtue of Statutory Instrument 62 of 2018 Dangerous Drugs (Production of Cannabis for Medicinal and Scientific Use) Regulations, 2018 (the cannabis regulations).[16]

The laws also regulate the general conditions for production including packaging, labelling and shipping. The regulations provide guidance on the production of medicinal and scientific use cannabis, and license must be obtained from the Minister of Health and Childcare. The licenses are valid for five years.

Previously, the production and use of cannabis was illegal and the possession of the substance carried a jail term of up to 12 years.

Licenses to grow are only for business owners that can prove citizenship or residency, which has led to an increase of partnerships between international producers and local farmers.

Applicants submit a form as prescribed by Section 5(1) of the Cannabis Regulations along with the prescribed statutory fee of US$50,000, and copies of the documents specified under PART II of the Cannabis Regulations. The sum of the fee has caused some controversy, as it is felt to be too steep for local farmers, while only locals or residents can apply for a licence.[17]

In June 2018, the government paused the medicinal cannabis programme to redraft some of the rules following issues that emerged relating to compliance issues with the necessary United Nations treaties and domestic accessibility problems.[18]

Marijuana Business Daily revealed the original law[19] defined how companies could become licensed producers and ship medical cannabis to 'authorised recipients'. While this was enough to create the framework for an export industry, the law did not establish how patients could become authorised within the country.

The original regulations were also almost identical to Canada's model, intended that way to help international companies familiar with Canada's system to eventually tap the new market, but this caused friction with businesses.

According to Trina Fraser, a business lawyer at Brazeau Seller Law:

> 'If you're not having deja vu, you should be, because many provisions in their legislation appear to have been copied directly from the ACMPR (Access to Cannabis for Medical Purposes Regulations, Canada's cannabis framework).'

The updated Statutory instrument 208 of 2019 of the Criminal Law Codification Regulations 2019 laid out further guidance on the growing, processing and supply of industrial hemp.

According to Rutendo Guvamatanga of law firm Manokore Attorneys, only certified individuals may acquire, possess supply, and cultivate industrial hemp on farms approved by the Minister of Lands, Agriculture, Water, Climate and Rural Resettlement.

> 'This development in the law clarifies the conflict between the cannabis regulations and the criminal code, which criminalised the possession of cannabis. Although the cannabis regulations rendered it legal to produce the drug, the criminal code still prohibited the cultivation, production and possession of cannabis, which resulted in a conflict between the two laws.'

Statutory Instrument 208 of 2019 removes this discrepancy, allowing those prescribed persons, who have been authorised by the Minister, to produce cannabis for medicinal and scientific purposes without any criminal implications.

In May 2019, Zimbabwe's government approved the country's first cannabis farm and production plant, at the Zimbabwe Prisons and Correctional Services' Buffalo Range prison in Chiredzi.[20] The prison was chosen out of convenience as the property already had tight security.

Industrial hemp

4.16 In September 2019, Zimbabwe further update its laws to allow farmers to grow industrial hemp for export, as previously the regulations only allowed the crop to be grown for medical and scientific uses.

Industrial hemp is a strain of a cannabis species grown specifically for industrial uses of its derived products. The fibre is used in textiles and paper, and it also produces edible seeds.

In October 2019, the country's first authorised hemp crop was planted at the prison in the capital Harare by Zimbabwe Industrial Hemp Trust. Six varieties of industrial hemp were planted.

Agriculture Minister Perence Shiri told guests at the launch:

> 'This project is the first of its kind in the history of our country. 'This pilot project will provide essential knowledge or information for the successful production of this crop. The benefits that will be derived from the production of industrial hemp are enormous and varied.'

AS AFRICA MAKES CULTIVATION PLAY, DOUBTS LINGER OVER STABILITY AND STANDARDS

4.17 Over the last two years, a handful of African states have enacted laws to regulate medicinal cannabis cultivation, with the aim of exporting to major European and American markets.

An influx of Canadian and European businesses has resulted in partnerships with local farmers, who can obtain licences. Optimism is high, but legal experts active in the relevant markets say it is early in the process and there is 'more talk than action' occurring.

Africa has the potential to become a major player in the global medicinal cannabis market, by virtue of its climate, environment, and experienced farming heritage, although questions persist over the region's political instability and the quality of the regulatory regimes drawn up.

The continent remains a huge black-market supplier, and approximately 38,000 tonnes is grown annually across the continent despite the fact cannabis is illegal in almost every African country.

The decline of tobacco has led to a fall in fortunes for already impoverished nations, as unemployment rises. Zimbabwe, Uganda, Swaziland and Lesotho are the prime African movers who consider cannabis as a way to replace tobacco production.

Several countries in the continent are in the process of updating (or in some cases, creating for the first time) medicinal cannabis laws that will create a framework for export.

Lack of accurate data

4.18 Private intelligence providers have published reports on the African market, but there is a dearth of data from the continent and it is difficult to ascertain the accuracy of these projections.

In 2018, Zimbabwe announced it was easing its historically strict drug laws in order to facilitate medicinal cannabis production, and received more than 60 applications inside the first four months. It later had to pause the project having run afoul of United Nations treaty agreements.

The country is experiencing one of its worst economic crises for decades, corruption amongst public officials is rife, and as in other areas of Africa, it will struggle to obtain quantities of water needed to grow the quantity and quality of cannabis required to service the EU.

Lesotho was the first African nation to legalise medicinal cannabis cultivation, and it has also had to tweak its regulations after becoming swamped with applications from North American and European firms trying to tap into its ideal climate and environment.

International firms are required to partner with local businesses if they want to acquire a licence and operate in Lesotho; however, reports from the country in late 2019[21] revealed domestic businesses were pricing out potential partners with their demands.

Lesotho and Zimbabwe were quick to spot the opportunity, but their administrations do not have the maturity, experience or resources to scale up and run a fully-functional medicinal cannabis regulatory regime as yet. The repeated alterations to the laws in 2019 is expected to continue through 2020.

South African fallout

4.19 In September 2018, South Africa decriminalised the use and cultivation of cannabis for private use; however, the decision was made by the judiciary and not the government.

South Africa's government was given until 2020 to enact the law and is currently drawing up a framework. Experts in the country are not confident the resultant laws will be 'business friendly' given the government's resistance to recreational cannabis use.

The impact of South Africa's decision is also likely to have ramifications for the tiny Kingdom of Lesotho, which it surrounds geographically, and neighbouring Swaziland, both of which have enacted laws to allow for the cultivation of medicinal cannabis and rely on South Africa for demand for much of their crop exports.

Through 2020, Uganda will also further flesh out its regulatory framework for medicinal cannabis production. In line with much of the rest of Africa, cultivation or use of cannabis in Uganda will remain a criminal offence.

ENDNOTES

1. A Short History of Lesotho (1993): Stephen J Gill, ISBN 10: 9991179364.
2. *Turning Cannabis Into Cash: Agrarian Change and Lesotho's Evolving Experience*: https://journals.openedition.org/echogeo/17612?lang=en.
3. INCB report 2007: https://www.incb.org/documents/Publications/AnnualReports/AR2007/AR_07_English.pdf.
4. *Lesotho planning overhaul of medical cannabis rules*: https://mjbizdaily.com/lesotho-planning-overhaul-of-medical-cannabis-rules/.
5. United Nations Office on Drugs and Crime World Drug report 2019: https://wdr.unodc.org/wdr2019/prelaunch/WDR19_Booklet_1_EXECUTIVE_SUMMARY.pdf.
6. EMCDDA Europe Drug Report 2019: http://www.emcdda.europa.eu/edr2019_en.
7. *Morocco seizes 'record' 27.3 tons of cannabis resin*: https://www.arabnews.com/node/1522671/middle-east.
8. *South Africa's highest court legalises cannabis use*: https://www.bbc.com/news/world-africa-45559954.
9. Minister of Justice and Constitutional Development and Others v Prince (Clarke, Stobbs and Thorpe Intervening) (Doctors of Life International Inc as Amicus Curiae); National Director of Public Prosecutions and Others v Rubin; National Director of Public Prosecutions and Others v Acton and Others: https://collections.concourt.org.za/handle/20.500.12144/34547.
10. Drugs Act: http://www.justice.gov.za/legislation/acts/1992-140.pdf.
11. Medicines Act: https://www.nda.agric.za/doaDev/sideMenu/fisheries/03_areasofwork/Aquaculture/AquaPolGuidLeg/Legislation/MedicinesRelatedSubstancesControlAct101of1965.pdf.
12. *Weeding out the old*: https://www.ensafrica.com/news/detail/1862/weeding-out-the-old/.
13. Comment on the Central Drug Authority's position statement on cannabis: http://www.samj.org.za/index.php/samj/article/viewFile/11036/7385.
14. *Decriminalising dagga 'a good idea'*: https://www.iol.co.za/news/decriminalising-dagga-a-good-idea-2066640.
15. Medicines Control Council CULTIVATION OF CANNABIS AND MANUFACTURE OF CANNABIS-RELATED PHARMACEUTICAL PRODUCTS FOR MEDICINAL AND RESEARCH PURPOSES: https://www.sahpra.org.za/documents/84a71af62.44_cannabis_growth_feb2017_v1_for_comment.pdf.
16. Dangerous Drugs Regulations 2018: http://www.veritaszim.net/sites/veritas_d/files/SI%202018-62%20-%20Production%20of%20Cannabis%20for%20Medicinal%20%26%20Scientific%20Use%20Regulations.pdf.
17. *Zimbabwe cannabis growers to pay high licence fee – reports*: https://www.news24.com/Africa/Zimbabwe/zim-cannabis-growers-to-pay-high-licence-fee-of-50-000-reports-20180430.
18. *Zimbabwe going 'back to the drawing board' on medical marijuana law*: https://mjbizdaily.com/zimbabwe-drawing-board-medical-marijuana-law/.
19. *Zimbabwe approves first license for private cannabis company*: https://mjbizdaily.com/zimbabwe-issues-first-license-private-cannabis-company/.
20. *Legal insight: The Cannabis Industry in Zimbabwe*: https://furtherafrica.com/2019/10/09/legal-insight-the-cannabis-industry-in-zimbabwe/.
21. *Locals in danger of losing out on lucrative cannabis industry*: http://lestimes.com/locals-in-danger-of-losing-out-on-lucrative-cannabis-industry/.

Chapter 5

Asia Pacific

AUSTRALIA

5.01 Drug laws in Australia are complex, and the picture is not unlike the US where states and territories are moving forward with regulation that runs counter to federal guidance.[1] Several of Australia's states are discussing the possibility of recreational cannabis markets.

Australia's federal government is primarily concerned with import/export and customs laws, and the state governments are usually the authorities that deal with regulating and enforcing their respective drug laws. Federal and state laws overlap with penalties for possessing, using, growing or selling cannabis, or driving under the influence of cannabis.

There are also laws that prevent the sale and possession of bongs and other smoking equipment in some states and territories. Penalties can include fines, imprisonment, rehabilitation orders and disqualification from driving. Certain states in Australia have passed laws to allow access to medicinal cannabis for very specific conditions.

According to the Australian government, cannabis is the country's most popular illicit drug.[2] In the 2017/2018 financial year, there were over 72,000 cannabis-related arrests made in Australia and 92% of those arrested were consumers.

Australia's states have very distinct identities, and are pursuing their own agendas. They have shown little inclination to partner up for the sake of lobbying the federal government, and as things stand, updates will occur in the towns and cities long before anything happens at national level.

In 2016, the Australian Parliament passed an amendment permitting cannabis to be legally grown for medical and scientific purposes for the first time.[3]

Medicinal cannabis

5.02 In February 2016, the Narcotic Drugs Amendment Act 2016[4] became law in Australia. It contains a number of significant alterations to the Narcotic Drugs Act 1967 and one minor update to the Therapeutic Goods Act 1989. In October 2016 the Narcotic Drugs Regulation 2016 was published, which adds a lot more detail.

The new Act defines a number of Commonwealth licences and permits that can be granted to allow the production of medicinal cannabis in Australia:

- A cannabis research licence/permit allows the holder to cultivate, produce; package, store and transport cannabis plants and/or resin for research purposes.
- A medicinal cannabis licence/permit allows the holder to do the same as a research licence, but for medicinal purposes.
- A manufacture licence/permit allows the holder to turn cannabis and/or resin into drugs for research and/or medical use.

Authorisation is a multi-step process. A licence is granted to an organisation on the basis of their background and capability. Both cultivation and manufacture activities must be individually licensed.

Manufacturers and cultivators must subsequently obtain one or more permits which will specify the amounts and types of cannabis/cannabis products to be cultivated and manufactured. The decision on the grant of licences and permits lies with the Secretary of the Department of Health.

More research needed

5.03 According to the Australian federal government.

> 'There have been very few well-designed clinical trials using medicinal cannabis, so there is limited evidence on its success in treating different medical conditions, or on effective forms and dosages.'

The studies that have been undertaken have focused mainly on epilepsy in children and adults, multiple sclerosis, chronic non-cancer pain, chemotherapy-induced nausea, and palliative care.

Evidence supporting the use of medicinal cannabis in the treatment of certain childhood epilepsies is strongest, according to the government:

> 'There is a significant need for larger, high-quality studies to explore the potential benefits, limitations and safety issues associated with medicinal cannabis treatment across a range of health conditions and symptoms. If more studies support medicinal cannabis use and provide evidence for particular forms,

dosages and administration methods, it is more likely that doctors will feel confident in prescribing medicinal cannabis over other approved options.'

Australian Capital Territory

5.04 The Australian capital Canberra became the country's first city to legalise marijuana following a landmark poll in September 2019.[5] Lawmakers in the Australian Capital Territory (ACT) voted to allow people aged 18 or over to possess and cultivate marijuana for personal use.[6] Ruling officials said it was time to treat cannabis use as a health issue, rather than a criminal one.

The new law is set to come into effect from 31 January 2020. Under the regulations, residents in the territory will be able to legally possess up to 50g (1.76oz) of marijuana, and cultivate up to two plants per person, or four per household.

The ACT became the first of Australia's six states and two main territories to legalise marijuana for personal use.

Under the ACT's previous law, growing one or two cannabis plants or possessing 50g (1.76oz) of cannabis carried a possible AUS$160 fine (US$108), while possessing more than that amount carried a maximum AUS$8,000 fine (US$5,000) or two years in prison (or both).

The ACT's new law clashes with national drug laws enacted by Australia's Parliament which prohibit the possession of marijuana. According to Australian media reports, the government may try to overrule the ACT's new law, potentially setting up a High Court clash.

In 2013, the ACT legalised same-sex marriage, but the decision was later overturned by Australia's highest court, which ruled that the ACT legislation was inconsistent with the national law.

New South Wales

5.05 In March 2018, Australia's health minister Greg Hunt announced that the New South Wales (NSW) government had 'taken a machete' to red tape, allowing for 'direct and immediate access' to medicinal cannabis.[7]

NSW has previously chosen to hold its own licence, and produces cannabis itself for research purposes. Medicinal cannabis organisations hoping to operate and distribute in NSW must also be licensed by NSW Health under the NSW Poisons and Therapeutic Goods Act.

Patients in NSW now require a single clinical assessment from the Therapeutic Goods Administration (TGA), where previously approvals were overseen by both the federal government and NSW Health, and could take weeks to be granted.

> 'New South Wales is now the national leader, we have had tremendous discussions with Tasmania and Victoria, and so I am hopeful that will make progress with them very shortly, but the benchmark has been set here and this is about saving lives and protecting lives, it's about giving people the capacity to go through their treatments. (Hunt)

The NSW Green Party is also attempting to reform recreational cannabis laws. The party has committed to introducing a private member's bill to legalise, license, and regulate recreational marijuana use within the first 100 days after the election, along with moving for a parliamentary inquiry into the legislation.

The group wants to allow NSW residents to grow up to six cannabis plants at home for personal use, as well as consuming it wherever it is legal to smoke tobacco. The Greens say the legislation would raise an estimated AUS$200m (US$137m) per year in additional tax revenue for the state government, via a mix of licensing fees, and reduced criminal prosecution costs.

Northern Territory

5.06 The Northern Territory has been reluctant to embrace cannabis, but this may change as officials consider the potential size of an industrial hemp sector. The territory has an ideal climate for outdoor production.

Updating laws to allow for industrial hemp production would bring the Northern Territory in line with the rest of Australia. Draft legislation[8] to legalise the growing of industrial hemp is currently in consideration by the Cabinet. A successful trial crop in the Katherine region that indicated the states climate conditions are going to give the NT a 'big commercial advantage'.[9]

The territory has not enacted rules to allow for the growing of cannabis for medicinal purposes, despite federal approval to do so.

Queensland

5.07 Queensland's Public Health (Medicinal Cannabis) Act 2016 was passed by the Parliament in October 2016.[10] The Act sets out a structure for the distribution of medicinal cannabis via a chain of licenced specialist doctors and pharmacists to patients. A state permit from Queensland Health is required to manufacture cannabis products in Queensland.

In October 2018, the first cannabis clinic in Queensland was opened by the Cannabis Access Clinic network, part of a broader move to make the drug more accessible to patients.

This clinic's launch was followed by an announcement from the Queensland government in November 2018 that it wants to increase patient access to medicinal cannabis by repealing laws that limit its prescription.

Victoria

5.08 Victoria enacted the Access to Medicinal Cannabis Act 2016 in April 2016,[11] which amended the Drugs, Poisons and Controlled Substances Act 1981. It was the first state to legislate for medicinal cannabis in Australia.

Under the new Act, an entity with a Commonwealth manufacture licence can apply to Health and Human Services (HHS) for a Victorian manufacturing licence. A holder of a manufacturing licence can only sell to HHS, who will then distribute via licenced pharmacists and doctors. Although the Act appears focused on childhood epilepsy, HHS will provide licenses for other conditions.

The Victorian government has heavily backed research initiatives for medicinal cannabis products, and set a target of more than 500 jobs in the industry in the next few years.

Attracting industry investment is a major component of the state government's Medical Cannabis Industry Development Plan, which unveiled in 2018. The plan outlines a strategy to grow Victoria's medicinal cannabis industry into an established agri-pharma sector, and would see half the country's legal marijuana supplied by the state in the coming year.

Victoria has welcomed numerous new cannabis businesses, including Althea Group, MediPharm Labs, Cann Group, and Cannvalate, which in 2019 purchased 100 acres of farmland in south-east Melbourne. Cannvalate wants to create the largest cannabis cultivation hub in Australia, and is building several facilities it will lease to four international companies who have already signed on.

Tasmania

5.09 The Tasmanian Government has developed a medical cannabis controlled-access scheme (CAS).[12] The scheme allows relevant medical specialists to be authorised to prescribe medical cannabis (unregistered cannabinoid products) in limited circumstances where conventional treatment has been unsuccessful.

All Tasmanian offences for cannabis cultivation, possession and use still apply. Exceptions to this are unregistered cannabinoid products prescribed and accessed under this scheme, and cannabis grown and cannabinoid products made under Narcotic Drug Act 1967 licenses issued by the Australian Government's Office of Drug Control.

The state began granting patients access to the drug in September 2017, but a year on, only seven patients had been prescribed medicinal cannabis products.

Tasmania is the only Australian state that does not offer an online application system to streamline the prescription process. The state's legislature has not kept pace with popular opinion, and recent polls indicate Tasmanians are broadly supportive of legalising recreational marijuana.

Western Australia

5.10 In December 2018, Western Australia opened its first medicinal cannabis-centric doctors' clinic in Subiaco. The practice is another extension of the Cannabis Access Clinics network.

The medical director of Cannabis Access Clinics, Dr Sanjay Nijhawan, said that the Western Australian Department of Health 'worked hard to streamline regulations and make access to treatment easier for patients in need.'

Any doctor in Western Australia can prescribe medicinal cannabis if they believe this treatment is suitable, provided they have the required Government approvals. Prescriptions for medicinal cannabis can be dispensed at any pharmacy in Western Australia.

The Department of Health WA claims there is only limited evidence of a variable quality that supports the use of medicinal cannabis, and the state is not as welcoming as other areas of the country.

WA police will also not entertain the possibility of recreational legalisation. In a submission last year to a Federal parliamentary inquiry into legalising cannabis, WA Assistant Commissioner Gary Budge said:

> 'the loosening of any restrictions on cannabis would have significant and far-reaching detrimental impacts on the community.

> 'Counterparts at the United States of America Drug Enforcement Agency have advised in places where cannabis has been legalised, it has enabled organised crime networks to either legitimise their cannabis businesses and/or continue to sell cannabis on the unregulated black market, where it remains cheaper and avoids being subject to tax.'

The federal view and treaty adherence

5.11 Following its decision to legalise recreational cannabis, Australia's capital territory drew the ire of the International Narcotics Control Board (INCB), the global drug law monitor. The INCB wrote to Australia's federal government asking for clarification over the laws, citing concerns they contravened at least three international conventions to which Australia was a signatory.

A copy of the correspondence obtained by *The Australian* newspaper[13] was sent to Australia's UN mission in Vienna, and forwarded on to the Department of Foreign Affairs and Trade and the Department of Health.

It suggested the ACT government's laws were in legal breach of the conventions the INCB upholds:

> 'The board has noted with concern recent reports regarding the legalisation of cannabis possession, use and cultivation in small amounts in the Australian Capital Territory, effective January 31, 2020.
>
> 'As the information does not stem from official sources, the board would appreciate receiving confirmation regarding the accuracy of these reports from your government.
>
> 'The board wishes to recall that cultivation, production and distribution of cannabis for non-medical purposes is inconsistent with the provisions of the 1961 convention as amended, in particular article 4(c), which requires state parties to limit the use of narcotic drugs exclusively to medical and scientific purposes.
>
> 'The board wishes to reiterate that the legalisation and regulation of cannabis for non-medical use, including in small quantities, would be inconsistent with Australia's international legal obligations.'

The INCB has previously criticised Uruguay, Canada and some US states for their efforts to legalise recreational cannabis, but it has had no impact on the decisions.

Australia's health minister Greg Hunt has asked the territory to explain its stance:

> 'The Australian government remains committed to the international drug control regime established by the UN international drug conventions, which do not support the legalisation of cannabis for recreational use.'

Australia's Attorney-General Christian Porter told ACT officials the cannabis laws were defective and poorly drafted, and would not provide a defence to overriding federal laws applying to cannabis use.

Next steps

5.12 According to Rhys Cohen, director of Consulting Australia:

> '2020 is going to be a big year. From the industry side of things, we're going to see some absolutely massive facilities complete construction. I expect we will also see several new global players set up shop in Australia. And the Narcotic Drugs Act – which sets out the license and permit scheme – will be amended in-line with the recommendations from its recent review. So, we'll probably see the cultivation/research/manufacture licenses be amalgamated into a single, generic license type.'

Cohen said terms of patient numbers, by the end of 2020 it is expected the country will issue approximately 10–20,000 approvals per month, as opposed to the current figures of less than 3,000.

> 'The number and variety of products available will continue to increase, and it's likely we'll see a few more domestically-grown cannabis products hit the market as well. This will all help to drive down prices, which are still too high for many patients.'

CHINA

5.13 China retains the death penalty for drug offences, and the country has a police-controlled approach to drug addiction treatment. Cannabis has been illegal since 1985, but despite this, the country is the world's largest producer of hemp,[14] and also the largest exporter of the product.

Ma (**麻** – the Chinese word for hemp) has been in use for thousands of years, so widely enough that the classic text Book of Odes, or Shi Jing (诗经), contains references to hemp use in the daily lives of Chinese people from the 11th to the 7th century BC.[15]

There is next to no chance that medicinal cannabis will be legalised in China, and certainly no recreational market has a chance of opening, however the country is moving toward a more structured policy for industrial hemp and export of CBD products.

Legal background

5.14 In 1985, the People's Republic of China joined the Convention on Psychotropic Substances and identified marijuana as a dangerous narcotic drug, and illegal to possess or use it.

The penalty for marijuana possession in China varies from various sources, but according to the Law on Public Security Administration Punishments, marijuana smokers shall be detained for 10 to 15 days and fined a maximum of 2,000 yuan (US$219).

China permits the sale of hemp seeds and hemp oil and the use of CBD in cosmetics, but it has not yet approved cannabidiol for use in food and medicines.

Companies can legally grow industrial hemp in Heilongjiang and Yunnan provinces, in China's northeast and southwest respectively.[16] China Daily reported early this year that rules to allow farmers to grow industrial hemp in Jilin province, next door to Heilongjiang, were drawn up in 2017. Hemp is also legally being grown in regions such as Anhui, Gansu, and Xinjiang.[17]

According to a Global Times report, China holds 309 of the world's 606 hemp-related patents, but due to legal restrictions, Chinese-made food and medicine containing CBD can only find a market outside of the country, in places like the US and the EU.

INDIA

5.15 Cannabis has been part of Indian life since recorded history began, and there is evidence of bhang, a mixture of cannabis and milk, used as an anaesthetic as far back as 1000 BC.[18] Despite its ubiquitous presence in Indian culture, and the fact you can buy it and drink it in the streets, cannabis, both medical and recreational, is illegal under Indian law.

In scenes similar to those playing out in South Africa and Mexico, Indian campaigners have increasingly taken the fight to the courts to argue criminalising the recreational use of small amounts of cannabis is against the constitution and disrespects Indian heritage.[19]

Initial attempts to get the law modified have failed, but the groups are heavily backed by public opinion and private funding, and are confident they can eventually force the courts to rule in their favour.

There are more realistic signs of movement in regard to medicinal cannabis, as in 2018 the government announced it was to conduct India's first human trials of cannabis-based compounds on a range of diseases and sicknesses.[20]

Growing cannabis for any purpose is illegal in India, except with explicit consent from the government, however hemp cultivation is legal for industrial purposes.

Legal background

5.16 Cannabis is dealt with under the Narcotic Drugs and Psychotropic Substances (NDPS) Act, 1985.[21] It states sale, production, consumption and trade of cannabis resin and flowers is prohibited. State governments have the right to shape rules pertaining to cannabis-related cultivation and sale, with respect to the ultimate purpose.

The Act defines cannabis as:

> 'the flowering or fruiting tops of the cannabis plant (excluding the seeds and leaves when not accompanied by the tops) from which the resin has not been extracted, by whatever name they may be designated.'

References to bhang were dropped from the Act as consumption of it is a central part of a lot of Hindu festivities. Bhang tablets, made from seeds, are on sale everywhere.

In 2017, India's government granted a medicinal cannabis research licence to the Council of Scientific and Industrial Research (CSIR), an autonomous institution.[22] It permitted the group to undertake research activities with respect to identification of the medicinal value of cannabis. The institute has a one-acre patch of land, technically the only patch of soil in the whole of India it is legal to grow cannabis.

In July 2018, the Uttarakhand government issued a licence to the Indian Industrial Hemp Association (IIHA) for commercial cultivation of industrial hemp.

The Uttar Pradesh government plans to issue research licences for cannabis cultivation, as of October 2019. And in February 2018, Indian goods company Patanjali Ayurved had announced it is researching cannabis at its Haridwar campus.

The Odisha government has also reportedly granted licences for medicinal consumption of cannabis-based products; Bhubaneswar-based Ayurveda medicines manufacturer Vedi Herbals has been granted permission by the state government and the ministry of AYUSH to manufacture and sell cannabis-based capsules.

It also has a doctor on board to assess a patient's medical history and prescribe medication accordingly.

Petition

5.17 The most prominent lobby group in India is the Great Legislation India Movement Trust (GLIMT). In July 2019, the campaigners failed in their most recent attempt to have the law overturned before the Hon'ble Delhi High Court.

The GLIMT was seeking to overturn the prohibition of cannabis in India, and force revisions to the Narcotic Drugs and Psychotropic Substances Act 1985 and the Narcotic Drugs and Psychotropic Substances Rules1985, which prohibit and criminalise the use of cannabis or industrial hemp and prescribe restrictions on activities related to it.

They argued that that various Sections of the NDPS Act, 1985 are in violation of Articles 14, 19, 21, 25 and 29 of the Constitution of India. The group said they were not seeking total legalisation of recreational use, merely to repeal the rules to allow for 'reasonable restrictions'.

The group said while enacting the NDPS Act 1985, the government did not take into account the positive effects of cannabis on human health and the history of use of cannabis in India.

The plea was dismissed by the Delhi High Court on 26 July 2019, and the Court asked the petitioners to pay a cost of INR10,000 (US$141), observing:

> 'it appears this petition is seeking direction to legalise cannabis for medical use. It can only be done by bringing proper enactment or amendment under the Narcotics Drugs and Psychotropic Substances (NDPS) Act. We are not inclined to grant the prayer.'[23]

According to Vikrant Rana, managing partner of one of India's top law firms SS Rana:

> 'As far as the use of cannabis for medical purposes is concerned, it is not allowed in India irrespective of the quantity used according to Section 2 (iii) of the NDPS Act, 1985. However, the Central Council for Research in Ayurvedic Sciences (CCRAS), a body under the Ministry of AYUSH, has announced the results of advanced research conducted on the possible use of cannabis as a restorative drug for cancer patients in November 2018.'

The CCRAS concluded that cannabis-based drugs can be effective in alleviating pain and other symptoms in cancer patients after chemotherapy and radiotherapy.

Social change

5.18 The twin strands of social evolution and pressure from groups representing patients. may finally be enough to force India's government to rewrite its cannabis laws.[24]

An extremely detailed report by Financial Express in India (link below) delves into the issue in much greater detail.[25]

Ram Vishwakarma, director of the CSIR, said he thinks further legalisation is likely to be a matter of time:

> 'Many countries are legalising cannabis for one purpose or the other, so eventually, India will have to follow suit as well. We can't say when and how though. That is under consideration with the central government.'

ISRAEL

5.19 Israel is a global leader in the medicinal cannabis field, and one of the main reasons is Dr Raphael Mechoulam. The 89-year-old president of the Multidisciplinary Center for Cannabinoid Research is known as the 'godfather of cannabis' for his discovery of the THC molecule in 1964.

Dr Mechoulam's team first discovered the endocannabinoid system, and his lab was the first to isolate the non-psychoactive compound CBD. A scientific revolution of cannabinoid studies ensued.

For more than 50 years Dr Mechoulam's laboratory has worked on the chemistry, pharmacology and clinical effects of cannabis (amongst other natural products).[26] It has isolated numerous cannabinoids, including the active constituent of cannabis, delta9-THC, and elucidated its structure. It has also identified endogenous cannabinoids in the pig brain.

Medicinal cannabis has been permitted in Israel since the early 1990s, and in many ways the country has been waiting for the rest of the world to catch up. Israel has the highest rate of cannabis patients in relation to the population anywhere in the world.

'Israel isn't just at the forefront of medical cannabis research,' said Swiss medical cannabis company Cibdol.[27] 'It is out in front by some margin.'

Such is their dominance in laboratory testing and technology, Israeli equipment manufacturers are in huge demand across the Americas.

According to Daniel Turgel, M&A partner at White & Case law firm in London and Tel Aviv:

> 'The Israeli market is very hot, with numerous technology firms looking to serve some of the big North American markets. Several Israeli companies have listed or considered listing in Canada. They were very quick to pivot and take advantage of the Canadian markets when they opened up.'

Background

5.20 On 25 December 2018, the Israeli Parliament (the Knesset) passed the 16th amendment to the Dangerous Drugs Ordinance that concerns the governance and regulatory aspects of exporting medical cannabis from Israel.

The amended bill allows provisions for future medical cannabis export. A government resolution is required to authorise export.

In January 2019, Israel's cabinet approved the law which allows exports of medical cannabis to increase state revenues and help the agriculture sector.[28]

The government estimates exports could raise tax revenue by 1bn shekels (US$273m). The bill imposes tough regulations on exporters and threatens jail terms and hefty fines for violations.

The law allows Israeli companies to export medical marijuana with an appropriate licence. The licences are issued by the Minister of Health with an appropriate recommendation from the police and a committee designed to review such applications. Anyone found to violate the terms of the licence will be fined the equivalent of US$19,887 or serve up to 24 months' imprisonment.

Eight Israeli agricultural companies who have set up operations similar to pharmaceutical companies for the production of medical marijuana lent their support for the law. The businesses have strict growing and quality control procedures to maintain the product, and Israel's climate makes it an optimal location for growing cannabis. Dozens of business owners have since requested government authorisation to export.

Domestically, cannabis is defined as a 'dangerous drug' in accordance with the Dangerous Drugs Ordinance [New Version] 1973[29] (Hebrew), and it can only be used for medicinal purposes.

Patients suffering with cancer, chronic neuropathic pain, post-traumatic stress disorder, colitis, Parkinson's, epilepsy, HIV/AIDS, Crohn's disease, multiple sclerosis, Tourette's syndrome, and terminal illness, are permitted to use medicinal cannabis.

Soon, the drug is expected to be approved for autism and fibromyalgia. The Health Ministry receives 300 applications per day for medical marijuana use, and there is a huge backlog for approvals.

In March, reforms by the Health Ministry forced the country's largest medical cannabis supplier to temporarily close as it relocates its farm, stranding at least 5,000 patients, and up to 9,000, without access to their medicine.

The legislative update was supposed to standardise rules and procedures to ensure that cannabis is produced, stored, transported, and distributed in ways that protect the quality of the medicine, according to the Health Ministry.

Cultivator Tikun Olam provides 15,500 people per month with medical cannabis, out of the approximately 38,000 who have prescriptions in Israel. It had to inform patients that due to the cannabis reform, which required it to move to a new facility, it was unable to provide cannabis in flower form (including loose flowers, pre-rolled joints, and pills filled with crushed flowers), although patients who use cannabis oil can could fill their prescriptions.

The company and the government (naturally) blamed each other.

Next steps

5.21 In April 2019, Israel partially decriminalised recreational marijuana use,[30] swapping fines for opening criminal proceedings against first to third-time offenders caught with 'a personal amount' of marijuana.

A version of the plan was first floated in early 2017 by the government's Anti-Drug Authority, and was approved by cabinet ministers in March of that year.

It is based on the so-called 'Portugal Model', which treats marijuana use as a public health issue akin to cigarette smoking rather than a criminal problem.

Israel's Ministry of Health has much more on medicinal cannabis,[31] including information on courses for doctors, and an information booklet and medical guide IMC-GCP sub-circular to the Ministry of Health Director (also called the 'green book', Hebrew only) which included a clinical methodology intended for the doctor treating with medical cannabis.

The document contains extensive information on the issue of medical cannabis and is meant to guide and assist in customising the treatment with medical cannabis.

JAPAN

5.22 Japan's zero tolerance drug laws are so strict they prohibit its citizens using cannabis even when outside the country. In 2015, two snowboarders who admitted smoking marijuana at a camp in Colorado (where cannabis use is legal) were suspended by their sports associations and also investigated by Japanese police.[32]

In fact, the tough laws forbid debates and research on the subject.[33] Drinks manufacturers Suntory and Japan Tobacco had to hire external consultants to carry out market surveys because their own staff were unable to taste cannabis-related products, or visit cannabis grow-ops or shops.[34]

Hideo Nagayoshi's book Taima Nyumon[35] (An Introduction to Cannabis), explains how the Cannabis Control Act is separate from the Narcotics Control Law, putting cannabis in its own category. It was implemented during the American Occupation after the Second World War, and goes further than simple criminalisation.

In order to please the US, which wished to export certain materials to Japan that had previously been created with hemp, the Japanese government expressly banned the use of cannabis for medicinal and other purposes.

Cannabis in Japan has been illegal since 1948, and use and possession can result in up to five years' imprisonment and a fine. Penalties for cultivation, sale, and transport are to ten years' imprisonment and a fine.

In 2016, the laws around CBD products, which contain almost no THC, were relaxed by Japan's Prime Minister Shinzo Abe, although companies were not allowed to tell anyone due to an advertising ban.

Abe's wife, the Japanese First Lady Akie Abe, may have had a hand in the decision, as she has repeatedly expressed her love for hemp products and posed for pictures buying Elixinol when the update was made public.[36]

Cannabis Control Act

5.23 The Cannabis Control Act regulates certain parts of cannabis plants, regardless of the THC content.[37] Leaves and flowers of cannabis plants are illegal; however, seeds and stems are legal.

There are two kinds of licence defined in this act: 'cannabis cultivator' and 'cannabis researcher'. The cannabis cultivator licence is issued to farmers that grow hemp to sell fibres and seeds. However, cannabis is regulated as a narcotic plant, and hardly any have ever been issued, mainly for pharmaceutical research.

Article 4 of the Act prohibits both the prescription of cannabis by doctors and the use of cannabis by patients. It is therefore impossible to evaluate the efficacy and safety of cannabis in Japan in clinical studies.

Medicinal cannabis

5.24 Asian countries on balance have the strictest drug laws of any continent, however there are signs medicinal cannabis may become more widely accepted by certain governments who are willing entertain research.

In March 2019, Japan approved the cannabis compound Epidiolex for clinical trials in epileptic patients with Dravet and Lennox-Gastaut syndromes. The decision was considered a major departure from general government policy and the first time such a product had gained approval.

The country prohibits cannabis-based agents overall, and as stated above, tightly monitored hospital trials are exempt from its Cannabis Control Act. Epidiolex is a plant-derived cannabidiol (CBD) which does not have the mind-altering effects characteristic of the THC.

The trials were announced recently by Japan's Ministry of Health, Labour and Welfare[38] officials during a meeting of the research and development agency Okinawa-Northern Task Force. It's unclear when the trials will begin.

Public perception

5.25 Between 2015 and 2017, the rate of cannabis use jumped from 1% to 1.4% with an estimated 1.33m people using the drug.

Police statistics for 2019 showed 3,008 people were arrested on charges related to cannabis in 2017, up 472 cases from the previous year and the highest annual figure ever recorded in Japan.[39]

The figures were most significantly higher in the 20–29 age bracket, with 9.4 arrests per 100,000 people, close to double the 5 per 100,000 people reported in 2014. Much has also been made of arrests among people below the age of 20, which has spiked to 4.1 arrests per 100,000 people, up from 1.1 per 100,000 people in 2014.

The number of cannabis-related arrests among adolescents has risen, and experts say this social shift is in line with global trends being played out in social media discussions, with some television personalities bucking Japanese culture to call for public debate.

Japanese youths arrested for cannabis smoking have said they were merely copying Western music groups, in comments that sparked alarm for their apparent nonchalance.[40]

Japanese authorities have given little shrift, and the topic still remains as taboo as ever in government circles. The country says its rigid controls on stimulants, amphetamines, and methamphetamines has prevented drug epidemics like those seen in Europe and the United States from taking hold.

A Ministry of Health report claimed that the rate of people who will try cannabis at some point in their life in Japan is almost 40% lower than that of the US and Europe.

CBD advertising ban

5.26 CBD was legalised in November 2016, but firms struggled to gain approval to market their products. In 2018, the first advertising campaign for medicinal cannabis oil in Japan went live following Australian producer Elixinol:[41]

> 'Japan has a very strong cultural connection with hemp, and its use by our people dates back to ancient times. Elixinol has been supplying hemp oil products to Japan for over three years, however up until now we have not been able to actively market the product range. Approval to commercially advertise our Hemp Oil Drops is a major win for the hemp industry and comes after many months of working with the relevant authorities to gain authorisation.' (Elixinol CEO Makoto Matsumaru)

Elixinol was able to get around the outdoor advertising regulations, which in this case are controlled by Toei Transport, owing to its conservative creative design, media reported.

In April 2019, Touchstone Essentials of North Carolina announced it had received approval by Japanese regulators to begin selling its full spectrum CBD-rich THC-free hemp oil product line to customers in Japan.

NEW ZEALAND

5.27 At some point during 2020 New Zealanders will head to the polls to vote on whether to legalise and regulate recreational cannabis. Should 'Yes' win, New Zealand would break with international anti-drug agreements to follow Uruguay, Canada, and several US states in opening a regulated adult market.

It would also be the first Asia-Pacific region to legalise both medicinal and recreational cannabis. Neighbour Australia is aligned with international controls on narcotics at the federal level, however, the country's capital state is to legalise recreational cannabis use in the near future, breaking with the rest of Australia's territories.

The legally binding New Zealand cannabis referendum will form part of the 2020 general election in the country, and the latest date it can be held is November. The Labour and Green party coalition government is 'committed to a health-based approach to drugs, to minimise harm and take control away from criminals'.[42]

Legal background

5.28 The cabinet has agreed there will be a simple 'Yes/No' question on the basis of a draft piece of legislation that will include:

- A minimum age of 20 to use and purchase recreational cannabis.
- Regulations and commercial supply controls.
- Limited home-growing options.
- A public education programme.
- Stakeholder engagement.

The decision to go to the public was made after the 2017 general election when a confidence and supply agreement between the Labour Party and the Green Party was struck. This agreement[43] was to 'increase funding for alcohol and drug addiction services and ensure drug use is treated as a health issue'. This included an obligation for the government to undertake a referendum on cannabis law reform.

According to Chlöe Swarbrick, a Green Party Member of Parliament:

> 'In line with a health-based approach, consumption will be limited to private spaces or to those that are licensed. We are also guaranteeing that there is going to be no advertising because the last thing we want to do is open the door to big corporates and invite another 'Big Tobacco' or 'Big Alcohol' and replace the black market with some big corporate control.'

The proposal also calls for a licensing scheme that would 'provide for safe spaces for people to use cannabis away from home.'

The primary and secondary goals of the proposed referendum, are outlined in the footnote link.

Primary objectives:

- To address the wellbeing of New Zealanders and harm reduction – the model should minimise harms associated with cannabis, such as health-related harm, social harms and harm to youth.
- To lower the overall use of cannabis over time through education and addiction services – with a particular focus on lowering the use amongst youths by increasing the age of first use;

- To raise revenue through the regulation of cannabis which should contribute to relevant health-related measures.

Secondary objectives:

- Disempowering the gangs and the illegal trade in cannabis.
- Lowering the prison population over time and lowering the number of New Zealanders (especially Maori) whose future opportunities are negatively affected by cannabis use charges.
- To ensure product safety and control of THC levels via legislation and regulation.
- To be consistent with the rule of law – the model should uphold New Zealand's constitution. It should also minimise opportunities for the illicit market and be clear and easy to follow.
- To be tailored and workable for New Zealand – the model should recognise and reflect New Zealand's cultural practices and the values of New Zealand society so that it can be accepted by New Zealanders.
- Fiscal sustainability – the model should seek to fund mechanisms that directly address cannabis-related harms, while also aiming to lower use over time.

Current punishments

5.29 Penalties associated with cannabis range from a NZ$500 (US$317) fine for possession to a 14-year jail term for its supply or manufacture. Cultivation of cannabis, including to sow or plant it, can, on indictment, result in a seven-year jail term, an immediate two-year jail term and/or a fine of NZ$2,000 (US$1,269) depending on the amount of product.

Medicinal cannabis

5.30 On 11 December 2018, the New Zealand Parliament passed the Misuse of Drugs (Medicinal Cannabis) Amendment Bill.[44]

This introduced an exception and a statutory defence for terminally ill people to possess and use illicit cannabis and to possess a cannabis utensil; provide a regulation-making power to enable the setting of standards that products manufactured, imported, and supplied under licence must meet. It also amended Schedule 2 to the [Misuse of Drugs] Act so that cannabidiol (CBD) and CBD products are no longer classed as controlled drugs.'

Previously, according to the government's explanatory note on the Bill, while there was 'a legal pathway for people to obtain cannabis on prescription from a medical practitioner, access to affordable cannabis products remains problematic for New Zealanders.'

The Bill was introduced in December 2017 following a commitment by the Labour Party-led government to make medicinal cannabis more available to people with terminal illnesses or chronic pain.[45]

The government hoped to increase the supply of quality medicinal cannabis over time, including New Zealand-made products.

As an interim measure until the legal regime for medicinal cannabis was in place, the Bill established a legal defence for the possession and use of cannabis so that certain seriously-ill people could use it without being criminalised.

Until the referendum, cannabis itself remains an illicit substance under the Misuse of Drugs Act 1975.

Medicinal products are available on prescription. Regulations, licensing rules and quality standards for the medicinal cannabis sector will be set on expert advice through 2020, following a consultation that ran in 2019.

The Ministry of Health consulted the public on the proposals for the medicinal cannabis regulations needed to support the scheme, between July and August 2019.[46]

Details to be set forth include how the government plans to enable the commercial cultivation of medicinal cannabis and the manufacture of medicinal cannabis products in New Zealand, and standards for medicinal cannabis products so that medical practitioners can prescribe them with more confidence.

The regulations are being developed to establish the regulatory system.

Public opinion and the case for 'Yes'

5.31 A January 2019 survey found that 60% of New Zealand residents would approve a referendum to legalise cannabis.[47] Only 24% of respondents voiced opposition to the policy and 16% were left undecided.

In March 2019, the Helen Clark Foundation was launched as an independent public policy think-tank based in Auckland, named after and encompassing the values of the former New Zealand Prime Minister. The Foundation released a detailed report in September 2019 entitled *The Case for 'Yes'*.[48]

It argues that the disproportionately adverse effects of current policies on cannabis use justify putting in place legalisation and effective regulation. Up to 80% of New Zealanders will use cannabis at least once before turning 25, making cannabis the most commonly used illicit drug in New Zealand, it reports:

> 'Yet cannabis remains an illegal drug, and prosecutions for possession and use alone continue for those unlucky enough to get caught. Our view is that the New Zealand government should adopt an approach to cannabis use which sees it as a health and social issue and not a criminal one. Regulation should seek to prevent the emergence of major corporate interests in the market which would have a profit motive to undermine public health objectives.'

This issue of large-scale international businesses moving in is a concern that has been echoed in other areas such as Uruguay, Mexico, Greece, Germany, and sections of Africa, where cannabis laws pertaining to both medicinal and recreational production are becoming more business-friendly.

Some countries are seeking to protect their fledgling domestic cultivation industries by forcing international (read, Canadian or US) businesses to partner with local firms in order to acquire licences.

The Foundation's report also looks at regulated commercial markets it terms the 'North American model', which allow for licensed retailers to sell cannabis to take at home or licensed premises to sell it for onsite use. A small amount of home growing is usually permitted alongside the commercial market:

> 'Licensing would make vendors accountable for the potency, packaging, and preparation of cannabis products. If people choose to consume legal cannabis, they would know with confidence what they are buying, how much, and how strong it is. Vendors would also become responsible for ensuring that they are not selling product to those under the lawful age.
>
> 'Legalisation in this manner would also allow the government to tax revenue from cannabis sales as it does for any other legal product. Strict controls on advertising and packaging could be applied, similar to those which apply to tobacco,' it concludes. 'Local communities should be consulted on the nature of service provision in their area.'

Should New Zealand vote to legalise, the early signs are promising that the forthcoming regulatory framework, building on the successes and failings elsewhere, could be one of the strongest to emerge in the coming years.

THE PACIFIC ISLANDS REGION

5.32 There are 24 countries, with an estimated 7,500 to 10,000 islands in Oceania, including Australia, New Zealand and the numerous Pacific Island Countries and Territories (PICT) of Polynesia, Micronesia and Melanesia.

It is an enormously diverse region of more than 34m people, speaking more than 1,200 languages and dialects. The Pacific Island states are made up of people of Melanesian, Micronesian and Polynesian backgrounds, and countries such as Fiji and the Solomon Islands include a large number of people of Chinese and Indian origin.

In this book we cover Australia and New Zealand in detail, as these highly-developed nations have their own rapidly-developing cannabis sectors. In contrast, the PICT faces many difficult challenges relating to poverty, political instability, and poor governance and infrastructure.[49]

The PICT neighbour drug producing countries in East Asia and high-demand consumer countries such as Australia and New Zealand, making them a prime drug smuggling route.

Cannabis is cultivated in many of the small islands in the region, and most reports conclude the product is consumed locally.[50]

The PICT approach to drug regulation is generally one of 'zero-tolerance' and prohibition, and harm reduction services rarely exist. A network, the Pacific Island Drug and Alcohol Research Network (PDARN), was created by the Burnet Institute and the Australian National Council on Drugs to improve outcomes for drug users across the region.

The Burnet Institute data estimates that there are approximately 1m frequent cannabis users in Papua New Guinea (PNG), and up to 350,000 daily cannabis users.

Cannabis use also appears to have become part of youth cultures in the PICTs. The Burnet Institute indicated an increasing number of unemployed 15 to 30-year-olds in Vanuatu who smoke cannabis recreationally.

Data on the islands is scarce, however. A report by Buchananan-Aruwafu6 on HIV risk and vulnerability in the Pacific has indicated that heavy cannabis use by young people in the Pacific is linked to poor health, accidents and violence, crime, unwanted and unprotected sex, teen pregnancies, STIs, and mental health problems.

VANUATU

5.33 Throughout 2018, stories emerged that the government of Vanuatu was considering legalising the cultivation of medical marijuana, as it sought to help the local agricultural sector and bring in much-needed funds.

Vanuatu's Council of Ministers released a Policy Direction on Cannabis,[51] which proposed to establish an 'ethical cannabis industry in Vanuatu'. It said it would grant five licences in the initial phase for a period of five years. Cannabis use would continue to be outlawed in Vanuatu; however, the crops would be exported for medical use to overseas markets.

The proposal was initiated by Vanuatu's former Agricultural Minister and set to be reviewed by the Minister for Agriculture, Hosea Nevu before being introduced into parliament for debate in the 2019 parliamentary year.

Amendments to Vanuatu's Dangerous Drugs Act were approved to allow medical marijuana, but government figures have urged caution and said it will take time for ministers to develop the necessary legislation for what is still largely an experiment.

Reports began to emerge in December 2018 that the government was working with an American company to trial a new experimental cannabis-derived drug on diabetics, given Vanuatu's epidemic-level numbers.

The company, Phoenix Life Sciences International, was headquartered in the US state of Colorado but relocated their operations to Vanuatu in 2019 to carry out clinical trials.

Phoenix Life's then chief executive, Australian-born Martin Tindall, said his company would target poorer nations and work with the Pacific Islands governments to conduct medicinal cannabis trials in areas where diabetes rates were of epidemic proportions:

> 'As the founder and CEO [of] an adaptive healthcare solutions company developing cannabinoid-based medicines, I have an intimate appreciation for the effects of federal prohibition. Unable to carry out research into cannabis-derived pharmaceuticals for diabetics in the US, we were forced to relocate our first production centre to the Republic of Vanuatu in the South Pacific.'

In June 2019, Prime Minister Charlot Salwai said Vanuatu had not committed to working with Phoenix Life Sciences, despite the government allegedly signing a memorandum of understanding with the company to do just that.[52]

The deal allegedly gave Phoenix Life exclusive rights to prescribe its cannabis-based product to treat diabetes, cervical cancer and autoimmune disease.

The alleged MOU would have made Phoenix Life the country's provider of national diabetes treatment over the next 25 years. It was also alleged the government had pledged 5,000 acres of land on the island of Santo for large scale cultivation of medical marijuana over 75 years. But Vanuatu Prime Minister walked back on the commitment and said no agreement had been struck.

In July 2019, Tindall was arrested and charged with securities fraud after setting foot in Colorado, according to Boulder County court documents. Phoenix removed him as CEO, and as of October 2019, Tindall was awaiting trial after being indicted by a grand jury for allegedly misleading investors.

Tindall proclaimed his innocence, calling himself a 'political prisoner'.

The Phoenix Life affair has proved a sobering reminder of the enormous complexities of conducting cannabis research and development in areas where laws are unclear, along with the compliance risks of cross-border activity and transactions concerning cannabis-related activities.

SOUTH KOREA

5.34 South Korea, like Japan, prosecutes its citizens for using cannabis in other countries where recreational marijuana is legalised.

Under the country's anti-drug laws, smoking and dealing marijuana is illegal with those found guilty facing up to five years in prison.

However, in November 2018, South Korea became the first Asian country to legalise medical cannabis,[53] eschewing a long-term policy of zero tolerance to any form of drug use. The highly conservative country expanded treatment options for patients with epilepsy and other rare diseases.

The Korean National Assembly passed an amendment to the Narcotics Control Act[54] to allow the medical use of cannabis under strict conditions. Prior approval is necessary and granted on a case-by-case basis.

The Ministry of Food and Drug Safety (MFDS) has established specific implementing regulations that procedure patients must follow to qualify.

Cannabis even for medical purposes remains strictly controlled with patients required to apply to the Korea Orphan Drug Centre, a government body facilitating patient access to rare medicines, after receiving a doctor's prescription.

Imports

5.35 In February 2019, South Korea announced it would allow imports of medical cannabis starting from the next month, as part of efforts to provide more treatment options for patients with rare diseases.[55]

Patients must also submit a physician's document stating that there is no alternative treatment in the country.

Under the Ministry of Food and Drug Safety (MFDS) regulations, only certain cannabis products licensed and marketed in specific countries will be permitted.

That list currently includes Sativex, Epidiolex, Marinol and Cesamet, which have been permitted in the United States, the United Kingdom, Germany, France and Australia.

Next steps

5.36 It's early days for the South Korean medicinal cannabis regime, but already the country has welcomed Canadian producer Canopy Growth. Such has been the draconian nature of South Korea's anti-cannabis stance for so many years, even small movements are considered significant, and this may serve as a bellwether for the rest of Asia.

SRI LANKA

5.37 Sri Lanka's people have grown and used cannabis socially for thousands of years, yet the drug is illegal and carries a criminal penalty. The ban was first introduced by British colonial occupiers who intended to promote tobacco instead.[56]

In 2018, the government announced it would begin cultivating cannabis for medical purposes,[57] and specifically for export to markets such as Canada and the UK, citing the British update to its own domestic medicinal cannabis laws in November 2018.

The health minister Rajitha Senaratne outlined plans for cultivation to take place across 100 acres of designated cannabis plantation land in the north-central Anuradhapura and Polonnaruwa districts.

Minister Senaratne said that cannabis should be allowed to use in Sri Lanka legally as an Ayurvedic drug, a popular form of medicine that has been handed down through the centuries.

When cannabis batches are seized by law enforcement, small portions are often allocated to Ayurvedic practitioners to develop into medicine. However, this has proved insufficient; 'by the time our native doctors get this cannabis, it is about four to five-years-old and it has lost its effectiveness,' Senaratne said.

Legal background

5.38 Sri Lanka is a signatory to all three UN Conventions on drug abuse and trafficking, namely Single Convention on Narcotic Drugs 1961, Convention on Psychotropic Substances 1971 and United Nations Convention Against Illicit Traffic in Narcotic Drugs and Psychotropic Substances 1988.

Legislation pertaining to drug control in Sri Lanka is the Poisons, Opium and Dangerous Drugs Act, the Penal Code,[58] Cosmetic, Devices and Drugs Act, Customs Ordinance and Indigenous Medical Act.

- The Penal Code (Ordinance No. 2 of 1983 as subsequently amended) in particular Chapter 14, which covers public health and safety;
- The Cosmetics, Devices and Drugs Act (Act No. 27 of 1980, as amended by Act No. 38 of 1984). The Act regulates the manufacture, sale, distribution, labelling and advertising of all commercial drugs;
- The Ayurveda Act (Act No. 31 of 1961 as amended by Act No. 5 of 1962) entitles ayurvedic physicians to obtain opium and cannabis for manufacture of their medicinal preparations;
- The Customs Ordinance (Ordinance No. 17 of 1869, imposes prohibitions and restrictions of both import and export of substances prohibited under the Poisons Opium and Dangerous Drugs Ordinance).

The Poisons, Opium and Dangerous Drugs Ordinance of 1935, which has undergone many amendments, is the principal statutory enactment to regulate drugs.

Overseas investment

5.39 In January 2019, one of Australia's top listed cannabis companies Creso Pharma announced an expansion into Sri Lanka. The company has signed a letter of intent with Ceyoka Health, one of Sri Lanka's main pharmaceutical distribution companies, to geographically expand the distribution of its products.

The partnership will initially focus on gaining the necessary regulatory acceptance for Creso's flagship medicinal cannabis product cannAFFORD 50, a throat lozenge that helps patients suffering chronic pain.

Dr Miri Halperin Wernli Creso Pharma CEO and co-founder said the company was excited to tap into Ceyoka's network of over 1,800 pharmacies.

THAILAND

5.40 Thailand has traditionally delivered some of the world's toughest punishments for drug use and possession, and the death penalty is still in effect.

Recreational cannabis is illegal, and will likely remain so for some time, but the first signs of a thaw in the country's tough stance appeared in 2016 when lawmakers began to update the Narcotics Act 1979[59] to deal with prison overcrowding.

The amendments also removed the immediate death penalty for drug dealers that often applied without giving the accused the opportunity to prove their innocence.[60] In another significant alteration, the wording of the code was updated to ensure drug users would not be automatically prosecuted as drug dealers.

On 24 November 2016, the National Legislative Assembly (NLA) approved the adoption of new amendments to Thailand's Narcotics Act. The updates were unanimously voted 196 'Yes' and 0 'No'. These reforms were published in the *Royal Gazette* on 15 January 2017, and took effect the next day.

In the last two years, Thailand has embraced medicinal marijuana and may even prove a leader in the Southern Asian market as the government intends to invest significantly in research.

The country's parliament voted in December 2018 to approve cannabis for medical use, making it the first in the region, with a top lawmaker calling it a 'New Year's gift' to the Thai people.[61]

Overcrowded prisons

5.41 Serious problems with an ever-increasing prison population was one of the main drivers of reform to the country's notoriously strict drug laws. Thailand has the largest prison population in Southeast Asia and the sixth largest in the world. It also has the highest rate of female imprisonment anywhere in the world, and this is mostly down to minor drug offences.

Two years of debate in the National Assembly centred on plans to cut penalties for possession, import/export and production for sale. The legislative amendments eventually passed also altered culpability calculations and replaced mandatory sentences in cases where the amounts seized exceed a designated threshold.

Individuals can now argue they were not intending to sell the drug as legal defence is given more of a chance to put forward evidence and arguments to contest the presumed supply offence, ensuring a steady stream of work for lawyers active in the region.

Medicinal cannabis

5.42 Thailand's junta-appointed parliament voted to amend the Narcotic Act of 1979 in December 2018, to legalise licensed possession of cannabis for medical purposes, as of 19 February 2019.

'This is a New Year's gift from the National Legislative Assembly to the government and the Thai people,' said Somchai Sawangkarn, chairman of the drafting committee, during the televised session.

Consumers will be able to carry specified amounts necessary for medicinal purposes, if they have a prescription or recognised certificate, the Bangkok Post said. Licences for production and sale of the product will be tightly controlled.

The also applies to kratom, a Southeast Asian plant that acts as a stimulant.

Peerapan Tungsuwan, partner and head of the Healthcare Industry Group of Baker McKenzie's Bangkok office, said that cultivation must be approved by the relevant government agency (Thailand's Food and Drug Agency) and during the first five years from the date that the Narcotics Act (No. 7), B.E. 2562 (2019) (the Act) came into effect (19 February 2019).

The applicant must be one of the following:

- A government agency that can research or educate people, or provide services on medicine, pharmacology, science, or agricultural science to facilitate medical or pharmacological benefits, or to protect against, suppress, and solve narcotics problems, or the Thai Red Cross; or
- The above-mentioned government agency, working in cooperation with a medical practitioner, a Thai traditional medicine practitioner, a higher education institution under the law regarding private higher-education institutions that have duties to conduct research and education on medicine or pharmacology, or agricultural practitioners who group together as community enterprises, social enterprises, or agricultural cooperatives.

The private sector can participate in research and development projects with government agencies only if they fall into one of the following categories:

- A medical practitioner, a pharmacology practitioner, a dental practitioner, a first-class veterinary practitioner, a Thai traditional medicine practitioner, an applied Thai traditional medicine practitioner, or a folk doctor under the Thai medicine profession law;
- A higher-education institution under the law regarding private higher-education institutions that have duties to conduct research and education on medicine or pharmacology; or
- Agricultural practitioners who group together as community enterprises, social enterprises, or agricultural cooperatives.

The Ministry of Public Health by the Narcotics Control Board is monitoring the performance of the measures by conducting evaluations. These are carried out every six months during the first five years from the date that the Act came into effect:

> 'The criteria to grant permission can be amended, if the board is of the opinion that the criteria should be improved and proposes that the Minister of Public Health review the permission criteria to make it more appropriate and up-to-date. Presently, there are no provisions that allow private sector entities to directly invest in cannabis. After the first five years, the law may become more liberal or more restrictive. It depends on the performance evaluation in the first five years from the date that the Act came into effect.' (Tungsuwan)

Future developments

5.43 Some of Thailand's politicians are looking at events in California and pondering if a similar market for recreational cannabis could ever appear in Thailand.[62]

It seems unlikely, and the country is in a 'transition period,' says Supachai Kunaratnpruk, a former senior official with Thailand's health ministry who is now overseeing medicinal research efforts.[63]

Cannabis plants are being grown in only a few government-approved greenhouses due to the ban on importation.

Doctors at state-run hospitals have been cleared to dispense a small batch of THC oils to select patients, and in August 2019 the government announced it was distributing about 10,000 bottles of cannabis oil hospital patients.[64]

Aside from the shortage required to serve such a market, the government remains wary of all-out legalisation, according to Supachai. He said there are concerns the burgeoning industry could become monopolised by one or two corporations, most likely foreign, that are focused on profits and not health:

> 'We can't let it fall into one set of hands, one big company. Our responsibility is to develop special Thai strains of world-class cannabis used in medicine. We want to cooperate with farmer co-ops. They grow it, we provide knowledge and it's all sold to the medical profession. That's the model.'

FROM HARDLINE TO FRONTLINE: ASIA-PACIFIC MAKES MEDICINAL CANNABIS STRIDES

5.44 The Asia-Pacific (APAC) region has the toughest drug laws of all the territories we cover in this book, with the death penalty still a deterrent in several countries. On the medicinal cannabis side, however, APAC is a world leader in testing.

North American firms have been slow to penetrate the EU market as manufacturing standards in the EU are stricter than in their domestic market. A solution appears in the advanced laboratory proficiency testing of Asian companies that have access to a large base of manufacturers and research laboratories.

The scientific base and research capabilities in several Asian countries is increasing, with Asian pharmaceutical, food, and biologics markets driving growth.

Cannabis laboratory testing regulations in various US states are also in the process of being toughened following a series of deaths linked to vaping. This will create further opportunities for Asian firms looking to enter new markets.

Slow progress

5.45 The region's mighty power China has welcomed its first international investment in cannabis-related businesses in the last year. Cannabis is illegal, but government permits allow hemp growers to operate in Yunnan, and Hong Kong-listed CBD CannAcubed became the first foreign company to successfully set up and establish a hemp cultivation and CBD production project in that region.

CannAcubed is the only cannabis company in China to be fully licensed across the entire value chain, including research and development, cultivation, storage and transport, production and processing, manufacturing, and import/export. The company grows the industrial cannabis hemp; strains of cannabis with less than 0.3% of the psychoactive substance tetrahydrocannabinol (THC).

China has launched government-funded studies into cultivation, although the People's Republic officially holds a position of total prohibition of cannabis. Anecdotally, local authorities have turned a blind eye to farmers growing their own low-THC varieties because it is an important source of income for the regions.

China is also increasing the number of patents it holds in relation to cannabis, according to the World Intellectual Property Organisation. Dr Luc Duchesne, an Ottawa-based businessman and biochemist, told market analysis site InvestorIntel: 'Because cannabis in Western medicine is becoming accepted, the predominance of Chinese patents suggests that pharmaceutical sciences are evolving quickly in China, outpacing Western capabilities.'

CannAcubed is headquartered in Singapore, another jurisdiction with traditionally strict drug-control laws, but manages to avoid the draconian laws by conducting all its operations in Yunnan.

Attitudes towards cannabis in China are shifting, but regulatory adjustment is likely to occur extremely slowly. The progress of early adopters such as CannAcubed will serve as a test case for Western firms considering the viability of the regulatory landscape.

Public vote

5.46 A referendum in New Zealand on the matter of legalisation of recreational cannabis will take place in 2020, and goes very much against the grain of the APAC region. Public support for 'Yes' is running high, and reflective of a wider appetite for reform of cannabis laws amongst the public of APAC territories than from the respective governments.

Australia's capital region has legalised cannabis for personal use, but similar to the situation in the US, the country's federal ban on non-medicinal or scientific purpose cannabis remains in place.

Medicinal cannabis is legal in Australia, however, and each of the states and territories are committing to more research in 2020, and an update of their laws to improve access for patients.

ENDNOTES

1. Australia Government Department of Health, Drug laws in Australia: https://www.health.gov.au/health-topics/drugs/about-drugs/drug-laws-in-australia.
2. Australia Government Australian Institute of Health and Welfare, Alcohol, tobacco and other drugs: https://www.aihw.gov.au/reports/phe/221/alcohol-tobacco-other-drugs-australia/contents/drug-types/cannabis.

3. *Medical marijuana legalized in Australia*: https://edition.cnn.com/2016/02/24/health/medical-marijuana-legal-australia-irpt/index.html.

4. Narcotic Drugs Legislation Amendment Bill 2016 [and] Narcotic Drugs (Licence Charges) Bill 2016: https://www.aph.gov.au/Parliamentary_Business/Bills_Legislation/bd/bd1617a/17bd034.

5. *A collection of CNN stories about the marijuana legalization debate:* https://edition.cnn.com/specials/us/marijuana-debate.

6. Drugs of Dependence (Personal Cannabis Use) Amendment Bill 2018: https://www.legislation.act.gov.au/b/db_59295/.

7. *Medical Marijuana Legalisation in Australia – the Current State of Play*: https://thegreenfund.com/green-states-a-state-by-state-guide-to-australian-cannabis.

8. *Industrial Hemp Bill Tabled In Australia's Northern Territory*: https://hempgazette.com/news/industrial-hemp-nt-hg0917/.

9. *Hemp industry wins the legal OK from NT Govt*: https://www.katherinetimes.com.au/story/6318832/hemp-industry-wins-the-legal-ok-from-nt-govt/.

10. Public Health (Medicinal Cannabis) Act 2016: https://www.legislation.qld.gov.au/view/pdf/2017-03-01/act-2016-053.

11. Access to Medicinal Cannabis Act 2016 No. 20 of 2016: http://www.legislation.vic.gov.au/Domino/Web_Notes/LDMS/PubStatbook.nsf/f932b66241ecf1b7ca256e92000e23be/1E1D95ECB3B1662ECA257FA100098BF7/$FILE/16-020aa%20authorised.pdf.

12. Medical Cannabis Controlled Access Scheme: https://www.dhhs.tas.gov.au/psbtas/publications/medical_cannabis/medical_cannabis_controlled_access_scheme.

13. *ACT dope laws 'flout UN statutes'*: https://www.theaustralian.com.au/nation/politics/act-dope-laws-flout-un-treaty-statutes/news-story/1a443da26779e4292dadfe34fb681ae7.

14. *Chinese hemp companies see fortune behind tight controls*: http://www.globaltimes.cn/content/1159846.shtml.

15. *Amid Regulatory Uncertainty and Global Demand, China's Hemp Industry is Booming*: https://radiichina.com/cbd-hemp-cannabis-industry-china/.

16. *Jilin to become the third province to deregulate industrial hemp cultivation:* http://www.chinadaily.com.cn/a/201902/18/WS5c6a972fa3106c65c34e9f18.html.

17. Hemp regulations: https://www.tsu.tw/edu/7161.html.

18. *Bhang-On! How India Romances Cannabis*: https://www.firstpost.com/india/bhang-on-how-india-romances-cannabis-6266301.html.

19. *Petition in court seeking to legalise cannabis for medical use dismissed*: https://www.thehindu.com/news/cities/Delhi/petition-in-court-seeking-to-legalise-cannabis-for-medical-use-dismissed/article28726994.ece.

20. *Human clinical trials of cannabis as medicine*: https://www.telegraphindia.com/health/india-plans-1st-human-clinical-trials-of-cannabis-to-treat-cancer-epilepsy-and-blood-disorders/cid/1676369.

21. Narcotic Drugs and Psychotropic Substances (NDPS) Act, 1985: http://lawcommissionofindia.nic.in/101-169/Report155.pdf.

22. *India's history of cannabis use encourages scientists to explore new ways of using it as a legal painkiller*: https://www.scmp.com/lifestyle/health-wellness/article/2179351/indias-history-cannabis-use-encourages-scientists-explore.

23. *Delhi HC Dismisses Plea to Legalise Cannabis For Medical Use, Imposes Rs 10K cost*: https://www.livelaw.in/news-updates/delhi-hc-dismisses-plea-to-legalise-cannabis-for-medical-use-imposes-rs-10k-cost-146703.

24. *Is India losing out on a ready-to-boom cannabis market by not legalising its use*? https://economictimes.indiatimes.com/industry/cons-products/tobacco/is-india-losing-out-on-a-ready-to-boom-cannabis-market-by-not-legalising-its-use/articleshow/66101561.cms?

25. *Is it right to outrightly ban cannabis cultivation?*: https://www.financialexpress.com/lifestyle/is-it-right-to-outrightly-ban-cannabis-cultivation/1568030/.

26. This 2007 interview with Addiction magazine is a fascinating dive into Dr Mechoulam's life and work on cannabis and does a far better job of bringing his work to life than this author ever could: https://onlinelibrary.wiley.com/doi/full/10.1111/j.1360-0443.2007.01795.x.

27. *Israel Is At The Forefront Of Medical Cannabis Research*: https://www.cibdol.com/blog/692-israel-is-at-the-forefront-of-medical-cannabis-research.

28. Israel approves medicinal cannabis laws: https://main.knesset.gov.il/Activity/Legislation/Laws/Pages/LawBill.aspx?t=lawsuggestionssearch&lawitemid=2010934.

29. Dangerous Drugs Ordinance [New Version] 1973: https://www.health.gov.il/LegislationLibrary/Samim_01.pdf.

30. *Partial decriminalization of public cannabis use takes effect Sunday night*: https://www.timesofisrael.com/partial-decriminalization-of-public-cannabis-use-to-come-into-effect/.

31. State of Israel, Ministry of Health, Cannabis for Medical Use and for Research: https://www.health.gov.il/English/Topics/cannabis/Pages/default.aspx.

32. *2 Japanese snowboarders suspected of using pot in Colorado*: https://mainichi.jp/english/articles/20160427/p2a/00m/0sp/004000c.

33. *Japan's war against medical marijuana*: https://www.japantimes.co.jp/news/2016/11/05/national/media-national/japans-war-medical-marijuana/#.XadLEy2ZPx5.

34. *Corporate Japan needs chance to have a view on cannabis boom*: https://www.ft.com/content/50fa13e0-86a9-11e9-a028-86cea8523dc2.

35. Taima Nyumon; Hideo Nagayoshi: https://keikobayashi.com/blog/?p=3727.

36. *Japan's First Lady Ushers In New Era of Hemp Acceptance by Purchasing Elixinol CBD Hemp Oil Product*: https://www.globenewswire.com/news-release/2016/07/08/854645/0/en/Japan-s-First-Lady-Ushers-In-New-Era-of-Hemp-Acceptance-by-Purchasing-Elixinol-CBD-Hemp-Oil-Product.html.

37. *International Association for Cannabinoid Medicines, Japan*: https://www.cannabis-med.org/index.php?tpl=page&id=314&lng=en.

38. Ministry of Health, Labour and Welfare update: https://www.mhlw.go.jp/index.html.

39. *Japan struggles with growing cannabis use*: https://www.dw.com/en/japan-struggles-with-growing-cannabis-use/a-44094855.

40. *Japan's Police Struggle to Curb a Sharp Increase in Cannabis Use*: https://thediplomat.com/2019/06/japans-police-struggle-to-curb-a-sharp-increase-in-cannabis-use/.

41. *Japan gets first outdoor billboard advertising medicinal cannabis*: https://www.mumbrella.asia/2018/05/japan-gets-first-outdoor-billboard-advertising-medicinal-cannabis.

42. New Zealanders to make the decision in cannabis referendum: https://www.beehive.govt.nz/release/new-zealanders-make-decision-cannabis-referendum.

43. Hon Andrew Little – Minister of Justice, Proactive release – 2020 Cannabis Referendum: https://www.beehive.govt.nz/sites/default/files/2019-05/Proactive%20release%20-%20Cabinet%20paper%20-%202020%20Cannabis%20Referendum%20-%207%20May%202019.pdf.

44. Misuse of Drugs (Medicinal Cannabis) Amendment Bill: https://www.parliament.nz/en/pb/bills-and-laws/bills-proposed-laws/document/BILL_75877/misuse-of-drugs-medicinal-cannabis-amendment-bill.

45. https://www.beehive.govt.nz/release/medicinal-cannabis-ease-suffering.

46. Medicinal Cannabis Scheme consultation: https://www.health.govt.nz/publication/medicinal-cannabis-scheme-consultation.

47. *60 per cent support for legal cannabis – new poll*: https://www.nzherald.co.nz/nz/news/article.cfm?c_id=1&objectid=12187654.

48. *The Helen Clark Foundation: The case for YES in the 2020 referendum on cannabis*: https://helenclark.foundation/wp-content/uploads/2019/09/the-case-for-yes-in-the-2020-cannabis-referendum.pdf.

49. *Young people and cannabis in the Western Pacific region*: https://cannabissupport.com.au/young-people-and-cannabis-in-the-western-pacific-region/.

50. IDPC, Oceania: https://idpc.net/policy-advocacy/regional-work/oceania.

51. *Vanuatu contemplates legalising marijuana*: https://www.rnz.co.nz/international/pacific-news/378816/vanuatu-contemplates-legalising-marijuana.

52. *Prime Minister says no firm commitment with controversial medical cannabis company*: https://dailypost.vu/news/prime-minister-says-no-firm-commitment-with-controversial-medical-cannabis/article_7ec6629e-9b59-596d-a16c-8896eb46868c.html.

53. Bill information: http://likms.assembly.go.kr/bill/billDetail.do?billId=PRC_V1E8A0T9Q1Z9I1H7H1U4E0Z9P6X1Z4.

54. Narcotics Control Act: https://elaw.klri.re.kr/eng_service/lawView.do?hseq=37716&lang=ENG.

55. *S. Korea to allow imports of medical cannabis starting in March*: https://en.yna.co.kr/view/AEN20190219002500320.

56. United Nations Office on Drugs and Crime, Sri Lanka report: https://www.unodc.org/pdf/india/publications/south_Asia_Regional_Profile_Sept_2005/13_srilanka.pdf.

57. *Cannabis cultivation under care of Army*: http://www.sundayobserver.lk/2018/04/15/news/cannabis-cultivation-under-care-army.

58. Poisons, Opium, and Dangerous Drugs Ordinance: http://www.nddcb.gov.lk/Docs/acts/25345.pdf.

59. NARCOTICS ACT B.E. 2522 (1979): http://www.thailawforum.com/database1/Narcotics-Act-part2.html.

60. Thailand Drug Laws: https://ilaw.or.th/node/4352.

61. *Thailand approves medicinal cannabis*: https://www.bbc.co.uk/news/world-asia-46679098.

62. *Green economy? Thai party Bhumjaithai campaigns on marijuana as cash crop*: https://www.scmp.com/news/asia/southeast-asia/article/2188251/green-economy-thai-party-bhumjaithai-campaigns-marijuana.

63. *Thailand is betting big on cannabis. Visit its first legal lab*: https://www.pri.org/stories/2019-08-06/thailand-betting-big-cannabis-visit-its-first-legal-lab.

64. *Thailand set to deliver first batch of medical marijuana*: https://www.reuters.com/article/us-thailand-cannabis/thailand-set-to-deliver-first-batch-of-medical-marijuana-idUSKCN1UR4LX.

Chapter 6

Emerging trends for businesses

IP AND TRADEMARKS

6.01 The number of global patent applications for cannabis and cannabis-related inventions has soared over the last decade, and lawyers believe the European market may become an even more fierce battleground in the coming years.

According to the World Intellectual Property Organization (WIPO), more than 11,000 cannabis-related applications have been filed in total since 1978 under the Patent Cooperation Treaty (PCT), with nearly 7,000 applications coming after 2008.

WIPO estimates cannabis IP has grown by 154% in the last decade, but the true number is almost certainly higher as firms use loopholes to obtain patents related to cannabis, such as growing or treating addictions, without expressly referring to marijuana in their application.

Concerns have been raised in areas such as New Zealand that large international firms are using their size and power to snatch patents and shore up their positions, while the emergence of 'patent trolls' is also causing concern that bad actors will monopolise existing knowledge and attempt to take popular strains out of play.

Businesses seeking to enter Europe's fledgling medicinal cannabis sector must consider the experiences of the North American market on intellectual property, said Toronto specialist life sciences patent attorney Micheline Gravelle Managing Partner at law firm Bereskin & Parr, as tussles over intellectual property have waged for several decades.

> 'Given the international competition in this hugely dynamic and commoditised industry, robust intellectual property protection will be absolutely crucial for European businesses looking to make their mark. As the market evolved in Canada during the 1990s, it was truly eye-opening to see such a patchy understanding of the basics of IP.'

Typically, large biotechnology companies with big budgets are well-versed in the art of protecting their innovations, but in the rush to bring products to market, smaller start-ups can find themselves falling short on the fundamentals.

Gravelle said active and rigorous due diligence was one of the most important aspects for any firm looking at the European market, which is projected to be worth hundreds of billions of dollars in the next decade:

> 'European companies also need to be especially mindful of the international nature of the industry. The 90-plus Canadian publicly-listed cannabis companies have a market value of about CA$31bn, but the top three filers of patents there are Swiss, US and British businesses.
>
> 'Although the Canadian industry is already maturing, it remains uncertain just how swiftly the European market will follow suit.'

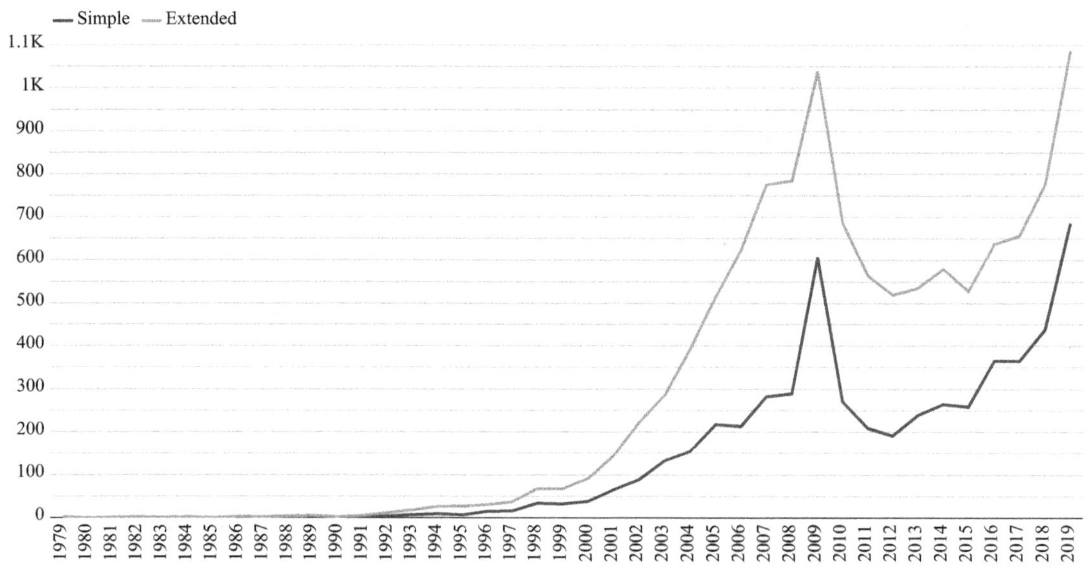

Source: World Intellectual Property Organization.
The data for 'simple' represents Patent Cooperation Treaty 'cannabis' patents, while 'extended' represents the number of PCT international patent applications that include 'cannabis', 'cannabinoid', 'phytocannabinoid', 'cannabidiol', 'cannabinodiol', 'cannabinol', 'tetrahydrocannabinol', 'tetrahydrocannabinolic acid', 'hashish', 'hash oil'.

The soaring number of patents is a direct result of the significant sums of money flooding into the sector. Legal cannabis sales are believed to have hit $10bn in the US in 2018, and are predicted to reach nearly $23bn by 2025, according to Bloomberg Intelligence data sourced from cannabis industry intelligence firm New Frontier Data. CBD sales are expected to quadruple over the next four years, from $535m in 2018 to more than $1.9bn by 2022.

Protecting IP is expensive, however, and the exorbitant cost is hindering the amount of research conducted in the medicinal cannabis space, which in turn causes doctors to shy away, said Dylan Kennett, M&A lawyer and leader of DLA Piper's EMEA cannabis practice:

> 'Most companies playing in the space are at least looking at developing or commissioning research. There is a time-lag before all these results come in, but any company worth their salt is investing in R&D. It's a big source of pride and marketing for them, as well. Once those begin to hopefully deliver favourable results, government will have difficulty justifying their position if the research is positive. It

would have been experimental research in the past, but now there is a proper industry behind it which can justify the costs.'

Big Pharma IP battles

6.02 One of the most active filers of cannabis patents is British firm GW Pharmaceuticals, a world-leading biopharma firm and creator of the first prescription medicine derived from the cannabis plant.

GW's intellectual property portfolio at 30 September 2018 included 82 patent families with issued and/or pending claims directed to plants, plant extracts, extraction technology, pharmaceutical formulations, drug delivery and the therapeutic uses of cannabinoids, as well as plant variety rights, know-how and trade secrets.

From these families, it owns and/or licenses 252 pending patent applications worldwide. Within the US, GW has 48 issued patents, with a further 39 pending patent applications under active prosecution. GW has an additional 563 issued patents outside of the US.

From those, it owns or licenses 252 pending patent applications worldwide. Within the US it has 48 issued patents, with a further 39 pending patent applications under active prosecution. There are an additional 563 issued patents outside the US.

The company disclosed it has been involved in several IP legal struggles over its landmark drugs, Epidiolex, which uses CBD oil to treat epilepsy, and Sativex, a mouth spray with trace amounts of THC and CBD used to treat, amongst other illnesses, multiple sclerosis.

In January 2019, US judges threw out GW's attempt to patent multiple cannabinoids for epilepsy treatment, following an eight-year battle. The US Patent Trial and Appeal Board, an administrative law body of the national patent office, denied patent US9066920B2, siding with petitioner Insys, a rival biotech firm.[1]

The patent, in dispute since 2010, is for 'the use of one or more cannabinoids in the treatment of epilepsy'. More particularly, for the use of one or a combination of cannabinoids, CBD oil, in the treatment of generalised or partial seizures.

The invention covers a method of treating partial seizures comprising administering cannabidiol (CBD) to a patient wherein the CBD is present in an amount which provides a daily dose of at least 400mg.

Of 13 claims, administrative patent judges Erica Franklin, Susan Mitchell, and Zhenyu Yang, said the first two were 'unpatentable' under US law, however the remaining 11 claims that were challenged remain valid, and potentially enforceable should GW decide to appeal.

GW's patent portfolio is extensive, running into the several hundred, with many aimed at using cannabis to fight diseases.

In 2018, the British company successfully lobbied the US Food and Drug Administration (FDA) to approve Epidiolex, its landmark cannabinoid-based oral solution for the treatment of seizures, becoming the first company in the world to gain FDA backing for a cannabis product.

According to GW's 2018 annual report, it spent more than £110m (US$141m) on Epidolex research and development in 2017 alone, as it invested heavily in attempts to have the drug approved in the US and push through it in Europe. It spent more than $100m on the drug in 2016.

GW said many of its competitors are undergoing the same fight to protect, defend and enforce intellectual property rights in foreign jurisdictions:

> 'The legal systems of certain countries, particularly certain developing countries, do not favour the enforcement of patents and other intellectual property rights, particularly those relating to pharmaceuticals, which could make it difficult for us to stop the infringement of our patents or marketing of competing products in violation of our proprietary rights generally.'

Cannabis patents in the US

6.03 The complex history of cannabis legalisation means securing IP rights is never straightforward, and in the case of the US, where most of the business activity is currently taking place, the situation is extremely messy.

In the US, cannabis firms cannot use federal trademark protection to shield their brand, as the drug is still illegal at federal level despite a number of states now allowing recreational use.

The issue of cannabis as a Schedule 1 narcotic has led to a situation where the Drug Enforcement Agency (DEA) refuses to downgrade cannabis under the Controlled Substances Act (CSA), yet the US government itself holds a patent on non-psychoactive cannabinoids, most notably CBD, as a medicine.

Patent 6,630,507, titled 'Cannabinoids as antioxidants and neuroprotectants' was issued on October 7, 2003, to the United States as represented by the Department of Health and Human Services.

There are three basic types of patent available for cannabis firms to apply for; utility, design, and plant. A fourth, provisional, is linked to utility patents.

Utility patents: By far the most common patent issued by the United States Patent and Trademark Office, approximately 90% of applications are for utility patents, and are issued for 20 years. A utility patent is intended to protect 'new and useful' inventions, such as a process, a machine, a manufacturing method, a composition of matter or a similarly new and equally useful improvement of an existing invention.

Smoking devices, or processes for extracting and purifying marijuana and its key ingredients for medical use have been covered with utility patents. It also concerns other cannabis technologies, both recreational and medicinal. The category is extremely broad, making it a popular litigation subject.

Design patents: Design patents are intended for new, original and ornamental designs that can be used on goods, such as the shape of a smoking device such as a pipe or a bong. They exclude parties other than the owner from using, making or selling the design. The patent is granted for a term of 14 years, and unlike the utility patent, requires no maintenance fees to be upheld.

Plant patents: Perhaps the most controversial in regard to cannabis are patents is issued for new, distinct variations of plants invented or discovered through cultivation, mutation, hybridisation or any other artificial process. The same exclusive rights are granted as with the other patents, but while the term lasts for 20 years there is no need to pay maintenance fees.

Cannabis IP in court

6.04 The first lawsuit over cannabis intellectual property appeared in July 2018,[2] filed by United Cannabis Corporation (UCANN) against Pure Hemp Collective (PHC), both Colorado corporations, in federal court.

The case concerned allegations that Pure Hemp's tinctures, gel capsules, vape pens, and other cannabis products infringe one or more claims of UCANN's patent for 'cannabis extracts and methods of preparing and using same' (US Patent No. 9,730,911).

'The case has major implications on two fronts,' said David Gold, of Cole Schotz PC:

> 'First, the enforcement of the UCANN patent specifically; and second, the overall viability of litigation concerning cannabis-related patents.'

At the industry level, Gold said, a decision to validate and enforce a rather broad patent could determine whether UCANN will be able to strong-arm anyone else in the industry using a liquid cannabinoid formulation containing 95% cannabidiol (CBD).

More broadly, it is the first infringement suit concerning a patent on a cannabis-related product that, while patented, is used with a federally illegal. There are questions over the ability of the court to hear the case, as a result.

> 'We're months, if not years' away from a decision on whether Pure Hemp infringed on UCANN's patent. That's going to require what's called 'claim construction,' where they're going to go through, and there's going to be demonstratives and scientists and experts that are going to get in and figure [the patent claim] out.' (Gold)

In April 2019, a Denver federal judge denied an early motion to dismiss several aspects of the lawsuit, allowing it to proceed toward a jury trial. It is a case everyone in the industry should be glued to.

According to Rod Kight, lawyer and author of the Kight On Cannabis blog:

> 'In fighting out over IP, the cannabis industry has reached an important milestone. Truly novel inventions should be granted protection from infringement,' he said. 'This incentivises and promotes advances in the field. However, patent 'land-grabs' that are broad in scope and based on inventions which existed but were not well documented are a blight on the industry and will stall advances.'

CANNABIS INVESTING AND THE PROCEEDS OF CRIME ACT 2002

6.05 British law firms have reported a significant rise in cannabis investing queries, particularly in relation to the regulated Canadian market, and what risks lie in drawing profits from an activity that is illegal under UK law.

It is a question that investors in any market outside Canada or certain US states will be pondering; will the investment in a legal and regulated cannabis entity trigger any criminal laws in my domestic jurisdiction?

According to David Rundle, counsel at WilmerHale law firm in London:

> 'Deregulation and changing societal attitudes present commercial opportunities: cannabis is big business and has become an attractive area for investment globally. The growing deregulation and (global) commercialisation of cannabis exposes a policy paradox that warrants reform: secondary legislation could be introduced to extend the scope of the statutory defence and thereby alleviate the burden on the regulated sector.'

The scope and application of the UK's Proceeds of Crime Act 2002 (POCA) has been drawn into sharp focus. POCA defines the proceeds of crime by reference to whether the predicate activity (criminal conduct) is lawful in the UK, not where it was committed.

'As such, revenue derived from a (legal) Canadian cannabis company, for example, would constitute the proceeds of crime,' said Rundle. Yet there has been no guidance from the Law Commission, the police, any of the UK's financial regulators or the government.

According to Jonah Anderson, a partner in the London office of White & Case:

> 'People want advice on cannabis investment, particularly regulated firms. There has been no guidance, or case law and there is no established way of dealing with it. For the moment, it's unclear, and from a commercial basis, things are rapidly expanding.'

Suspicious activity

6.06 The main issues revolve around interpretation of money laundering laws and the POCA, said Anderson. Regulated firms, such as banks and other financial firms, are obliged to have in place anti-money laundering systems and controls and to file suspicious activity reports (SAR) when they suspect or have knowledge of improper transactions.

The UK is by far the largest reporter of SARs in the EU, attributed to London's enormous financial services sector which dwarfs the rest of the bloc, and each year, approximately half a million SARs are made.

The proceeds of crime are defined as 'criminal property' under s 340 of POCA. Property is criminal property if it represents a person's benefit from criminal conduct. Criminal conduct is conduct which constitutes an offence in the UK, or would constitute an offence if it occurred there.

Businesses that facilitate these sorts of investments – banks, brokers and investment houses – may also be drawn into the wrangle, according to Nicola Finnerty, partner at Kinglsey Napley:

> 'They may be entering into arrangements concerning the proceeds of crime,' she said. 'Further, Canadian citizens who work for a cannabis production company and visit the UK or who decide to invest in the UK, for example in the UK property market, may also find that the source of their funds comes under scrutiny.'

The 'Spanish Bullfighter' problem

6.07

> 'This broad approach to criminal property can cause problems, particularly in relation to conduct outside the UK. For example, killing bulls may be lawful in Spain, but not England, so if a Spanish bullfighter takes his professional winnings or salary and attempts to purchase real estate in London, then he risks committing a money laundering offence under POCA.'
>
> 'Cannabis investment is the new Spanish bullfighter problem, and there is no government guidance or case law on the implications of investing in a cannabis business in an overseas jurisdiction where it is legal to do so.'(Anderson)

In the UK, a safe harbour exists in relation to money laundering, known as the consent regime. If a SAR is made seeking consent from the UK's National Crime Agency (NCA) to undertake a certain activity that may otherwise be considered money laundering, and the firm which filed the SAR receives express consent from the NCA, or consent is deemed, then there is no risk of committing an offence.

The consent regime is not quick or easy, however and for businesses conducting a lot of transactions it becomes difficult to manage commercially.

> 'The consent regime is extremely relevant for the cannabis industry. There has been a huge amount of interest in overseas investment in regulated Canadian cannabis businesses, but very little regarding investment in 'hash cafes' in Amsterdam, when essentially the same issues arise.' (Anderson)

Managing risk

6.08 Canada is a much larger market than Amsterdam, however, with greater scale production, and the direction of travel is that the Canadian model may be adopted in other jurisdictions.

> 'For investors in legal cannabis production in Canada, under s 340 of POCA, one could argue that the investment in the business would satisfy the definition of criminal property. 'On this view, the production, distribution and supply of cannabis in Canada would be a crime if it occurred in the UK, and would result in a benefit, and thus engage the UK money laundering regime.' (Anderson)

On this interpretation and in that situation, businesses are now considering how they manage that risk.

> 'If one takes the view that the proceeds of crime may be received, or otherwise dealt with, a regulated firm would be expected to make a SAR seeking consent, whereupon the NCA will review it and respond. As yet, the NCA has not issued guidance about cannabis investment. Anecdotally, the approach the NCA takes is to neither grant nor refuse consent, and instead the reporter may take legal advice and rely on deemed consent.' (Anderson)

Overseas conduct

6.09 The NCA has been silent on the matter, and ongoing reform of the SAR regime has been broadly criticised by legal experts including the Law Society.[3]

The Law Commission's remit regarding its review of SAR reform did not include cannabis investment, but it has recommended that the issue be addressed by the provision of guidance or the expansion of the narrow exemptions to the regime. An Order covering overseas conduct exemptions does exist, but it is old, badly drafted and not particularly helpful, according to Anderson:

> 'Is overseas investment in cannabis production, which is legal in the jurisdiction in question, going to be of interest to law enforcement generally? It seems unlikely, but because of the potential application of the money laundering regime, it is an issue that has emerged.'

While law enforcement may show little interest in SARs regarding investments in legal cannabis businesses in Canada or elsewhere, lawyers said regulated firms will need to demonstrate that they have considered the issue and dealt with it appropriately.

Paying the bounty

6.10 According to Anderson:

> 'Some years ago, there was a focus on the application of the money laundering regime to ransom payments to pirates who had kidnapped hostages. The concern was that paying the pirate was a substantive money laundering offence under s 328 of POCA because the payment of the ransom was an arrangement which facilitated the acquisition by the pirate of the proceeds of crime.'

The Supreme Court later clarified the breadth of the s 328 offence in a case which had its roots in fraud. The effect of this decision was that a ransom payment would not be caught by the s 328 offence because the ransom payment was not criminal property when it was paid and the arrangement operated on it.

> 'The funds instead became the proceeds of crime in the hands of the pirates, as it represented their benefit from kidnap for ransom. The issue therefore fell away and it may be that a forthcoming case has a similar indirect effect on cannabis investment.'

ENDNOTES

1. Insys Development Company, Inc. v. GW Pharma Limited, 2019 WL 101791 (2019).
2. United Cannabis Corp. v. Pure Hemp Collective Inc. (D. Colo. 2019).
3. Law Commission consultation on SARs reform – Law Society response: https://www.lawsociety.org.uk/policy-campaigns/consultation-responses/law-commission-consultation-on-sars-reform-law-society-response/.

Chapter 7

Conclusion: Time for international reform?

7.01 This snapshot of the fluctuating cannabis laws around the world shows the international agreements that have framed cannabis regulation and provided the backbone for prohibition over the last 60 years are dissolving.

In the next 12 months, Mexico and South Africa will have opened regulated recreational cannabis markets, with Luxembourg expected to do the same in Europe. Australia's capital territory has announced its intention to regulate, and New Zealand's population is expected to vote 'Yes' in a cannabis legalisation referendum later this year.

Countries and territories across four different continents are breaking UN drug treaty agreements to pursue their own agendas in the name of public health, crime reduction and personal freedoms.

It is a state of affairs made even more remarkable by the fact they are in lock-step with the world's largest economy, the architect of, and until recently the main enforcer of, global narcotics laws, the US.

The deviations are equally as profound inside the regulated sphere. Traditionally uber-conservative areas such as South Korea, Japan, Thailand, and the Philippines have opened the door to medicinal cannabis and CBD products. Business cases for cannabis-derivatives and the possibility of new international partnerships now exist in countries where even five years ago the mention of marijuana would be taboo.

Governments, and this includes UN-level representatives, have said the paucity of research and data is behind the reform lag, but as we have seen, this is in contradiction with the UN's own health committee, and is at odds with the amount of trials currently taking place.

As exciting as it may be for some, there are repercussions for countries ploughing ahead with their own regulatory regimes, and without some form of international control and agreement, the cannabis sector cannot realistically hope to straddle global boundaries.

PEOPLE POWER

7.02 The first countries to open adult recreational cannabis markets did so for two reasons: to take back control from organised crime; and to better educate their citizens about the health impact of cannabis use.

A regulated market in theory allows governments to monitor the quality and strength of products, and control who can access them and how. It stops people seeking out dealers who can push other drugs on them, and frees up police resources. Canada and Uruguay used this as justification, and Luxembourg is making similar noises.

In the US, however, citizens have forced ballots on their states to overturn cannabis consumption laws, and this hyperlocal trend looks set to continue. In Mexico and South Africa, the top courts have forced the governments' hands and sided with consumers. Rulings handed down state it is unconstitutional for the authorities to prohibit individuals from using small amounts of cannabis in their own homes or other designated private places. Argentina's court ruled this way ten years ago, leading to decriminalisation, but governments today are deciding to go further and open legalised marketplaces.

It is a telling development that some 60 years on from the signing of international treaties, the law has evolved to frame these agreements as outdated and incompatible with personal freedoms.

DIVERGENT STREAMS

7.03 The twin streams of medicinal and recreational cannabis are heading in very different directions, and a unique set of obstacles exists for the individuals and businesses active in both to negotiate.

There is growing optimism that medicinal cannabis can strengthen national healthcare offerings, and provide relief for the extremely sick where everything else has failed. Many patients and their families are hopeful they will soon not have to exhaust all other options in order to access help.

Almost every government, health authority, and police agency debating the matter is united in their message that for this to happen there desperately needs to be more research done on cannabis' potential as a medicine.

It is a simple Catch-22. The R&D shortfall is because the plant has been classified as one of the most dangerous substances known to humanity, and its status has not been reviewed since drug scheduling began during an era of strict prohibition.

Should the UN drugs committee approve the recommendations put forth by the United Nations health committee and remove cannabis from Schedule IV to the 1961 Single Convention on Narcotic Drugs, this will ease the pressure on researchers.

HARMONISED STANDARDS

7.04 For its part, the EU has already recognised this problem, and is taking steps to ensure medicinal cannabis is covered by harmonised regulation. It remains to be seen what policymakers will draw up in 2020; however, taking what we already know about the harmonisation process, it would not be too difficult to imagine what the end guidance may say.

The first step is to create a common technical language used by all actors in the sector, which the EU has committed to. This will allow lawmakers to define the requirements that are then handed down to national regulatory authorities.

Harmonisation will also allow for the development of unique testing and manufacturing standards, and perhaps the EU will attempt to draw up a framework for sustainable cannabis production.

Given the strides the EU has made through its data protection mandate in creating a framework that is now being copied elsewhere, perhaps the bloc can also one day lead the world in cannabis R&D, sustainability, and environmentally-sound cultivation standards.

Advancing medicinal cannabis frameworks within the international system, and allowing countries to work together legally at least gives the chance of consistency, which is not the case when we consider how recreational markets are mushrooming.

HYPER-COMMERCIALISATION

7.05 The brisk growth of non-medicinal, adult recreational cannabis markets, particularly in the US, has captured the imagination of big business. Should Congress lift the federal prohibition ban on cannabis, all bets are off as to how quickly other major developed nations follows suit.

It is tempting to think in terms of 'when, not if' this will occur, but federal approval is by no means certain, and the current levels of hype and frenzy within the sector are doing more harm than good. An over-commercialised market carries significant risks, as we have seen with almost decades of unrestricted activity from the tobacco and alcohol industries.

Regulation of these two products has begun to tighten in the last 20 years, and there are lessons for the cannabis industry to learn about how products considered dangerous are marketed sold.

The matter is more complex when we consider how the compound CBD has become so wildly popular (to an extent there are now pet food supplements containing it) all over the world, even in areas where cannabis possession can still result in the death penalty.

Could the inescapable presence of CBD normalise cannabis to extent it downplays the public's perception of risks of a very powerful drug? Or could it even derail the progress of the research everyone is crying out for? CBD is not psychoactive, and for the most part can only be considered a food supplement and not a medicine, but does the man or woman in the street know the difference?

When considering why major pharmaceutical companies are reluctant to commission full-scale medicinal cannabis trials, perhaps the answer lies in the risks of conducting billion-dollar research and going through the regulatory process only for a CBD dietary supplement company to undercut them in the market.

The excitement of cannabis and cannabis businesses has also begun to seduce investors, and more clarity is needed from financial authorities outside of Canada on where funds and individuals stand.

We have covered the UK in these pages, but the situation will be playing out in any jurisdiction in the world where investors are looking at cannabis businesses in Canada and the US states as a way of providing returns.

Similarly, for businesses, the IP and patent battlegrounds are beginning to heat up in Europe, and companies are advised to take heed of the trends appearing in North America around trademarking and patenting, as they are surely bound to make their way over.

DIRECTION OF TRAVEL

7.06 This book details developing cannabis laws, and in doing so chronicles the changing attitudes towards the drug in every corner of the world. We have observed how the accelerating process of national reforms has taken cannabis policies beyond the boundaries of what the outdated international conventions can accommodate.

On the current path there is a real risk of even greater fracture between nation states; the international treaty agreements designed to protect us have been undermined by the actions of Canada,

Uruguay and the US states. Today, Mexico, New Zealand, and Australia's capital territory, along with Luxembourg, the Netherlands, and several Caribbean jurisdictions stand ready to follow.

In breaking such agreements, these countries are on a weaker footing when they call out, for example, the human rights violations of Saudi Arabia, Afghanistan, Russia or Hungary.

Given the US's pro-cannabis tilt, and the speed at which states are approving legislation to allow recreational marijuana, it is extremely unlikely the US will be making any effort to sanction its neighbours Mexico and Canada, or pressure other countries to take similar action. If anything, their success in this endeavour is likely to make the US more tolerant of cannabis trade.

Globally, the direction of travel is towards either decriminalisation, or regulation and control. Prisons are increasingly overcrowded, public opinion is shifting, cannabis is being viewed through the prism of health rather than crime, and courts around the world are less inclined than ever to hand criminal records to otherwise law-abiding citizens over cannabis offences.

Perhaps there is a need to reclassify the cannabis plant altogether, and explicitly allow countries to regulate it, or to alter the conventions to allow the legal regulation of cannabis. Neither of these options are on the immediate horizon, but given how far things have moved in the last 12 months, and the number of active and driven parties building out the global cannabis industry, it would be foolish to rule them out.

Index

[All references are to paragraph numbers]